The Decision-making Process of Meetings, Congresses, Conventions and Incentives Organizers

Table of contents

Acknowledgments

This study was prepared by Mr. Bruce Redor (GainingEdge) in partnership with Marketing Challenges International on the commission to the European Travel Commission (ETC) and the World Tourism Organization (UNWTO).

This study is part of ETC's ongoing Market Intelligence Programme and was carried out under the supervision of Mr. Vincent Nijs and Ms. Louise Derre (Visit Flanders), Ms. Cristina Salsinha (Turismo de Portugal), Ms. Jennifer Iduh and Ms. Stefanie Gallob (ETC Executive Unit) on behalf of the ETC Market Intelligence Group (MIG) and in collaboration with UNWTO's Tourism Market Trends Programme: Ms. Julia Baunemann, Mr. Michel Julian and Mr. John Kester.

We would like to acknowledge the contributions of all institutions and experts involved in the interviews and collection of best-practice examples for the completion of the study.

We also want to place on record our sincere gratitude to all and one of the experts of Gaining Edge that contributed to the elaboration of this study.

Foreword

The Meetings industry continues to thrive while experiencing fastest growth in the tourism sector and thus generating millions of revenues. As the one of the main purpose of travel worldwide, this industry has received increased attention from both countries and cities, particularly from emerging destinations, which are considerably and successfully investing in the development of venues, transportation and accommodation infrastructures, and facilities with the aim of attracting business events. With new destinations entering the meetings, congresses, conventions and incentives (MCCI) market, competition for market share in Europe and worldwide has become vigorous. In addition, a changing and more technological environment is making innovation and dynamism key elements for a successful MCCI destination.

In this framework, it becomes core for tourism professionals to achieve an in-depth understanding of this growing sector and its segments, as well as the key reasons concerning meting planners' choice of a destination to hold meetings, conventions, congresses and incentives events.

ETC and UNWTO understand the importance of the MCCI industry for the tourism sector and therefore embrace the elaboration of a study that lays the foundations of a better-understand of the overall decision-making process of meetings, congresses, conventions and incentives organizers in order to provide professionals with an optimum knowledge to excel in the sector.

Aimed at Destination Management Organizations (DMOs), National Tourism Organizations (NTOs) and National Tourism Administrations (NTAs) the study offers a wide-ranging overview of the meetings, conferences, congresses and incentives segments and a comprehensive analysis of planners' needs and expectations with respect to destination and venues choice.

Once again ETC and UNWTO are pleased to publish another practical and useful tool for their members based on the strong cooperation between both organizations and which we believe is the best response to address challenges and make the most of the opportunities provided by the MCCI industry.

Taleb Rifai
Secretary-General,
World Tourism Organization (UNWTO)

Peter de Wilde
President,
European Travel Commission (ETC)

Executive summary

MCCI industry overview

- The Meetings, Congresses, Conventions and Incentives (MCCI) industry is part of the greater tourism sector and includes three different segments: association conventions and congresses, corporate meetings and corporate incentive programmes;
- The industry is a key driver in assisting organizations in their efforts to reach strategic business objectives and effectively communicate with their members, employees, customers and partners worldwide;
- Although the landscape is continuously changing, trend analyses reveal a sense of optimism that attendance and budgets will increase in the near future in all segments and in all geographic regions;
- More and more destinations are investing resources in this growing industry because they recognise its potential to create positive economic and social impact;
- Most governments' economic development plans include business events as these provide a range of strategic 'beyond tourism benefits';
- The MCCI industry is a vector for connecting leading experts, sharing knowledge and know-how, encouraging exchange of ideas and engaging professionals in the development of business and opportunities; and
- There is a need for increasing focus on establishing business networks to facilitate the integration of the MCCI industry.

Analysis of segments and profiles

The three MCCI segments have different objectives and characteristics.

Association conventions and congresses

Characteristics:
- Associations, which are generally not-for-profit organizations, organize annual, biannual or multiyear conventions and congresses, which are key revenue generators for the association;
- Association conventions and congresses can either be international, regional/transnational or national and can include an exhibition related to the subject of the convention;
- The segment is seen as tri-polar in terms of rotation activity, figuring Europe, Africa and the Middle East as one pole, the Americas as a second pole and Asia and the Pacific as a third pole;
- Association conventions and congresses have the longest lead-time, which is the time for organizing the event, taking an average of 3 to 6 years. This is due to the scale of the events,

the increasing competition between associations and the large number of players included in the process. International conventions and congresses have the longest lead times, whereas regional, national and government meetings have a shorter lead-time;

- Associations in the fields of medical sciences, technology and science dominate the segment, as these sectors have more associations and bigger budgets;
- Association conventions and congresses are generally large, with an average 500 pax per event, and produce high spending, generating significant economic benefits for the host destination; and
- These events generally take place in specifically designed convention centres, hotels with meeting facilities and increasingly in universities.

Key trends:
- Dominated by Europe and North America, the association conventions and congresses segment is experiencing a shift towards emerging destinations, which are investing in infrastructure and technology;
- As the Baby Boomers retire, the new generations X and Y are taking over the industry, focusing on return on investment (ROI) and using new technologies. Therefore there is important investment made in young future leaders;
- As the industry continues to adapt to its changing environment, associations need to re-evaluate what participants consider as 'value' and need to focus on doing more with less, favouring quality over quantity;
- As participants want associations to maximize opportunities for learning and exchange during and after conventions and congresses, and because of the recent boom in handheld communication devices, associations are increasingly integrating technology and social media to engage participants and members throughout their events;
- Because of reduced spending by participants and increased focus on ROI, associations are trending towards regional rotation. There is a trend towards using second-tier destinations where associations benefit from lower costs and more personalised service and can engage local communities;
- Concerns over safety and economic, social and political stability are pushing associations to conduct risk adversity studies to assist in the final choice of destinations;
- There are growing interest to build new alliances and partnerships between associations with compatible or complementary business interests and goals. These partnerships allows for associations to share resources, risk and rewards, and the overall enhancement of the meeting experience;
- Besides establishing corporate social responsibility internally, associations are responding to external sustainable development challenges, which affects their overall decision-making; and
- As the segment expands and becomes more globalized, participants and members are putting more and more pressure on associations to underline their demands for changes of technical or regulatory standards. Associations are therefore increasingly pressured to influence the policy and regulatory environment, which in turn allow associations to gain more members and build strategic alliances.

Key players: conventions and congresses are generally organized with in-house management, however some either outsource the organization to a professional conference organizer (PCO), under certain circumstances, or directly ask association management companies (AMCs) or destination management companies (DMCs), event management companies (EMCs), which provide management services for the organization of the events.

Drivers: the growth of new industries is triggering new market opportunities and the growing ease of access and affordability of destinations are also driving demand.

Barriers: the increasing competition amongst associations, is forcing associations to be innovative and adapt to new demands, and growing security concerns and sluggish economic growth are affecting the segment.

Corporate meetings

Characteristics:
- Corporate meetings are high profile and a communicating vehicle for conveying important messages about the company;
- Typical planning cycle ranges between 2 to 6 months, much shorter than for association conventions and congresses;
- There are two types of corporate meetings, internal and external meetings;
- Internal corporate meetings are organization focused to discuss firm infrastructure, human resources, technology, procurement, operations, sales and other internal activities. These include annual meetings, team building, planning and training courses amongst others. Internal meetings are generally smaller groups making decisions on short-term lead times. The pharmaceutical/medical sector, the financial services/banking sector, and the IT/telecommunications/electronics sector host internal meetings the most frequently. These meetings have little to do with destination selling as they are generally held near corporate locations using internal resources; and
- External corporate meetings are more focused on business or 'market facing'. The aims are generally about managing supply chain relationships or enhancing customer relationship management but can also be used as market promotional meetings for product launches. External meetings are demand-focused and engage a large global audience. For these meetings, corporations are more focused on the destination and aim to impress and use larger venues including conference and convention centres and meeting facilities in hotels.

Key trends:
- In the wake of the global financial crisis scrutinising budgets more closely has been an integral part of corporations' priorities in order to respond to changes in demand. Corporations are also focusing on assessing the outcomes of their investment by measuring ROI of their meetings;
- Demand for corporate meetings is increasing, however this trend is expected to increase mostly within regions. And, while the number of meetings being held and the number of participants has been slowly growing, this is expected to change as corporations aim to gain efficiency; and
- Because participants are time-constrained, there is a growing demand for secondary and closer-to-home destinations, and an increase in the number of virtual meetings. Cost savings for the corporation and reduced travel time for participants are a driving force for this trend.

Key players: internal corporate meetings are generally organized by in-house corporate planners. However, the bigger external corporate meetings, can be complex and engage a large number of intermediaries. Some corporations seek support from corporate meetings/incentive, third party planners and hotel national sales offices, which help with the operational and logistical elements of the event.

Drivers: the segment is driven by increasing budgets and, as demand for emerging destinations increases the segment expands into new markets and finds new opportunities. Moreover, regional trade agreements are driving demand for B2B meetings between partner countries.

Barriers: as corporations react to the changing environment, it needs to quickly and strategically respond to an increasing use of virtual meetings, and the demand for shorter-haul destinations and shorter meetings. Recent economic instabilities have also increased pressure on corporations to focus on ROI.

Incentive programmes

Characteristics:
- The nature of incentive programmes is mainly to reward employees and suppliers to enhance their satisfaction and performance, which in turns ensure better returns for the corporation. These programmes are increasingly recognised across companies;
- Similarly to corporate meetings, incentive programmes have a very short lead-time, ranging on average between 6 to 12 months;
- The decision-making process is largely dependent on three main areas, including the logistical criteria, the financial criteria and the emotional criteria, the latter relates to the employee's experience;
- Incentive programmes are meant to be highly entertaining and authentic experience, therefore planners look for destinations that are unique and can offer a wide range of activities. For this reason emerging destinations are becoming more and more popular, including Asia and South America, however destinations such as the Caribbean, North America and Europe remain top choices; and
- Corporations want incentive programmes to be high quality. Locations are therefore high quality hotels or resorts, four or five stars, which including meeting facilities.

Key trends:
- These programmes are mainly recreational but corporations are increasingly adding meeting components for tax benefits, and offer additional value in terms of communication between employees;
- After adopting cost-cutting measures due to past economic conditions, per-person expenditure has been affected and awards shifted from group to individual awards. As a result corporations are focusing on adopting several measures to offer participants more value-for-money;
- Similarly to association conventions and congresses and corporate meetings, incentive planners are increasingly incorporating social media and new technologies to promote their events, especially to assess the success of the programmes and collect feedback; and
- As incentives gain recognition, there is growing demand for unique experience and the additional 'wow factor'. Moreover companies are increasingly offering wellness components to programmes to improve employee health/fitness.

Key players: depending on the aims and needs of the corporation, incentive organization may be outsourced to organize the programme, or simply be organized by in-house corporate travel agents, Incentive agencies, travel fulfilment companies, Destination Management Companies and Event Management Companies can assist with the preparation of budgets, activities, team-building, assistance for visa, travel insurance and other managerial components.

Drivers: corporations are increasingly recognising the importance of incentive programmes and are therefore investing the necessary resources, which is in turn driving demand incentives.

Barriers: because budgets are highly dependent on the corporation and thus on the state of the economy, they can vary from one year to another. This can become a challenge for organizers, as they need to manage costs without compromising on quality.

The decision-making process of MCCI organizers

MCCI planners' decision-making varies across segments and countries.

Association conventions and congresses

- **What planners want:** to engage delegates and make the event a platform to support ideas and communication within the industry;
- **Key criteria:** decisive criteria influencing destination choice can be separated into two categories, first the basic criteria, which includes cost and size of meeting facilities as most important, second the 'added value' criteria, including advocacy for subject matter, membership recruitment and local presence as most important, once basic factors are met;
- **Decision makers:** final decisions are mostly made either by the executive, the board or the committee;
- **Intermediaries:** local chapter assistance, PCOs, DMCs and third party planners are the most common intermediaries used for the organization of conventions and congresses;
- **Key trends affecting lead times and decision-making** include organizational resources and characteristics, such as knowledge or budget, and the quality of information channels; and
- **Role of convention bureaux (CBs):** CBs support associations with the bidding process, developing ambassador programmes, and assisting planners with logistical, operational and strategic activities of the event. Association meeting planners use CBs the most.

Corporate meetings

- **What planners want:** desire to provide quality and high profile events which is largely dependent on the nature of the meeting – internal or external, as planners aim to provide successful returns such as increased loyalty, better relationships, product launches, educational meetings and ROI;
- **Key criteria:** once basic needs are met, the most important being destination appeal and access, corporate meeting planners underline that destinations with local presence are preferred;
- **Decision makers:** top management or sometimes event committee take final decisions;
- **Intermediaries:** procurement departments are having a much stronger influence on site selections; yet key intermediaries include DMCs and hotel national sales offices; and
- **Role of CBs:** CBs are less solicited for corporate meeting planning, however CBs can bring valuable help in creating first contact between corporations and event companies and offering information and support throughout the organization of the event.

Incentive programmes

- **What planners want:** incentive programmes are aimed at recognising performance, increasing sales, improving employee loyalty, amongst others;
- **Key criteria** include destination appeal, unique experience and the desire to offer the additional 'wow' factor. Key decision-making criteria go hand in hand with the aims of the corporation's communication strategy;
- **Decision makers:** similarly to corporate meetings, top management or event committee mostly take final decisions;
- **Intermediaries:** incentive houses, travel fulfilment companies, corporate travel agencies and DMCs are common intermediaries; and
- **Role of CBs:** CBs can assist planners with information and guidance throughout the organization of the incentive programme.

Convention bureaux' best practices

- Differences are particularly observed between mature markets and developing destinations. While cultural and business differences can sometimes bring difficulties to working abroad, convention bureaux appear to be a perfect steppingstone for engaging in and organizing MCCI events;
- Governments can play an important role in the development and success of the MCCI industry through financial support and policy developments; and
- CBs are key players in developing the MCCI industry. Some best practices include:
  - Clearly defined business development strategy;
  - Strong support from government institutions;
  - Close working relationships with MCCI partners;
  - Strong marketing/branding strategy;
  - Presence in global markets; and
  - Investment in research and development, and innovation.

European convention bureau landscape:
- The European landscape is very diverse including local/city CBs, which are the most important, national CBs and Europe is the region with the most regional, on a national context, CBs; and
- Best practices: German Convention Bureau, Serbia Convention Bureau, Vienna Convention Bureau, Prague Convention Bureau.

American convention bureau landscape:
- The North American landscape is very developed and represents the biggest number of CBs and the biggest budgets. The Latin American landscape, on the other hand, is still working on portraying a different image, dealing with issues of security and instability; and
- Best practices: Tourism Vancouver, Greater Bogota Convention Bureau.

Asian convention bureau landscape:
- The Asian landscape still includes a large number of developing countries; nonetheless successful examples of CBs are quality examples for future CBs; and
- Best practices: Malaysia Convention & Exhibition Bureau, Singapore Exhibition & Exhibition Bureau.

Introduction

The ETC/UNWTO study on the decision-making process of meetings, congresses, conventions and incentives (MCCI) organizers, is valued as an important step for understanding and developing strategies for Europe and other parts of the world.

Witnessing the growth of this key economic sector over the years, various studies such as the 2013 ICCA survey *A Modern History of International Association Meetings 1963–2012,*[1] Advito's 2015 annual *Industry Forecast,*[2] American Express's 2015 industry forecast[3] or the 2014 *MPI Meeting Outlook survey,*[4] clearly indicate optimism for the industry.

The global MCCI industry, dominated by Europe and North America, continues to grow in many markets across all segments. The association conventions and congresses segment, dominated by Europe is witnessing a shift towards emerging nations, primarily driven by investment in new facilities and technologies. Corporate meetings are witnessing marginal growth, despite a rise in virtual meetings, led by a rebound in Asia and the Pacific and emerging destinations. And the incentives segment is witnessing growth led by a rise in corporate budgets, demand for new offerings and value-for-money packages.

The purpose of this comprehensive study is to provide a better understanding of the MCCI industry and the way meeting and event organizers make decisions. The findings of the study will feed into the ETC's long-term strategy 'Destination Europe 2020' and will provide an input for NTO activities in the MCCI segments. The objectives of business events are wide reaching and the benefits are far greater than the tourism spend alone. These 'beyond tourism benefits' are varied and include a convergence between the world's leading experts – international knowledge, expertise and best practices – and local sector researchers and practitioners in the same fields.

The report is divided into three phases. The first phase offers a strategic review of the MCCI industry, setting base for the following two phases by defining the MCCI segments: association conventions and congresses, corporate meetings and corporate incentive programmes and by presenting an exhaustive taxonomy and segment overview. The second phase captures relevant insights, analysing the decision-making processes of MCCI organizers and offering a clear overview of typologies of decision-making processes for each segment. The third and final phase benchmarks and presents best practices in national and local tourism organizations (convention bureaux), entities that act as important players in the development of destinations' MCCI industry.

1   International Congress and Convention Association (2013b), *A Modern History of International Association Meetings 1963–2012,* ICCA, Amsterdam.

2   Advito (2014), *Industry Forecast 2015* (online), available at www.advito.com (08-06-2015).

3   Sherry, Y. (2014), *2015 Global Meetings and Events Forecast, American Express Global Business Travel* (online), available at: www.imexamerica.com/media/517556/Yma-Sherry-2015-Global-Meetings-Trends.pdf (08-06-2015).

4   Meeting Professionals International (2014), *MPI Meetings Outlook,* spring edition, MPI.

In order to provide a comprehensive picture of the decision-making processes in the area of meetings, congresses, conventions and incentives, primary and secondary research was carried-out, focusing on the European market and with comparisons from the North American and Asian markets. Primary research was conducted in two phases. First surveys were sent to 300 people, receiving 120 answers. Second, phone interviews were conducted in two sets. The first step of the phone interviews, which included 25 participants, aimed at gaining a deeper understanding of planners' decision-making processes. And the second set of phone interviews, aimed at identifying which criteria were most important for decision-making once basic criteria are met. The primary research targeted a representative sample of planers in Europe, North America and Asia.

As the MCCI continues to grow, reflecting on these findings can offer additional valuable information for the development of strategies for European destinations.

About this study

The European Travel Commission (ETC) and the World Tourism Organization (UNWTO) commissioned a comprehensive study on the decision-making process of meetings, conventions, congresses and incentives planners. The purpose of the study is to gain meaningful information on the dynamics of a growing segment in the overall tourism sector and to allow ETC member countries to gain an insight on organizers' expectations and needs and the factors influencing the decision-making process. The insights obtained from the study will feed into the development of ETC's long-term strategy "Destination Europe 2020".

The study has the following four main objectives:
1. Achieve a better understanding of the meetings, congresses, conventions and incentives industries in the form of an exhaustive taxonomy and segment overview;
2. Provide a map of the market conditions including key players;
3. Outline the expectations and needs of organizers and in particular their decision-making process; and
4. Provide best practice examples from selected National Tourism Organizations (NTOs), public congress bureaux, city or regional tourist boards or other relevant.

Phase 1
Strategic review

Chapter 1

MCCI industry overview

As an introduction to the study, the purpose of phase 1 is to provide a strategic review of the meetings, congresses, conventions and incentives (MCCI) industry, through an exhaustive taxonomy and segment overview, in order to achieve a better understanding the meetings, congresses, conventions and incentives industries.

The strategic review describes the different segments, the market landscape for each, event and venue types, roles and activities of key players, relevant markets and provides the key elements that define the decision-making processes. Whenever possible, it provides key statistical information on each of the three segments: association conventions and congresses, corporate meetings and corporate incentives.

In the wake of the global financial crisis in 2008–2009, a consensus is forming that meetings, events and business travel will continue to remain critical drivers assisting organizations in their efforts to reach their strategic business objectives and effectively communicate with their members, employees, customers and partners worldwide.

More and more destinations are investing resources in this growing sector because they recognise its potential to create positive economic impact. This is particularly true in the developing world, where there has been a massive development boom in hotels, convention centres, fully-integrated facilities, transportation systems and the like, in order to attract business events.

As the MCCI continues to grow in many markets around the world, there is increased competition for market share, and it becomes crucial to understand the key factors that influence decisions about where to hold meetings, conventions and incentives.

This is a strategic issue for European destinations, particularly in the light of the increasingly competitive environment in the MCCI industry.

Key messages:
- As part of the broader tourism sector, the MCCI industry is finding growing recognition around the globe;
- Composed of three distinctive categories including associations conventions and congresses, corporate meetings and incentives, the industry supplements the economy through visitors spending, social contributions and is a catalyst for economic and intellectual engagement;
- The increased recognition and understanding of the importance of the MCCI industry is stimulating investment and engaging countries in becoming more attractive for business events;

– The association conventions and congresses segment is less influenced by economic instabilities, but is experiencing some changes in participants' demand and competition between associations;

– The corporate meetings segment is sensitive to the rising usage of virtual meetings;

– The incentive segment is growing, as corporates understand the importance of motivational rewards;

– All three segments are experiencing a number of changes, to which key players need to react to, in order to respond to new demands; and

– The recovering economy coupled with rising supply and demand from emerging countries are stimulating growth, however cautious spending due to economic uncertainty and changes in demand and technology are a source of concern for the industry.

1.1 Description and background of MCCI industry

The tourism sector includes leisure and business tourism. Today the MCCI industry is finding increasing recognition across the globe and is gaining market share. For the purpose of better understanding key areas of the industry the three main segments of association conventions and congresses, corporate meetings, and corporate incentives, need to be defined. Destinations increasingly understand the importance of hosting these meetings as they represent a vital form of global engagement – both economic and intellectual. MCCI is thus becoming part of economic development strategies. Understanding what key trends and players influence the industry is essential for developing better services, which fulfil the needs of the ever-changing environment.

Figure 1.1   **MCCI industry within the tourism sector**

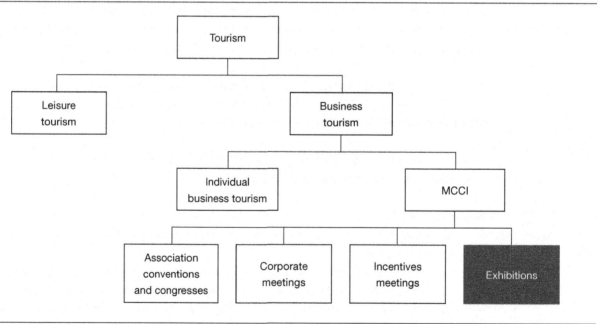

1.1.1   The meetings industry: definitions

The meetings industry comprises four components – association conventions and congresses, corporate meetings, incentives and exhibitions. The meetings industry (sometimes referred to as the meetings, incentives, conferences and exhibitions – or 'MICE' sector) includes: activities based on the organization, promotion, sales and delivery of meetings and events; products and services that include corporate, association and government meetings, corporate incentives, seminars, congresses, conferences, conventions events, exhibitions and fairs.[1]

Among the four key components – association conventions and congresses, corporate meetings, incentives and exhibitions, this report focuses on the three first segments of the industry, yet the following table offers a description for each segment.

The decision-making process of the exhibition segment is fundamentally different from the other segments. The key elements driving decision-making are access to the market and the quality of infrastructure. Given that this segment widely differs form the others, the study will review the decision-making process in the meetings, congresses, conventions and incentives (MCCI) segments.

---

1   World Tourism Organization (2006), *Measuring the Economic Importance of the Meetings Industry – Developing a Tourism Satellite Account Extension,* UNWTO, Madrid.

Table 1.1   **Meetings industry components**

Association conventions and congresses	Corporate meetings	Incentive programmes	Exhibitions
Definitions			
– Meetings/conferences-congresses hosted by associations and multilateral bodies; – These events are designed for discussions and information sharing; and – Government meetings (included as a subset).	Corporate meetings/seminars/events organized on an ad-hoc or periodic basis (does not include in-house meetings).	– A global management tool that uses an exceptional travel experience to motivate and/or recognise participants for increased levels of performance in support of organizational goals; and – It can be clubbed with a meeting or offered as travel only.	– A global mB2B and B2C events, where products and services are displayed; and – These events facilitate product launches, buyer-seller meetings and market entry.
Information availability			
– Global regional and country level statistics on number of international association meetings from the ICCA, UIA and IAPCO; and – Qualitative information on trends, drivers/barriers and determinants.	– Global corporate/government meetings statistics available from American Express Meetings forecast and Reeds; and – Qualitative information on trends, drivers and barriers and key determinants.	– Qualitative information on trends impacting incentive travel, drivers and barriers, and key determinants (information on global /regional market size is not available); and – SITE and IRF offer statistics.	– Global and regional statistics on exhibition space from UFI; and – Qualitative information on trends, driver and barriers, and key determinants.

Notes: IAPCO = International Association of Professional Congresses; ICCA = International Conventions and Congresses Association; IRF = Incentive Research Foundation; SITE = Society for Incentive Travel Excellence; UIA = Union of International Associations; UFI = Union of International Fairs.

Source: Compilation based on International Congress and Convention Association (2014).

1.1.2   Detailed description of segment and sub-segments

Segmentation is a process by which the market is divided in the distinct parts that behave in a similar way or have similar needs.

There are several attributes that can be used in the process of the market segmentation:
- Event type:
    - Association conventions and congresses;
    - Corporate meetings; and
    - Corporate incentives.

- Organizational type:
  - Association conventions and congresses – clients are professional, business, trade associations;
  - Corporate meetings and incentives – clients are companies and corporations; and
  - Governmental meetings – clients are governmental institutions on a different level.
- Geographical region:
  - Local;
  - National;
  - Regional or transnational level; and
  - International.

In the context of this report, segments are defined in terms of event type.

Association conventions and congresses

Associations are typically not-for-profit organizations devoted to education, industry development and influencing government policy as it relates to the industry. The Convention Industry Council (CIC) defines associations as an organized group of individuals and/or companies who band together to accomplish a common purpose, usually to provide for the needs of its members. These organizations usually organize annual, biannual or multiyear conventions (also known as congresses or conferences); one can speak about professional, business, trade, political, social, educational, scientific, religious, and other conventions and congresses, each with their individual objectives. A wide range of professions have associations; the most lucrative in terms of the numbers of associations, their size and spend are medical – 17%, technological – 14% and scientific – 13%.[2]

Association conventions and congresses consist of international governmental organizations and international non-governmental organizations (associations).[3]

The primary source for information on the international association conventions and congresses market is derived from the International Convention and Congress Association (ICCA). ICCA maintains data on international association conventions and congresses that meet the following criteria: the meeting being attended by at least 50 participants, it is organized on a regular basis, lasts for a minimum of 2 days, has at least 40% of the participants from overseas and must at least rotate to 3 different countries.[4]

The Union of International Associations (UIA) also analyses international meetings market, however the criteria used differs from ICCA's. There is a significant overlap between the two sets of data, the main difference being that UIA's events includes those held in a fixed location, whereas all of ICCA's events must rotate.

Association conventions and congresses have a relatively long lead-time; it is not unusual to find lead times of 5 years or more. Moreover, it is estimated that a growing minority of about 25–30% of

2   International Congress and Convention Association (2013b).

3   Ibid.

4   International Congress and Convention Association (2013a), *2013 Country and City Rankings,* ICCA, Amsterdam.

the decision-making processes no longer include an official bidding procedure, but have "central initiator" who selects the location and venues based on pre-determined and strict criteria.[5]

Dominated by Europe and North America, the association conventions and congresses segment is now seeing a shift towards emerging nations, primarily driven by investment in new facilities and technology and upgrading of tourism infrastructure. Along with the world's interest in engaging in emerging markets, generation change is a key driver in this growth. As Baby Boomers retire, Generation X and Y are taking over. They are connected and ROI (return on investment) focused. Associations are becoming more and more globalized and seeking engagement in new markets and in the developing world.

Additionally, the association world is now seen as tri-polar in terms of the association conventions and congresses' rotation policies, i.e., with Europe, Africa and Middle East as one pole, the Americas as the second pole followed by the Asia and the Pacific. This means that there is more competition around the globe concerning where association conventions and congresses will take place. The rotation of associations is generally based on two factors, either because of potential for future, or because of events happening in that area.

Figure 1.2   **The tri-polar world for association conventions and congresses**

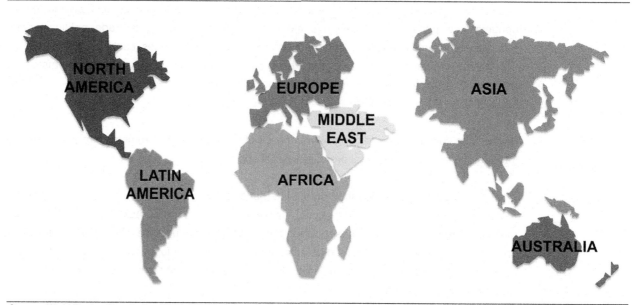

Source: World Tourism Organization (2012), *MICE Industry – An Asia-Pacific Perspective*, UNWTO, Madrid.

Europe still remains the most popular region attracting the highest number of meetings per region in 2013; however the percentage of meeting organized there has marginally dropped since 2009.

---

5   International Congress and Convention Association (2013b).

Figure 1.3   **Global and regional association conventions and congresses industry, 2003–2013**

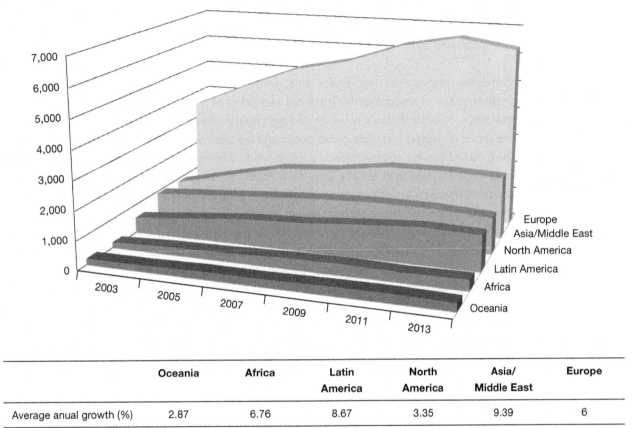

	Oceania	Africa	Latin America	North America	Asia/ Middle East	Europe
Average anual growth (%)	2.87	6.76	8.67	3.35	9.39	6

Note: North America includes México; Latin America includes the Caribbean, Central and South America.

Sources: International Congress and Convention Association (2013a).

Usually, association conventions and congresses are regular meetings organized by associations in specific destinations destination. Association conventions and congresses bring together members with common professional, scientific or social interests. They can be national, regional or international, can be large or small and use meetings for educational reasons and as a way for their members to network. Many international association conventions and congresses also included an exhibition related to the subject of the convention. In most instances these meetings are also key revenue generators for the association.

Association conventions and congresses are frequently large and produce high numbers of delegates, hotel room nights and spending. Since many delegates are international visitors, these events generate significant economic benefits for the host destination. Industry studies have consistently shown over time that the international association market has grown moderately from year to year, and has been relatively stable over the past few decades in relation to other visitor markets. Association conventions and congresses tend to be the component of the business tourism market least affected by economic fluctuations and world events.

Corporate meetings

For the purposes of this report, corporate meetings are defined as meetings held for planning and organizational purposes, excluding any incentive element. If a meeting has an incentive element, it is considered an incentive programme.

Corporate meetings are high-end events, which are direct contributors to communicating a positive image of the company. There are two types of corporate meetings, internal meetings that focus on organizational activities and are usually small scale, and external meetings which are aimed at a larger and more global public and are used as a tool for communicating directly to the group of interest and customers, such as product launches. The corporate meeting segment uses large budgets and usually aims to impress. Because large corporate meetings can be complex, involving larger groups and more intermediaries companies often outsource some of the organization to other meeting planners. On the other hand, internal corporate meetings are generally organized by in-house corporate planners and use their own resources to hold meetings. Major markets, population centres and corporate headquarter cities are the most popular destinations for corporate meetings. The benefit to corporate meetings is that they plan meetings with shorter lead times, and represent a very high spending, lucrative end of the market.

Information and data about corporate meetings can be more difficult to access, however comprehensive reports are available from IAPCO and American Express, amongst others. In 2013 IAPCO handled a total of 3329 global corporate meetings.[6]

The changing environment and evolving industry affect the corporate meetings segment. The global financial crisis has pushed planners to be more vigilant with their budgets and has triggered them to focus more on return on investment of their events. The segment is generally experiencing growth, however American Express and Advito respondents are expecting this growth to be mostly within regions. And, as MCCI industry continues to evolve, corporate meeting participants are demanding for 'closer to home' destinations and a better integration of new technologies and social media; and experts view that the market will rebound led by Asia and the Pacific, emerging and BRIC[7] destinations.

> "The number of corporate meetings will grow steadily in 2014, rather than spectacularly".
>
> Advito (2013), *Industry Forecast 2014*

Incentives

Incentives are events planned by corporations who reward certain employees (usually sales people and/or distributors) for high levels of performance. They are very lucrative events, as they can involve large numbers of people, being entertained at large expense and often scheduled with relatively short lead times. Incentives often focus on "sun and sea" destinations, or cities that have

---

6   International Association of Professional Congress Organisers (2013), *Annual Survey 2013,* IAPCO, Freshwater.

7   Advito (2014).

'EIBTM Trend Watch Report Indicates Growth for 2014' (2014), *International Meetings Review,* 18-11-2014 (online), available at: www.internationalmeetingsreview.com (08-06-2015).

BRIC countries are: Brazil, Russian Federation, India and China.

world leading destination appeal for activities like shopping, sightseeing and entertainment, yet there is a growing trend towards destinations which offer cultural experiences. At the same time, the cities in question must have highly developed incentive products to be successful.

The concern of international healthcare meetings evolving to meet the pressures to become more transparent, more educationally effective and still remain financially viable, take integral part of what is known as the Pharma code. As medical business events become more modest, delegates are also experiencing cuts in their sponsorship and financial support. As a result, the Pharma code is steering incentives away from resort type destinations, and increasing the trend for incentives to incorporating a meeting component to their programmes.

In a period of crisis, the incentive market is strongly affected. Research from relevant institutions reveals some of the latest trends on the incentive market. Indicators widely suggest that the incentive market recovered slightly in 2013, though not as much as other parts of the MCCI industry.[8] Planners are feeling more positive for 2015.[9] Trends show that the Asian market has been flourishing, while western markets have been sluggish. Reflecting the caution that characterised corporate spending, Advito's research (2013)[10] – the consulting arm of BCD Travel, the world's third-largest travel management company (headquartered in Dallas and operates around the world) – suggest that incentives also changed in the following ways:

– The average number of nights per trip has fallen from 6.5 to 4;
– Almost the only incentive trips which have survived are those with a well-defined ROI, such as a sales scheme;
– Although still very desirable, trips are less extravagant than in the past;
– Primary target destinations tend to be domestic or shorter haul international. However, there is a growing interest and activity in longer haul international, downgrading from business class to economy. In some cases, hotel standards have moved one tier down, from luxury to upper-upscale;
– There is now nearly always a business element to the trip, such as discussions about corporate strategy and direction; and
– There may well also be a "corporate giving" or corporate social responsibility (CSR) element to the trip, such as a team-building project that supports a local charity or community.

Some views on incentive travel market:

> "The programmes are still motivating. They're still creating experiences that are memorable and meaningful. But some of the incentives that were there before, like round-trip transfers or room gifts, aren't there anymore."
>
> Melissa Van Dyke, President, International Research Foundation

---

8 QRA Analytics (2013), *IRF Pulse Survey – Fall 2013*, International Research Foundation, 16-12-2013 (online), available at: (online), available at: http://theirf.org/research/irf-full-pulse-survey---fall-2013/99/ (08-06-2015).

9 van Dyke, M. (2015), *Rebounding the Recession: 10 Trends Paint A Picture of The Future of Incentive Travel 2015*, International Research Foundation, 07-02-2015 (online), available at: http://theirf.org/research/rebounding-the-recession-10-trends-paint-a-picture-of-the-future-of-incentive-travel-2015/87/ (08-06-2015).

10 Advito (2013), *Industry Forecast 2014* (online), available at: www.vdr-service.de/fileadmin/der-verband/fachthemen/studien/advito_industryforecast2014.pdf (08-06-2015).

"We will witness a radical shift in technology applications, growth in global service companies and also significantly higher expectations of channel participants from the incentive or loyalty initiative".

David Sand, President, Society for Incentive Travel Excellence International, December 2013[11]

"Whether it's taking the five senses and applying them to meeting design or appealing to multiple generations in a single event space, today's planners are keenly aware that incentive travel experiences go much deeper than excursions and entertaining speakers".

Melissa van Dyke, President, International Research Foundation, 2015[12]

Summary of segments and MCCI industry

Leisure tourism and the MCCI industries, although sharing some common infrastructure (e.g., airlines, hotels, and restaurants) have different characteristics and needs. Both have their own distinct features and require different approaches and expertise.

Table 1.2   **Comparisons between leisure tourism and business events/MCCI**

	Leisure tourism	**Business events and MCCI**
Audience	Consumers/general public, priority by geographic markets, tourism segmentation and propensity to travel.	Associations and corporations, priority by Head Offices locations, business centres and opportunities.
Supply chain	Wholesalers, consolidators, travel agents, online booking systems, inbound tour operators.	PCOs, DMCs, exhibition management companies, event management companies, corporate agents, incentive house.
Product	Attractions, tours, shopping, restaurants, retail, accommodation.	Venues, event management, accommodation, transport, technology plus tourism.
Motivators	Destination appeal, fun/self-actualisation.	Strength of local industry and host (local association), infrastructure, capacity, business-to-business opportunities, professional development, alignment with organizational goals.
Core competencies	Marketing, product packaging and promotion, servicing.	Sales, lobbying and promotion, negotiation.
Participants	Leisure travellers/tourists.	Delegates, exhibitors, trade visitors, high corporate achievers, professionals and business people.
Market approach	Advertising, public relations, e-marketing, collateral support, packaging, press and trade actions.	CRM, direct sales, bid process, media and public relations, event promotion.

11 Society for Incentive Travel Excellence (2013), *The Annual Analysis and Forecast for the Motivational Events Industry,* SITE (online), available at: www.siteglobal.com (09-06-2015).

12 van Dyke, M. (2015).

In some destinations, tourism bodies (ministries or national or local tourist offices) have responsibility to develop the MCCI industry. Some other destinations establish convention bureaux that are independent entities, which can report to the tourism ministry or economic development ministry. In 0, best practices of local, regional and national convention bureaux will be elaborated. In addition to supplementing the local economy through direct visitors spends as tourism does, the MCCI industry is also considered a catalyst for economic and intellectual engagement. This is especially true in the case of hosting international association conventions and congresses which provide opportunities to learn from, as well as to form research and trade links, with the world's thought leaders who converge at the hosting destination.

Table 1.3   **Key characteristics of the segments**

Types	Markets	Needs
Association conventions and congresses		
– Trade;	– International rotation; and	– 72% under 500 pax;
– Professional;	– Regional rotation.	– Good air access;
– User groups; and		– Adequate plenary and meeting space;
– Federations.		– Sufficient room blocks near venue (4- and 5-star);
		– Destination appeal;
		– Experience local suppliers (ground operators);
		– Value;
		– Strong local host; and
		– New market reach.
Corporate meetings		
– Business meetings;	– Multinational corporation (MNC) headquarter cities; and	– 89% under 500 pax;
– Seminars/training;		– Integrated facilities;
– Retreats;	– National.	– Accommodation;
– Team building;		– Quality hotels;
– AGMs;		– Quality food;
– Launches; and		– High level service; and
– User groups.		– Golf, team building.
Incentive programmes		
– High-end leisure;	– National;	– Destination appeal;
– Incentives with meeting component;	– Regional; and	– Fully integrated hotel and meeting space;
	– International.	– High quality 4- and 5-star facilities;
– Team building; and		– Unique venues;
– Sectors: Insurance, IT and electronics, automotive, pharmaceuticals, etc.		– High quality food and service;
		– Activities – themed events, golf, team building, unique and high quality experiences;
		– Ease of access; and
		– Cost competitive.

1.1.3   Global and regional trends affecting segments

The global environment

The global business event industry is recovering from the slump caused by the recession, driven primarily by Asia, Middle Eastern, South American and emerging economies. Companies are cautious about spending on business events and demanding more personalised and value-for-money offerings, which is resulting in new opportunities and potential for the business events industry in emerging economies.

The global business events industry, dominated by Europe and North America, is witnessing recovery across all MCCI segments:

–   Association conventions and congresses segment, dominated by Europe, is witnessing a shift towards emerging nations, primarily driven by investment in new facilities and technology as well as new market engagement and membership growth;

–   Corporate meetings are expected to witness marginal growth, despite a rise in virtual meetings, led by rebound in Asia and the Pacific and emerging destinations; and

–   Incentives segment, is expected to witness stabilising budgets, increasing for some, led by rise in corporate budget, demand for new offerings and value-for-money packages.

Asia, Middle East, Africa and South America witnessed strong growth in the number of international conventions and congresses, despite the contraction in number of conventions and congresses globally. Essentially, emerging players, particularly China and Brazil, are taking initiatives to become popular MCCI destinations. Cities in emerging countries such as Dubai, Beijing, Shanghai and Istanbul have enhanced their infrastructure capabilities for business events and are aggressively promoting themselves as destinations for business events. Convention bureaux both at a national and city level are expected to play a key role in bringing new events.

Moreover, with economic recovery, the business events market is shifting towards a sellers' market; however, companies are increasingly focusing on ROI while selecting a destination. The duration of business events and number of participants/attendees have seen a decline and a similar trend is expected in the short-term across all segments of the MCCI industry.

Companies are increasingly focusing on value-for-money deals, either by choosing closer to home destinations, shifting to 4-star hotels, or conducting virtual meetings. Additionally, consumers are showing increased preference for personalised offerings across MCCI segments. The *2014 Global Meetings and Events Forecast*[13] and the Advito *Industry Forecast 2014*[14] confirm that business events are staying close to home. For example, corporations based in Europe will hold events on the continent, and in countries that are close geographically. Compliance, cost, and travel time are all noted as top drivers of this trend, as companies likely continue to seek alternative ways to control costs and reduce time away from office.

Finally, international associations are targeting emerging countries for holding their meetings, as they expand their membership base in new regions, such as Eastern Europe, Asia, Africa, and

---

13   American Express Meetings & Events (2013), *2014 Global Meetings and Events Forecast* (online), available at: www.congreswereld.nl/files/documents_upload/documents_upload_2013/2014_Meetings_Forecast_FINAL_US.pdf (08-06-2015).

14   Advito (2013).

Middle East. MNCs, looking to target consumer base, are also focusing on establishing their business networks in these economies through exhibitions and meetings. Corporate Social Responsibility (CSR) and environmental impact, as key criterion for choosing destination, provides ample opportunities to some countries.

1.2   Overall drivers and barriers

Drivers	Barriers
A recovering global economy, along with the rising supply and demand from emerging economies are driving growth for the global business events industry:	However, cautious spending by corporates due to economic uncertainty, changes in technology, and global inflation remain as primary areas of concern:

Drivers

A recovering global economy, along with the rising supply and demand from emerging economies are driving growth for the global business events industry:

- **Recovering global economy:** post the economic crisis, the global economy is recovering, with the global GDP witnessing 3.1% year on year growth in 2014, a slight increase in growth rates in 2013;

- **Increasing demand from emerging economies:** corporates from emerging economies such as BRIC and Middle Eastern countries are increasing their spend on business events;

- **Increasing investment by emerging economies in the business events industry:** emerging economies, such as China, Brazil, the United Arab Emirates (Abu Dhabi and Dubai) and Qatar, are investing in attracting more business events to their respective countries, which is driving the growth in global business events industry; and

- **Need for business networking:** increasing focus on establishing business networks, particularly in emerging countries is driving demand for face-to-face interaction among business professional, which is facilitated by business events.

Barriers

However, cautious spending by corporates due to economic uncertainty, changes in technology, and global inflation remain as primary areas of concern:

- **Economic uncertainty:** despite economic recovery, corporates are still uncertain about the global economic outlook (particularly in Europe) and are cautious about allocating significant budgets to business events;

- **Declining attendance:** the attendance of overseas delegates/participants/visitors in business events has witnessed a declining trend, post the economic recession, which is expected to continue in the short-term; and

- **Increasing costs:** hike in hotel prices, air fares, and suppliers' costs are expected to have a dampening effect on the growth of the business events industry.

1.3   Social contribution of MCCI

MCCI or business events, deliver a return on investment far beyond the significant direct visitor expenditure. This is because of the diverse nature of professions and industries that conduct business events covering both public and private sectors, particularly the areas of medical research, science, technology and industry, which account for about 53% of all international association conventions and congresses.[15] Business events are an integral part of most governments' economic development plan providing a range of strategic benefits including:

- The opportunity for export and trade promotion, and investment;
- The ability to lift the regional and international profile of the city and nation as a centre of innovation and expertise in specific fields;
- The development of local knowledge and expertise through education and training provided by business events;

---

15   International Congress and Convention Association (2013b).

- The engagement with the international business and professional community, developing business networks and opportunities;
- The encouragement of knowledge exchange to achieve world best practices; and
- The initiations of programmes and legacies that benefit communities in general.

The below figure summarises the "virtuous circle" of positive impacts that the development of the business events sector can have on a destination.

Figure 1.4   **"Virtuous circle" of social impact on business events for destinations**

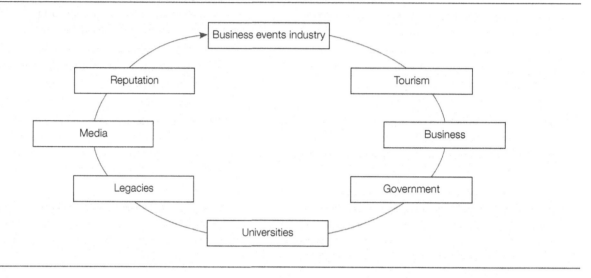

Figure 1.5 illustrates how participant and non-participant spending on meetings, travel and tourism and other meetings-related commodities affects the defined industries, which in turn, contributes to value added and additional spending by other industry suppliers.

Figure 1.5   **Spending and value added**

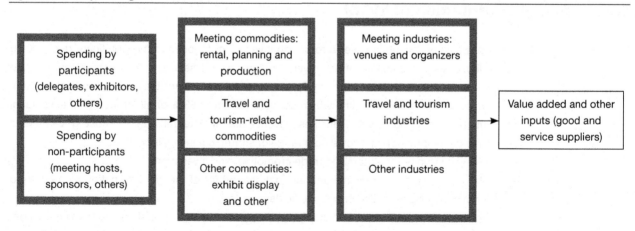

Source: Pricewaterhouse Coopers LLP (2014), *The Economic Significance of Meetings to the U.S. Economy – Interim Study Update for 2012,* Tampa (online), available at: www.conventionindustry.org (02-10-2015).

1.4   Economic contribution of MCCI

The implications of the trade effects from business travel are. Trade not only generates income for companies but also advances economic development by lowering prices, creating economies of scale, allowing countries to focus on areas of comparative advantage, spurring innovation and creating competition. The causality works in both directions: while business performances does influence travel budgets in the short term, there is long-term impact of business travel on overall business performance. In other words, business travel, as a catalyst of global trade, plays a significant role in driving faster GDP growth, improving standards of living and creating jobs.

Figure 1.6   **Relationship between business travel and trade**

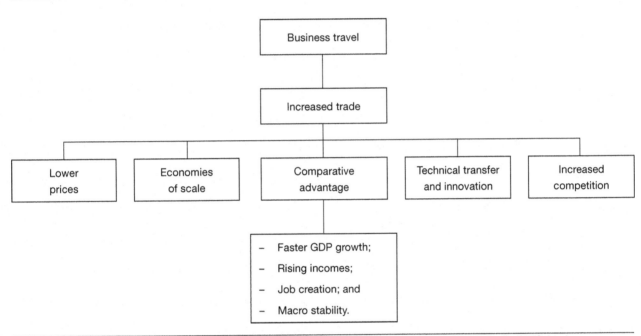

Source: World Travel & Tourism Council (2014), *Travel and Trade Linkages: Analysis of trends worldwide & within Asia-Pacific*, WTTC, London.

Differences across regions are partly determined by the industry composition of countries within each region. Typically, emerging markets, which are receptive to growth in key productivity sectors, see stronger response to business travel.

The World Travel & Tourism Council report[16] shares an extensive analysis of the benefits of business travel on the economy, mainly through trade. Globally, the study identifies that, on average, business travel yields high ROI and suggests that travel does generate trade over time.

---

16 World Travel & Tourism Council (2014).

Table 1.4   **Trade and business travel by country**

Country	Inbound business travel vs. imports causality (% confidence)			Outbound business travel vs. exports causality (% confidence)		
	Correlation	Travel causes trade (%)	Trade causes travel (%)	Correlation	Travel causes trade (%)	Trade causes travel (%)
United States of America	0.87	95	26	0.65	82	86
Canada	0.92	100	99	0.85	98	87
United Kingdom	0.54	65	85	0.61	95	80
France	0.49	57	85	0.63	61	92
Germany	0.97	90	81	0.69	60	98
Italy	0.52	99	100	0.17	58	99
Spain	0.20	75	99	0.74	91	80
Japan	0.91	97	53	0.40	74	92
China	0.32	92	95	0.67	90	99
Russian Federation	0.83	50	90	0.52	100	95
Brazil	0.57	100	100	0.98	88	87
India	0.72	84	66	0.46	99	58
United Arab Emirates	0.42	83	49	0.82	95	64
Singapore	0.70	96	94	0.74	83	53
Hong Kong, China	0.67	95	100	0.43	86	78

Source: World Travel & Tourism Council (2014).

Chapter 2

Association conventions and congresses: analysis and profile

This section provides a detailed description of the segment of association conventions and congresses, identifying characteristics, key trends, players, decision-making processes, the supply chain and other main areas of activity. It includes an overview of key trends in Europe, North America, Asia and other Regions.

2.1 Characteristics and activity

2.1.1 Event types

Association conventions and congresses are separated into international/global, regional/transnational, national and government meetings. Hereafter is a description of each meeting type.

International

International association conventions and congresses include meetings organized by international organizations and non-governmental organizations. New generations X and Y, along with increasing interconnectedness, access to social media and new technologies, are affecting the distribution of the association segment. Europe remains one of the leading regions of the world for association conventions and congresses, not only in number of events held, but also in overall growth. As the world slowly separates into a tri-polar area – in terms of the conventions' rotation policies – international association conventions and congresses are experiencing more competition around the globe.

Regional/trans-national

Regional association conventions and congresses are the first level of transnational association conventions and congresses and represent a very large market in some parts of Europe, especially if countries in the same region have strong cooperation policies in business, science, or education. A good example is Scandinavia with large number of Scandinavian association conventions and congresses rotating around Scandinavian countries. There are some other examples: Baltic countries, Balkan countries, Danube region etc. Also, within the European or international associations there are chapters organized on the regional level. Very often they have their chapter meetings within the specific region.

National

National association conventions and congresses are organized on country level. Local associations are far more likely to use secondary destinations than main or capital cities. Local associations may be more cost conscious, and usually their meetings will be somewhat smaller. In addition, they are interested in road networks, rail and transportation links as well as air access.

National association conventions and congresses generally rotate around the country. In that case, a smaller destination with a solid reputation and suitable infrastructure should be able to attract and secure these kinds of meetings.

Government meetings

Government meetings are events at which attendees are civil servants, elected officials or service providers to government entities. Additionally, governmental conferences are technical or political events between governments with the aim of discussing national or international topics. The table below identifies the main characteristics of government meetings.

Table 2.1   **Government meetings characteristics**

Types	Markets	Needs
– Meetings;	– State governments;	– Price sensitive;
– Training and education;	– Federal governments;	– Mainly 4- and some 5-star accommodations;
– Seminars;	– Regional governments; and	
– Functions and dinners; and	– G2G, G2B and G2C meetings.	– Conference, meeting, seminar and event space;
– Conferences.		– Training education rooms (20–50 pax); and
		– Secure venues.

Sources: International Congress and Convention Association (2013b).

International Association of Professional Congress Organisers (2014), *Members' Annual Review 2014,* IAPCO, Freshwater.

There are few statistics about the government meetings market. According to IAPCO, the trend for government meetings was increasing steadily until 2011, before declining in 2012 and 2013. According to IAPCO's annual member survey, the number of government meetings IAPCO members managed fell 14% between 2011 and 2013. 352 governmental meetings were national and 257 international.

Figure 2.1 **Number of government meetings, 2008–2013**

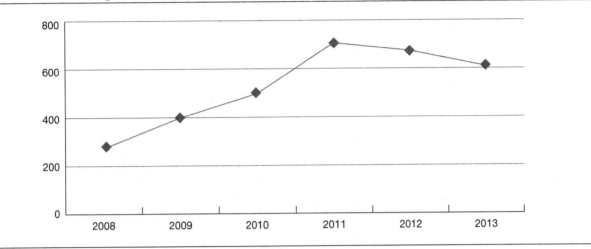

Source: International Association of Professional Congress Organisers (2014).

2.1.2 Subjects of meetings

Generally speaking, the order of the top-10 most popular subjects has been relatively stable all over the decade. The most popular subject by far is still medical science. Second preferred subject over the past ten years has been technology, which went up in popularity over the decade. Although the relative popularity of both industry and education has been fairly stable, Industry subject matter saw a minor decrease and education went up a bit in popularity closing the gap between them.

Figure 2.2   **Number of subjects of meetings for association conventions and congresses, 2004–2013**

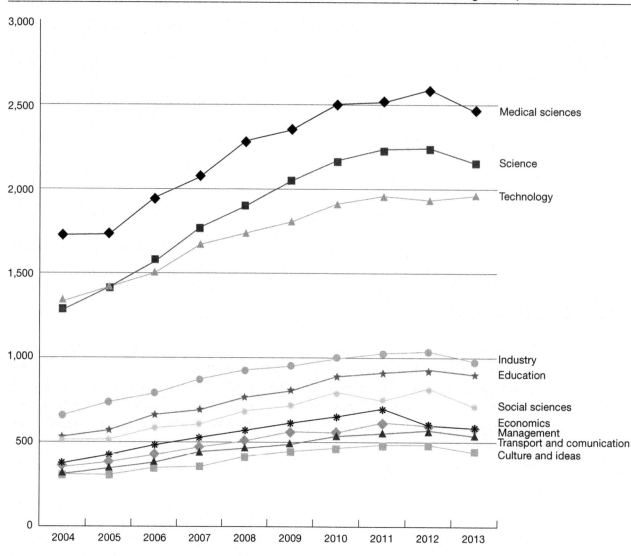

Sources: International Congress and Convention Association (2013a; 2013b).

2.1.3   Venues used

Over the last decade the usage of meeting facilities in hotels has been gradually increasing at the expense of the conference/exhibition centre. Hotels first took over first place as most popular venue in 2005 and have managed to retain first position with almost 43% market share in 2013. Despite the decrease in popularity over the past decade, the conference/exhibition centre is still the second most favourite venue, however universities are rapidly closing the gap. The decrease in usage of conference and exhibition centres is linked to the average downsizing in numbers of participants and shortening of meetings in general. This is also due the development of fully integrated resorts and large scale hotels with on site meeting facilities, and multiple breakout rooms, that are better equipped to handle association conventions and congresses. Fully integrated facilities can provide competitive meeting packages and minimise need for logistical costs and multiple contracting with venues and hotels. The usage of other venues has remained relatively stable throughout the decade. Other venues include castles, boats, theatres etc.

Figure 2.3   **Venues used for association conventions and congresses, 2002–2013 (market share, %)**

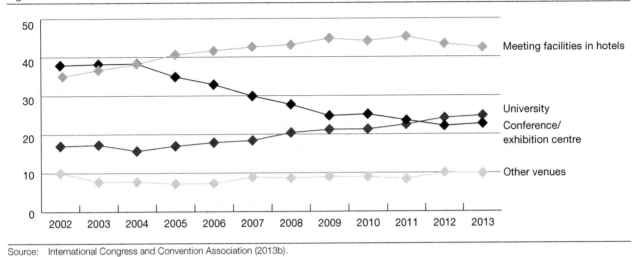

Source: International Congress and Convention Association (2013b).

2.1.4   Activity

Number of association conventions and congresses per region

The allocation of conventions and congresses per regions has been fairly stable over the years. With a majority of 54% of conventions and congresses in 2013, Europe attracted the highest number of conventions and congresses. Both North America and Europe are gaining in popularity, putting an end to the trend of decrease in their market shares ever since 2003. Latin America has also gained in relative popularity with its market share steadily increasing throughout the decade. Despite ups and downs Asia and Middle East have seen a rise in relative popularity over the past decade increasing its competitiveness, whilst Europe and North America have experienced overall declines over the period. Africa and Oceania have stayed rather stable over the years.

Figure 2.4   **Number of conventions and congresses per region, 2002–2013 (market share, %)**

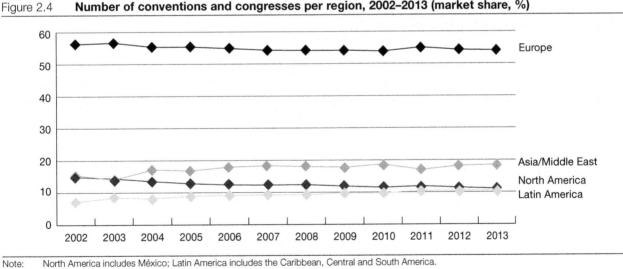

Note: North America includes México; Latin America includes the Caribbean, Central and South America.

Source: International Congress and Convention Association (2013a).

Number of conventions and congresses per country

The 2013 country top-10 showed little change in the number of conventions and congresses per country, with the top-6 repeating their rankings, led by the United States of America, Germany and Spain. The United States of America holds a strong position with a new record of 829 conventions and congresses. Both Germany and the United States of America have been retaining first and second position over the past ten years, with Germany narrowing the gap. Moreover, France, Italy, Spain and the United Kingdom always held places in the top-10. It is interesting to note that two "BRIC" nations, China and Brazil, have moved into the top-10 in 2013.

Table 2.2   **Number of conventions and congresses per country, 2002, 2006 and 2013**

	2002		2006		2013	
	Number of meetings	Rank	Number of meetings	Rank	Number of meetings	Rank
United States of America	599	1	712	1	829	1
Germany	326	2	484	2	722	2
Spain	297	5	436	6	562	3
France	293	6	413	4	527	4
United Kingdom	320	3	430	3	525	5
Italy	301	4	347	5	447	6
Japan	219	7	264	8	342	7
China	134	13	285	7	340	8
Brazil	117	17	228	11	315	9
Netherlands	175	9	236	10	302	10

Source: International Congress and Convention Association (2013b).

Number of conventions and congresses per city

Trends in the number of conventions and congresses per city show that Paris has always held strong advantage. Moreover, next to Vienna and Barcelona only Singapore has managed to attract a number of conventions and congresses that allowed it to be always among top-10 cities in this ranking. Berlin and Lisbon also appear to hold stable positions in the ranking.

Table 2.3   **Number of conventions and congresses per city worldwide, 2002, 2006 and 2013**

	2002		2006		2013	
	Number of meetings	Rank	Number of meetings	Rank	Number of meetings	Rank
Paris, France	93	2	174	1	204	1
Madrid, Spain	52	18	75	20	186	2
Vienna, Austria	76	5	159	2	182	3
Barcelona, Spain	101	1	105	8	179	4
Berlin, Germany	78	4	122	4	178	5
Singapore, Singapore	63	12	131	3	175	6
London, United Kingdom	72	6	112	5	166	7
Istanbul, Turkey	35	32	81	14	146	8
Lisbon, Portugal	61	15	83	13	125	9
Seoul, Republic of Korea	72	7	103	9	125	10

Source: International Congress and Convention Association (2013b).

Number of participants

Across all the different regions, there is a clear trend that international association conventions and congresses are getting smaller over the years (2003–2012).

Figure 2.5   **Average number of participants worldwide, 2003–2013**

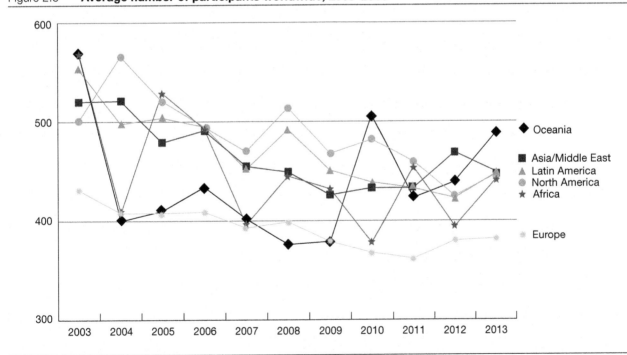

Note: North America includes México; Latin America includes the Caribbean, Central and South America.

Sources: International Congress and Convention Association (2013a; 2013b).

The average number of participants per conventions and congresses reached its lowest point of the past decade in 2011. Since the beginning of the decade the average number of participants per conventions and congresses dropped each year, with exception of the small revivals in 2006 and 2008, continuing the trend of international conventions and congresses getting smaller. The latest trends from 2013 show some slight increase in the average number of participants, yet the general trend of smaller size conventions and congresses is still visible. This is partly due to a greater number of breakout niche events and also due to the development of regional conference markets.

Figure 2.6   **Average number of participants in association conventions and congresses, 2013 (%)**

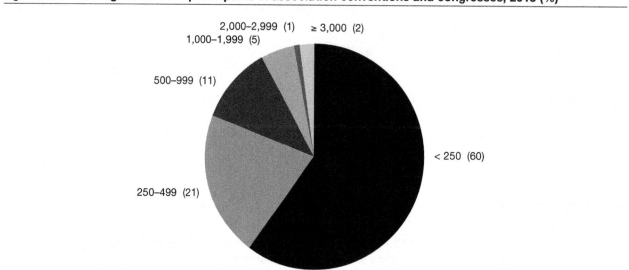

Source: International Congress and Convention Association (2013a).

Despite average meeting sizes getting smaller, the Total Number of Participants has increased exponentially due to the increase in the number of conventions and congresses.

Figure 2.7   **Total number of meetings, 2002–2011**

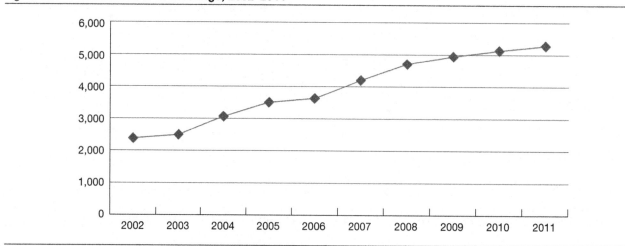

Source: International Congress and Convention Association (2013b).

2.1.5 Duration of events

Frequency of events

By far the largest number of international conventions and congresses is held annually. Furthermore, the relative number of biennial meetings (meaning they take place every 2 years) is gradually dropping over the years (23% in 2010 to 21% in 2013). Generally speaking, it can be said that the relative number of conventions and congresses taking place less often than once a year (e.g., every 3, 4 or 5 years) is decreasing.

Figure 2.8 **Frequency of association conventions and congresses, 2013 (%)**

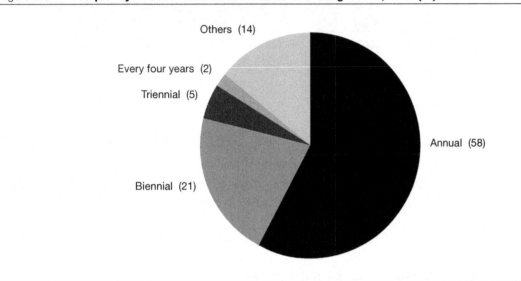

Source: International Congress and Convention Association (2013a).

Average duration of conventions and congresses

There is a trend of gradual decline in average length of conventions and congresses. The average in 2013 was 3.7 days. Although the trend seems to have levelled out this is likely to partially be due to the fact that conventions and congresses that last longer have a longer lead-time and are therefore sooner obtained for statistics purposes. This is partly due to economic conditions where budgets are tighter and time away for delegates is also getting tougher. Delegates are getting time poor and have greater access to data, information and education than ever before.

Figure 2.9   **Average length of association conventions and congresses, 2004–2013 (days)**

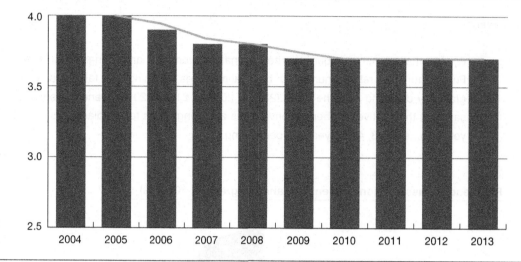

Sources: International Congress and Convention Association (2013a; 2013b).

Rotation of events

The percentage of conventions and congresses that have been rotating worldwide has been decreasing gradually over the past 10 years. Although the world/international is still the biggest rotation area, it is losing ground to meetings rotating in regional areas (of which Europe is biggest, followed by Asia).

Figure 2.10   **Number of events by rotation area by region, 2004–2013**

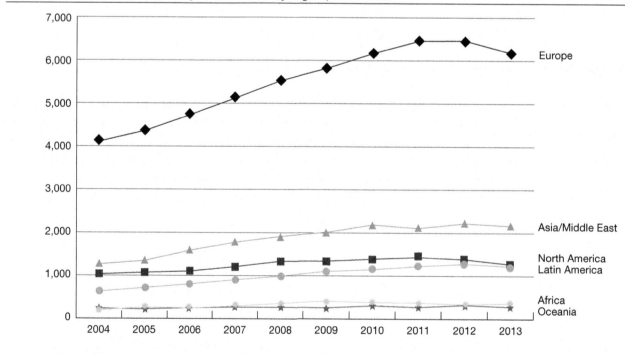

Note: North America includes México; Latin America includes the Caribbean, Central and South America.

Sources: International Congress and Convention Association (2013a; 2013b).

The Europe rotation area is still the second biggest and its market share shows a slow but steady increase throughout the decade as does Europe/North America. Moreover, the Africa/Middle East rotation area has seen an increase in number of conventions and congresses and in number of events that rotate within Latin America, is also experiencing a steady increase since 2006. The number of events, which rotate within Asia and Asia and the Pacific both seem to be stabilising over the past 4 years around 6.1% and 2.9% respectively. This is partly due to the emergence of regional headquarters (HQs) in emerging regions. Destinations are also providing incentives for international associations to set up regional chapters and HQs, i.e., Singapore or Dubai.

2.1.6   Average budget and spend

Meeting revenue here is interpreted as the income that comes mainly from registration fees of participants. Conventions and congresses expenditure on the other hand is costs incurred by participants, where a significant portion is spent on the registration fee.

Figure 2.11   **Aggregate income and expenditure by delegates in the world, 2004–2013 (USD million)**

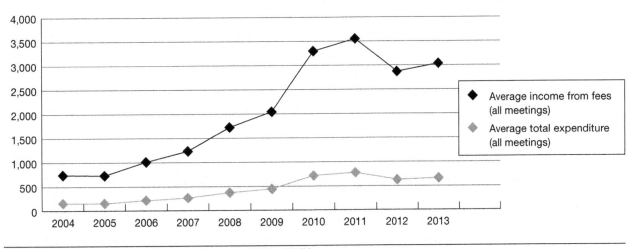

Sources: International Congress and Convention Association (2013a; 2013b).

It can be observed that the participant spending increases again, after the 2011 decrease likely due to general cautionary response to the global economic situation.

Factors that may influence the average fee per delegate per conventions and congresses are: increase of conventions and congresses with less participants (50–149 participants) and decrease in length of events.

2.1.7   Importance of exhibitions at conventions

It has been stated previously that the annual event organized by associations is one of the most important sources of revenue for these organizations. Many associations organize exhibitions as part of their major events, and this aspect of event management can be a significant source of additional income. This is particularly true when the subject matter of the conventions and congresses includes a significant technical component. Many medical conventions and congresses include a large trade show as part of the event.

In the wake of the global financial crisis, many associations have been looking for more ways to develop "non-dues revenue" in order to weather the storm, and as a result the exhibit/trade show aspect has become more and more professionalised.

In addition, the presence of exhibition space can therefore become a significant factor in the choice of a venue, or in the choice of a destination depending on the total meeting/exhibition capacity of its major venue and the potential marketplace for buyers and sellers.

Unfortunately, the exhibition/trade show component of association conventions and congresses is poorly documented in the MCCI literature. There is a wealth of information about conventions and congresses, and about large exhibitions/large trade shows (for example at the large *Messe* across Germany), but the segment attached to conventions and congresses has been overlooked.

A recent survey by the Professional Convention Management Association reveals that 29% of meeting planners are expecting exhibitor growth from 2014–2015 and that the segment has also been generally growing over 2013.[1] However, this survey is focused heavily on the United States market.

2.2   Association conventions and congresses key trends

2012 and 2013 brought optimism back to the conventions and congresses and events industry as associations embark on plans that were initially put on hold during the recession. In 2014, the desire to grow of conventions and congresses and programmes remains; but the uncertainty of the global economy and the financial situation in Europe in particular, is forcing association meeting planners around the world to proceed with caution.

Besides budget challenges, recent studies and literature have revealed further key trends in conventions and congresses that have influenced the market and will likely play a big part in shaping the characteristics of the market in the coming years.

---

1   Russell, M. (2014), 'Convene's 23rd Meetings Market Survey', *Convene,* March 2014, Professional Convention Management Association, p. 43–60 (online), available at: www.convene-digital.org (08-06-2015).

2.3 Perception of value: the new consumer

Meeting budget squeezes remain and will become a financial reality for time to come. Associations are required to now 'do more with less', and many are taking a strategic approach in reviewing the planning and design of their meeting events so as to eliminate unnecessary expenses.[2] Besides having to meet challenges on budgeting issues, associations have to re-evaluate what is considered of 'value' to participants.

The dropping of event attendance of up to 20%[3] is not just due to a squeeze in participant spending. Participants' perception of value has changed significantly – there are increasing demands for active exchange and implementation of knowledge as well as B2B opportunities, which is beyond the usual social networking and educational purposes.

Members and participants want associations to use meetings or conventions and congresses as a platform to support the idea of 'communities of practice' where they can learn more from one another during the event and rely on each other for professional support in a collaborative environment (The National Convention Centre, 2012). The meeting then becomes an effective bridge between the local association and a wider community, engaging even the most distant members.

Such 'communities of practice' are integrated in meetings through the involvement of experts, specialists or practitioners from all over the world to be first introduced to one another during the event, before they embark on a collaboration of a shared task either virtually after the event, or through discussion boards and newsgroups.

This indicates a clear trend toward higher quality association conventions and congresses instead of large quantity with no content or value.[4] So this means associations have to provide valuable content to participants all year round, from playing an organizer role to more of a facilitator or even publisher role.

2.3.1 Content capture/distribution with use of technology

With the amount of content available online and the ability to watch a speaker present virtually, the incentives for participants to travel to attend an association convention and congress has changed over the past years. So it is no surprise that participants want associations to do more in maximising opportunities for learning and information exchange during and after conventions and congresses – through the use of technology.[5] Associations are probably aware of this trend since this has been quite a common feedback, but incorporating technology and/or social media into meetings have been unclear for many meeting planners, and they are also unaware about how to do it effectively.

---

2   INCON (2012), *Fourth Annual INCON Survey of the Global Association Conference Market,* INCON.

3   International Congress and Convention Association (2013a).

4   Meeting Media (2013), *HeadQuarters Magazine* (online), available at: www.headquartersmagazine.com.

5   INCON (2012).

The explosive global use of smartphones and supporting mobile apps are probably key drivers of this trend as participants are taking their own initiative to tweet, blog, post on Facebook, or 'check in' with their own content and opinions relating to the event.[6]

As more associations understanding the need to extend the reach and lifecycle of their meetings, and expand the learning exchange to more people, some of them are currently adopting options that are easily available for integrating technology or social media – from something as easy as Twitter hashtag related to an event, to creating speaker videos, audios and visuals over the web on demand after the association conventions and congresses. Moreover, the emergence of Hybrid Events, combining traditional and new technological applications to stage meetings and events is likely to help transform the association conventions and congresses' landscape.

The fast changing landscape of technology will have a heavy influence on developing forms of knowledge and education transfer, which not only changes the design of a typical association convention/congresses but also the extensiveness of connections that could be made between participants, hosts, speakers, and even sponsors.

2.3.2   Higher expectations of returns on investment (ROI)

Although there are many benefits from association conventions and congresses that are hard to quantify, there is an increasing need for associations and meeting planners to measure the returns on investment (ROI) nonetheless in order to effectively demonstrate their value and relevance to members and participants. Similar to the earlier trends mentioned, members are demanding more value than ever at a time of budget restrictions and cost-containment, so associations are now pressed to demonstrate what could be considered as 'value' and healthy returns. Furthermore, associations are seeing fewer profits[7], so measuring ROI enables them to identify what could be unnecessary expenses and what could be done to attract more participants and revenue.

Some of the common ROI indicators,[8] which many associations are using include:

Table 2.4   **Return on investment (ROI) indicators**

ROI indicators	Description
1. Total attendance	One of the most obvious indicators for associations to know they are doing something right, although it will not tell the whole story.
2 Registration fee from participants	This has been an important indicator for associations for the past years as registration fees (i.e., revenue) have become increasingly one of the primary objectives, and forms a significant bulk of the revenue gained from the event.
3. Response and feedback	Although responses from participants could be fairly inconsistent, it has been a useful way to gather feedback on the quality of event (e.g., programme content and relevance) that are over and beyond the economic aspects.

6   American Express Meetings & Events (2013).

7   International Congress and Convention Association (2013a).

8   Meeting Metrics (2014), *Meetings and Events ROI,* White Paper (online), available at: www.meetingmetrics.com (08-06-2015).

ROI indicators	Description
4. New client leads or contacts gained by participants	This has been an increasingly popular and effective method to measuring ROI as it lies in the quality of leads generated which can be as simple as securing new contacts/names of any other information that benefits the participant.
5. Quality of participants	It has been increasingly common for associations to publish testimonials by participants commenting specifically on the 'quality of other participants' in the event. Getting the right audience is what participants want to strike. The right relationships, which are aligned with their objectives.
6. Learning objectives	This comes from responses from the participants, and establishes a clear indication of whether programme objectives have been met. With participants being keen to be engaged all year round, such survey findings on participants' learning expectations and outcome have to be done both pre- and post- event although most associations are currently doing this right only after event ends.
7. Development of new revenue streams and initiatives	Associations have witnessed some decline in their revenue, and are looking at potential new revenue sources. Besides driving sponsorship numbers and staging concurrent exhibitions (or increasing exhibition numbers), associations are exploring new partnerships, introducing innovative ideas, and expanding into new markets or sectors that are potential new revenue streams.
8. Press/ media coverage	More associations are recognising the positive impact of press and media coverage, and are making this ROI one of their primary objective to drive awareness and performance.
9. Membership growth	A successful association convention or congress event could result in membership growth for the associations, although it could be a gradual progress through continuous engagement. This is an indicator often used by associations who bundle event registration and membership registration together.

All of the above indicators have their place in determining the ROI of association conventions and congresses. Although most associations are not using all of them at the same time, they do utilise a combination of these methods to provide the best outcomes, or rather, the best report card they could show to their stakeholders.

2.3.3   Meeting rotation and selection of destination

There is a clear trend towards regional meetings, where the proportion of meetings that rotate worldwide has been decreasing.[9] Even for association conventions and congresses that do rotate worldwide, there is also a trend where instead of taking 6 to 10 years to return back to the same region, this duration or length of 'waiting time' has been reduced. In other words, there is a general push for meetings to stay 'localised' or 'regionalised' due to two main reasons:

1. **Reduced spending by participants:** the trend towards regional meetings (i.e., within between countries on same continent) implies reduced travel costs, especially for associations whose majority of members come from certain regions. Participants would want to get to and from events affordably and conveniently, so this will definitely influence meeting destinations and locations among other things;[10] and

2. **ROI emphasis over destination selection:** as earlier mentioned, associations are increasingly emphasising on ROI or outcomes of their meetings, rather than destinations

---

9   International Congress and Convention Association (2013a).

10   Sherry, Y. (2014).

alone. The UIA International Association Survey on meeting issues (2013)[11] stated that most respondents do not have a rigid official policy on destination selection or meeting rotation; but rather, it is dependent on case-to-case basis or preferences.

There is increasingly a trend for associations to go for lower costs, smaller destinations that provide personalised service and unique options. In these second-tier cities, meeting planners can afford to splurge because the basics are more affordable. They also receive more attention from the convention bureau, as they are often perceived as the biggest show in town.[12] Participants also benefit from the cost savings and also the fact that they are more focused on the programme than rushing out to catch the sights. In most cases, the important choice for meeting planners is not whether they ultimately select a 'first-tier' or 'second-tier' city, but one that fits the meeting's objectives.

Based on these trends, the key source market for European destinations is the European continent, which boasts the largest concentration of associations on a global scale.

2.3.4   Geographic shift in meetings

The changing environment is also triggering a shift in meeting locations around the globe. For the year 2014, Canada and the United States of America was expected to be relatively flat while Europe, Central and South America, including Mexico, may have even seen slight declines in the total number of meetings. Asia and the Pacific continues to have predicted increases, even though there may be a decline as well in the rate of increment compared to past three years.[13] More than 40% of planners interviewed by American Express[14] seek companies formalising their meetings programmes in one or more BRIC countries, expense policy compliance being at the top of their list.

2.3.5   Risk adversity and safety

Most associations conduct a destination feasibility study with various indicators to assist the final choice destination; and increasingly, concerns regarding safety and security as well as economic and political instability are expected to have a higher impact on the success of the association conventions and congresses.[15]

Some of the recent incidents driving safety and security concerns include political unrest which is happening in Cairo (Egypt), Jordan, Cambodia, Republic of Korea and the Democratic People's Republic of Korea, the Russian Federation and more recently Thailand. The general uncertainty has driven more events to Gulf destinations such as Abu Dhabi and Dubai, as well as parts of Asia.

---

11   Union of International Associations (2013), *2013 Associations Survey – International Meeting Organization and Issues – Final Report,* UIA, Brussels (online), available at: www.uia.org (09-06-2015).

12   Meeting Professionals International (2014).

13   American Express (2013b), *Press Release,* October, available at: http://about.americanexpress.com/news/pr/releases.aspx.

14   Sherry, Y. (2014).

15   'EIBTM Trend Watch Report Indicates Growth for 2014' (2014).

The threats of terrorism, riots and even natural disasters impacting on general participant safety have been paramount for association consideration.

Natural disasters such as the tsunami and earthquake in Japan, Hurricane Sandy in North America, storms and earthquakes in China, and floods in the Philippines have resulted in several association conventions and congresses being delayed or cancelled. The infrastructure damage and economic instability that often results from such events tend to deter participants from attending the meetings even if the latter were to proceed. This inevitably affects the turnout and revenue of the association convention/congress.

Meeting planners will continue to err on the side of caution by choosing destinations that they perceive to be 'safe', and this will continue to influence their meeting destination choices in 2015 and beyond.[16] To avoid some destinations being unnecessarily overlooked, convention and visitor bureaux (CVBs) and destination management companies (DMCs) may need to increase their education efforts to counteract any misinformation regarding certain destinations and locations.

2.3.6   Forging partnerships and alliances

One of the significant trends common to all associations in recent years (and till this date) is their interest to build new alliances and partnerships or extend existing ones. It is estimated that more than 60% of the global associations have planned or are actively doing this.[17] A strategic alliance usually materialises when both associations have compatible or complementary business interests and goals. So it is more common to see this amongst trade associations who have heavier business agendas, rather than professional associations/societies.

For trade associations, the interconnectedness of many industry sectors means that it is increasingly difficult for one association to be the sole 'voice' of that industry. For example, multinational companies in the consumer sphere have to cover an enormous range of issues from food safety, plastics and packaging to hygiene, biotechnology, consumer protection etc. No association can claim to be an expert in all these fields, so it comes as no surprise that associations are increasingly building alliances to leverage on one another's expertise, work together on an ad hoc basis, and reach out to wider audience and community.[18]

Establishing partnerships has several benefits, which comes either in the form of shared resources, shared risks and rewards, encouragement of event co-location, or enhancement of the meeting experience as participants get to meet and learn from more new people.

---

16 Sherry, Y. (2014).

17 Meeting Professionals International (2014).

18 Association Trends (2013), *Association mergers: Where are they headed now?* (online), available at: www.associationtrends.com (08-06-2015).

2.3.7   Trust in capabilities: from outsourcing to in-house management and local support

Majority of the world's associations (an overwhelming 84% of them) organize their meetings by themselves – either through their voluntary members, committee, or their in-house event management team.[19] Some international associations still retain their long and happy relationships with their professional convention organizers (PCOs), while many others still prefer to keep event management in-house.

Now, there has been a third development: in these cash-strapped times with higher ROI expectations – associations are not only organizing their own events, they are also reaching out for local support directly to ensure smooth arrangements, good attendance for their event, and to gain better understanding of the local industry and context. Associations often approach the destination's convention bureau for the local support or for referrals to good local PCOs, which are companies that specialise in organizing conventions and congresses.

Some associations with established in-house management services are even helping smaller associations/societies to organize their meetings. They do so for three main reasons:
1.   Save money and earn a small profit for themselves;
2.   Facilitate co-location with their partners' events (cost savings through economies of scale such as venue hire). This allows both parties to reap the benefits effectively; and
3.   More control in stimulating growth of event, and synergise co-locating events to attract more participants.

The staging of parallel meetings (or co-location of similar events) allow registrants from different associations to attend one another's sessions –providing an avenue for cross-fertilisation of ideas and also to attract more high-profile speakers since this arrangement makes better use of their time.

Trends include the development of cluster events, combining separately managed conferences, exhibitions and other ancillary events, such as public forums, i.e., International Water Week in Singapore.

With greater development in partnerships with local support and in-house management of partner's events leading to co-location will become ever more common – which is good news to convention centres and host cities as they will see additional participant numbers which such cooperation brings.

---

19 Union of International Associations (2013).

2.3.8 Sustainable framework within organizational model and corporate social responsibility (CSR)

A sustainable association is an organization that generates growth, profitability, and member value by integrating principles of sustainable development throughout the association.[20] Although associations are non-profit in nature, they are still required to generate surpluses, which can be reinvested in initiatives, programmes and services designed to fulfil the organization's mission.

With falling membership and associations increasingly facing challenges in retaining existing members, more associations are revisiting their organizational model and setting a sustainability framework to rethink their issues (limited resources, shrinking revenue, market unpredictability, etc.) as opportunities instead. Taking a proactive approach to fast changing realities they are facing now ensures their continued relevance to the member communities they serve. Some of the top-3 actions they are taking to ensure sustainability at the moment are:

1. Exploring new market/sector opportunities;
2. Reducing expenditure; and
3. Increasing non-member revenues.

The common concern amongst associations is that they do not have enough resources to grow, so to achieve the above three points, many are instilling good governance, recruitment and engagement of talent, and better optimisation of resources when organizing events (e.g., using local suppliers, inviting more local/regional members to participate).

Besides establishing a sustainable framework internally, associations are also responding to external sustainable development challenges. Industry associations in particular have been developing approaches for their industry sector members to advance corporate social responsibility (CSR) and sustainable development – albeit frequently with a focus on some specific facet of CSR. For example, many of the collectively-oriented initiatives have tended to focus on the environmental protection element of CSR. The key reasons why associations have been moving into this direction are:

– Industry sustainability: associations can assist members to advance along the sustainability party so that their industry concerns becomes more sustainable;

– Helps in attracting and retaining members: such sustainability and CSR programmes increases value and relevance of association to current and prospective members; and

– Builds positive government and NGO relations: associations are in a better position to contribute positively to regulatory initiatives by government and other agencies and to engage constructively with NGOS and other stakeholders

Builds industry reputation and brand: an association's CSR and sustainability programme demonstrates the sector's commitment to sustainable practices and leadership, hence building more positive stakeholder relationships with customers, communities, NGOs, and others. It basically enhances the sector's social license to operate and grow.

---

20 *Trends in International Association Meetings from North America 2015 Survey Report* (2014), Marketing Challenges International Inc., March 2014 (online), available at: https://gallery.mailchimp.com/620ef227ca4419ebb370f38d4/files/ Association_Survey_2015_MCIntl.pdf (08-06/2015).

CSR and green concerns are hot topics. A majority of 53% of INCON partners answering the survey[21] stated that they gave preference to venues, hotels and suppliers that have detailed environmental policies in place to reduce waste generation and recycle waste materials. Green modes of transport for delegate transfers between hotels and exhibition halls are promoted by a 77% majority of partners where possible, such as walking or using public transport. A 67% majority of partners favour exhibitors who minimise packing materials and use recyclable or reusable products.

A majority 83% of partners agree that a concerted effort is being made to keep marketing collateral online and avoid printing the conference abstract books, hand-outs etc. by issuing delegates with USB sticks, CD-ROMs or making data accessible online. A majority of 63% of events organizers recognise that large-scale events do not have to have huge climate impact and are making efforts to become low carbon or even carbon-neutral.

2.4   Emerging trends and forecast

2.4.1   Towards constant innovation and engagement

Associations are now looking to overcome several challenges – from budgetary regulations, falling membership numbers, thinning revenue margins, to tougher competition in the market and dropping participation figures in their events. Although most are still figuring out how to meet each challenge, there is one thing certain: they would have to constantly innovate or adopt a forward-looking approach in order to grow their association or even survive in the market.

This has resulted in some emerging trends which although are not yet commonplace, they will soon shape associations' business strategies and approaches:

–   **Continuous engagement with members and participants:** one can see more associations generating and presenting news and industry content to members in a much more interactive way, with much of the content actually generated by members themselves. This takes place not only during an event or meeting, but pre and post event. This process alone allows for participation in associations anywhere in the world, providing a globalized member engagement experience worth pursuing and paying for;

–   **Hybrid events:** majority of the associations (about 62% of them) do not have an exhibition or do not regularly organize one in conjunction with their conference.[22] Now to increase revenue streams, associations are looking at hybrid conferences and meetings where they incorporate exhibitions, technical tours, business matchmaking or hosted buyers programmes, and even virtual components. The hybrid version, though slightly more difficult to execute, allows a much richer, and often global, speaker participation process, and in turn attracts a larger pool of participants, allowing engagement throughout the year especially when there is a virtual component included.

    Other associations are welcoming public attendance in their conferences or events. This has proven to enliven the show for both professional conference participants as well as exhibitors. It also fulfils the association's advocacy role and mission; and

---

21   INCON (2012).

22   Union of International Associations (2013).

– **Leveraging on Web 2.0 and Mobile Apps for greater purposes:** it was mentioned that many associations have jumped on the bandwagon of using technology to capture information and distributing them to member's pre and post event (e.g., a video of a speaker that is uploaded on the website after event ends). However, few have yet to effectively leverage on mobile apps and web to deliver high-quality and cost-effective educational programmes that could be 'sold' to members either in the form of an online or app service, publication, or research report. Content can also be jointly created with members through the use of these technologies, which creates a greater sense of ownership amongst members.

Besides using the web or mobile app to interact and engage with members/participants to create indirect revenue streams, they are ideal platforms for associations to build their branding in today's crowded media marketplace. Associations can conduct quick polls, rapid surveys, online/app voting and social meeting to obtain feedback of what members are interested in, and create peer-to-peer viral marketing. It would help build communities of interest across sectors, which will give associations new opportunities to connect with new markets, potential members and partners. New technology applications are also being introduced to engage the next generation of members and association conventions and congresses participants.

2.4.2   Investing in future leaders

If associations are to be sustainable, they must attract and retain younger members who not only represent the future of the association, but also will become the future leaders in their profession or industry.

The realities of stagnating membership numbers and socio-demographic changes (where the older core group of individuals retire or become less active) are fast catching on with associations. The latter must redress this by attracting the younger generation, and some have started incorporating 'student' membership in their policy to achieve this objective. The intention is to accompany these student members throughout their professional career.

However, today's association leaders are often ill-equipped to understand the needs of the younger generation, which grew up in a digitally connected world – what they want and need in their career development. Hence the development of appropriate education tools and services relevant to this group remains at infancy stage. Nonetheless, more associations are recognising the importance of attracting new younger members who could actively help to grow and develop the association if it is meant to thrive in the future.

2.4.3   Influencing the evolving policy and regulatory environment

The purpose and value of associations comes primarily from the latter's ability to influence the policy and regulatory environment. It could be regulation that affects the nation, or the particular industry or profession; but it is all about being able to set the 'gold' standards for what they believe in.

As members and participants become more globalized with higher expectations, they are putting pressures on associations to highlight their demands for application of certain technical or regulatory standards to be applied wherever possible to minimise the barriers they face (e.g., trade barriers, or professional workplace barriers).

Associations are often slow in doing this as they have limited resources. But to gain more members and be seen as a thought leader, many are building strategic alliances with other industry associations (often on an ad hoc basis) to present a unified voice to regulators to achieve better policy frameworks.

It is hence important for regulators/government agencies to work collaboratively with associations so that the latter can be seen as more flexible, responsive, and interactive with their respective stakeholders. It is only when associations are perceived as the authoritative voice of their industry will they become a trusted source of information and expertise – which in turn will naturally help to drive meetings and participation numbers.

2.5   Key players: service offerings

2.5.1   International associations

International Associations are not-for-profit or non-government organizations. These are most often membership-based where Europe has the largest proportion of associations with many located in the United Kingdom, Switzerland, Benelux, Germany and France. The United States of America has the second most number of association headquarters and there are an increasing number also based in Asia (Singapore; Hong Kong, China; Japan). Associations would normally appoint a congress committee or nominate the executive council to vote and decide on the next conference destination. Some associations will allow the general assembly of members to cast their vote.

2.5.2   In-house meeting planner

Some of the larger associations have their own in-house events unit or meeting planner that will plan and organize their conventions and congresses. The in-house meeting planner is an employee of the association and will report to the executive director of the association. They will review the bid submissions and provide an assessment of the destinations to the board/executive committee/council for their decision. At times the in-house meeting planner may provide a recommendation on the destination that best meets the bid criteria.

In Europe, there exists a non-profit organization called Associations Conference Forum (AC Forum) that provides a platform for information exchange amongst peers working and facing the same challenges in the association conventions and congresses industry. Today AC Forum includes 28 members, and includes some of Europe's most prestigious associations.

2.5.3   Professional conference organizer (PCO)

Professional conference organizers (PCOs) is a company, which specialises in organizing conferences. A full service PCO will provide a full range of conference management services including conference registration, financial management, sponsorship and event marketing, speaker management, handling abstracts, venue and supplier liaison and management.

Moreover, a PCO will often be engaged by a national or international association to organize their conventions and congresses. Core PCO's are less likely to engage the full services of a local PCO but may engage them for partial services.

PCOs provide assistance to local associations in bidding for international conventions and congresses:

– Collating association conventions and congresses proceedings, papers and publications;
– On-site registration for association conventions and congresses;
– Marketing and communication for attracting delegates;
– Arranging speakers for association conventions and congresses; and
– Coordinating with DMC and other local service providers.

Local PCOs in a particular country may be used by associations to provide meetings management support once that particular country has been selected for a future meeting, or they may be asked by local member of the association for assistance at the bidding stage, in return for guarantees they will win the contract for organizing the event if the bid is successful. Which elements of the PCOs range of services are used will depend upon the in-house expertise of the association.

A local PCO will almost never get involved in providing strategic advice; they will be employed for a one-time event only, but their range of services goes beyond that of Destination Marketing Organizations (DMOs). Additionally, association relationships with AMCs, DMCs and PCOs are conducted on a commercial basis.

Role of core professional conference organizers (PCOs)

A growing number of PCOs work with international associations as outsourced organizers of the association's meetings programme around the world or within a particular region, with a multi-year contract. This type of PCO is known within the meetings industry as a 'core PCO'. Some Associations Management Companies offer similar support as part of their portfolio of services. International associations may outsource the meeting planner role to a PCO that will be contracted for a set number of years to organize their conference no matter where the conference may take place. Aside from organizing the conference the core PCO may play a pivotal role in the bid process i.e., sending out the tender to bid, assessing the bid, conducting site inspections of the shortlisted cities and putting forward their assessment to the decision-making body (board/ congress committee, council). They are key influencers but not normally the decision makers.

A core PCO may manage a conference remotely or appoint a local PCO or DMC to assist with certain aspects of the conference or logistics.

2.5.4   Association management company (AMC)

Association management companies (AMCs) are for-profit enterprises whose primary business is serving as headquarters and providing contracted full service management to two or more volunteer-governed organizations. An AMC provides: experienced staff; expertise; and efficiency (office space and equipment). The AMC client keeps its name, board, website, etc. and pays a fee for the services of the AMC.

Association management companies manage the affairs of the association. Some associations will outsource their secretariats to an AMC who will look after the day-to-day operations of the association such as governance, budgets, membership, education, meetings and events. An AMC will most often provide conference management services as part of their support to the association so they act like a core PCO. Examples of AMC/PCO companies include MCI and Kenes.

2.5.5   Local hosts

To facilitate an international conference most often there is a requirement for the local member/chapter of the international association to become the local host organization. This is most often a national association of the host country. Their role varies but generally it will include sending the official invitation to the international association to express their interest in hosting the event and to set up a local organizing committee. The local organizing committee can perform different roles such as secure local sponsorship and support for the conference, help market the conference within the country/region, assist in securing local speakers develop scientific content from the regional community, assist with social programmes and provide volunteers on site for the conference.

The local host may or may not have financial obligations such as underwriting the cost of the event, share the surplus and/or loss. The local host may appoint a local PCO to manage a conference on their behalf.

2.5.6   Destination management companies (DMC)

A professional services company possessing an extensive local knowledge, expertise and resources, specialising in the design and implementation of events, activities, tours, transportation and programme logistics for conferences and incentive programmes. They often also have access to a ready supply of temporary staff both skilled and unskilled.[23]

Where an international association has an in-house meeting planner and/or core PCO in place they may engage a DMC in the host country to assist with transport and logistics. DMCs and PCOs play a similar role for corporates as for associations:
–   Deciding budget;
–   Support in finding sponsorship;
–   Consulting for destination selection;

---

23 International Congress and Convention Association (April 2014b), *International Association Meetings: Bidding and Decision-making*, ICCA, Amsterdam.

- Designing of association conventions and congresses collateral;
- Arranging accommodation and transportation;
- Arranging foreign exchange;
- Providing travel insurance;
- Providing audio visual and staging;
- Photography and video coverage, and webcasting; and
- Providing security.

2.5.7 Event management companies

Event Management Companies are responsible for organizing a specific event or a component of a conference such as a welcome reception or gala dinner. They are often engaged by corporations to manage events such as product launches, awards nights or gala dinners.

Associations, corporations, government agencies and/or PCOs may either engage an event management company or organize an event themselves.

2.5.8 The role of convention bureaux

In essence, a convention bureau (CB) exists where there is a "storefront" for clients to go to and a "back of house" which delivers full bureau functionality. In all convention bureaux that full functionality consists of a public-private partnership, with the involvement and support of both government and the local MCCI industry. The main focus of a convention bureau is to find a way to attract association conventions and congresses and how to approach associations to encourage them to organize their meetings within the destination. The services provided by convention bureaux include support in bidding preparation, connecting conference owners/organizers to the appropriate service providers and event planners, offer networking opportunities, and, in more general terms, support associations in organizing their event. Some of the main areas of focus are:
- Destination sales and marketing;
- Bidding support;
- Event planning advice and assistance;
- Event marketing support;
- On site event support;
- Product and service selection;
- Government liaison;
- Product development;
- Sales tools;
- Ambassador programme (programmes to secure local hosts); and
- Industry training.

National convention bureaux (NCBs)

National convention bureaux (NCBs) play an important role in strengthening a country's MCCI offerings globally. They conduct marketing and promotion campaigns, act as one-shop-stop, and provide technical support. Globally, several countries are establishing or have recently established national-level convention bureaux to strengthen their business event offerings. Conventions bureaux are increasingly providing financial support, or in some cases subvention, to attract business events to their destinations.

Table 2.5   **National convention bureaux (NCBs)**

Destination marketing	NCBs globally promote its respective country for holding meetings, incentives, conventions and exhibitions.
Support in bidding	– NCBs provide support to regional or city convention bureaux in bidding for key events through activities such as document preparation and presentation; and – For international events, NCBs promote the entire country as venue and highlight its key destination.
Financial support	In some cases, NCBs provide financial support to organizers through programmes such as subvention, or help generate funds for the business event.
Maximising attendance	NCBs work with convention bureaux (CBs) to generate maximum delegate attendance at events that have been secured, through advertising and association channels.
Generate business leads	Help develop business leads and share them with CBs for securing the contracts for events.
Education and research	– NCBs actively dissipate knowledge, and educate its members and other stakeholders; and – They conduct industry research to gauge existing opportunities and trends, and maximising business based on the outcome.
Information point	– NCBs act as common information point for organizers and venues, providing advice and support in arrangements; and – They also build liaison with other stakeholders such as hotel suppliers and airlines.

Regional convention bureaux (RCBs)

On a broader level, regional convention bureaux are non-governmental organizations funded by its members' subscription, receiving financial support from the region or any national government. Regional convention bureaux refer to regional on a national context. The bureaux' primary role is to promote the region as an ideal and enticing destination for the MCCI industry. More objectives, stated by the AACVB include:[24]

– To strive towards regional cooperation in developing the region's potential and in promoting the region as an ideal convention destination;

– To stimulate intra-regional conventions, especially those that can be rotated among member countries;

– To encourage the formation of national, state/province or city convention organizations to enhance members' convention-hosting capabilities;

– To be instrumental in professionalising the convention industry by developing sound professional practices in the solicitation and servicing of meetings and conventions; to initiate training programmes to achieve this objective; and

– To facilitate the exchange of information through the establishment of a comprehensive regional convention data bank, to serve as clearing house of information on the regional convention industry.

---

24 Asian Association of Convention and Visitor Bureaus (2014), *Background and History,* AACVB (online), available at: www.aacvb.org.

Local convention bureaux (LCBs)

Emulating the roles of national convention bureaux (NCBs), local convention bureaux (LCBs) primarily focus on the development of business events industry in their respective province, city or region.

Table 2.6   **Local convention bureaux (LCBs)**

Destination marketing	Promotes, on a national and international level, cities or regions as destinations, using different media and channels.
Business events bidding	– CBs either directly bid for business events or provide support to local venues for bidding; and – They also help prepare bid documents, request for proposals (RFP), and help build strategies for successful bids.
Event support	Give help in business events planning and provide support in organizing business events: – CBs establish information booths and provide visitor guides; and – They collaborate with local stakeholders, to create a smooth experience for visitors.
Boosting attendance	CBs help maximise attendance at the planned events through promotions, pre-event marketing, and communication using appropriate channels.
Financial support	– CBs, in some cases, provide financial support or help generate funds for making events successful; and – They also help in financial planning and event budgeting.
Facilitating information	– CBs help build contacts and network, and provide relevant information to organizers and suppliers; and – They organize site inspections, and help organizers in identifying right suppliers.

2.6   Decision-making: buying processes

The decision-makers vary enormously from association to association, with big implications for the overall shape of the decision-making process, and also for the relative importance of different decision-influencing factors. There is also a wide range of both formal and informal decision-influencers who can play a significant role in the process.[25]

The list of influencers also differs enormously from one association to another. Table 2.7 identifies a possible list of decision-makers along with the decision-influencers – which includes all decision makers plus the following – however this list is not representative of the entire association segment's decision-making process:

---

25   International Congress and Convention Association (April 2014b).

Table 2.7   **Decision-makers and decision-influencers in the buying processes for conventions and congresses**

Decision-makers	Decision-influencers
– Single volunteer leader (e.g., President; Chairman);	– Hired consultants;
– Single association executive (e.g., CEO; Secretary-General);	– Core PCO, in-house meeting planner;
– Full Board of Directors;	– Association management company (AMC), secretariat, CEO, Congress Committee;
– Executive Board;	– Sponsors;
– Congress Committee (either a formal grouping or set-up ad hoc to make a particular decision);	– Business partners, councillors;
– Representative of association sub-groups (or in the case of a federation, the constituent organizations' nominated representatives);	– Association staff (especially meetings department); – Past members of board of Directors, other national and regional representatives, national association councillors;
– National representatives;	– Members who have recently hosted the association conventions and congresses, other members;
– Official delegates at General Assembly; and	– Respected senior figures related to the association, councillors, board members, high profile members, other members;
– All members (e.g., via online referendum).	– Association leaders from other international associations with similar size/profile of events (many associations executives trust the views and experience of their peers with regard to recently used destinations/venues);
	– Politicians;
	– Celebrities;
	– News media (negative stories especially relating to security issues can have big influence); and
	– Other decision-influencers such as family, relatives, friends.

Source: International Congress and Convention Association (April 2014b).

2.6.1   Internal association objectives

Whilst logistics typically determine which destinations have the capacity to host the association's events, and financial factors play a critical role, the vast majority of international associations have important internal objectives, which they have to balance against these considerations. These internal objectives relate to the associations Mission and its future capacity to deliver long-term benefits to its members and stakeholders.[26]

Generally speaking, suppliers who invest in research to understand these factors will be in a much stronger position to work in partnership with international associations and to deliver more effective events.

Associations may also wish to differentiate between long-term tactical objectives, to set out the priority order of objectives, and to identify local association chapter objectives distinctly from global association objectives.

26 Ibid.

2.6.2   Channels

While expos and business networking are key channels used to target decision makers on the demand side, online media, such as emails and social media, have become key channels to reach delegates and visitors.

Business events expos

Expos are organized for organizations, in a specific industry, to showcase latest products and services and also to examine recent trends and opportunities. There are a growing number of business event expos taking place in key regions around the world where destinations, products and services are vying for the attention of association, government and corporate decision makers.

> "EIBTM was as always, a tremendously beneficial event, I made a number of great new contacts and was able to flesh out several new agreements as a direct result of my time in Barcelona".
>
> Jim Walker, President, Crossing Boundaries, an exhibitor at EIBTM, 2012

ibtm° world   ijmex Frankfurt 19–21 April 2016   AIME WHERE INSPIRATION BEGINS

Business networking

Networking is an activity, which enables like-minded individuals to recognise, create or act-upon business opportunities. Networking events often take place at conferences and trade exhibitions designed to bring suppliers and buyers/decision makers together.

> "Sometimes we get leads for a prospective convention from convention bureaux or convention centres, however at times, prospective clients [associations] also approach us through reference of the previous clients (word-of-mouth)".
>
> Director of a Europe-based PCO, May 2013

Direct post and e-mails

> "Online channels, such as websites and e-mails, have become a key channel to reach delegates and visitors, particularly for international delegates".
>
> Management Director of a PCO, February 2013

Social media

Social media has become a particularly important communication tool to connect with the younger generations, however there is still a more traditional generation that require more established and traditional forms of communication. Traditional forms of communication such as print and face to face are often used to reach to key decision makers that are generally members of the older generation. The MCCI industry is still grappling with how to combine traditional and new communication tools to best communicate with their diverse communities.

"A tsunami of connectedness, driven by social, mobile and virtual, will ultimately enable the attendee engagement experience. Facebook, LinkedIn and Twitter are mainstream, making integrated event marketing the new normal for event professionals".

Peter Micciche, CEO, Certain Inc, March 2013

2.6.3   Key determinants

Association conventions and congresses destination selection is often driven by concentration of members; however, factors such as subvention schemes provided by the convention bureaux also act as an important determinant.

Key determinants for association conventions and congresses destination selection

Generally speaking, international associations conventions and congresses favour destinations, which offer the following:
–   Active membership of the association at the proposed destination;
–   Appropriate combination of meeting facilities, including IT and technical services;
–   Financial and non-financial support, i.e., subvention;
–   International, regional and local accessibility to/from destination and convention and congresses precinct;
–   Safety and security, i.e., political and economic stability, delegate safety, safety from terrorist attacks, crime;
–   Shopping and entertainment for delegates, i.e., opportunities for pre and post tours, social programmes;
–   PCOs and support services in the city;
–   Hotel stock and facility package;
–   Destination appeal;
–   Local experience and expertise;
–   Strength of local industry, i.e., amount of innovation, research and development in the country/region;
–   Business-to-business opportunities, i.e., new market opportunities;
–   Legacy, i.e., extent to which association can achieve its core mission and goals;

–   Cost competitiveness; and
–   Minimising risk against financial loss, political instability, local competency.

Active membership

Association meeting planners consider active local and regional membership at the proposed destinations before selection of destinations, as it directly impacts the attendance at the association conventions and congresses.

Meeting facilities and technical support

Association conventions and congresses attract a large number of delegates therefore the meeting space offered by destinations plays an important role in destination selection. Moreover, support services provided at the destinations including PCOs, DMCs and IT services, are an important determinant.

The size, type of building: historic/modern, capacity, location, layout, quality, in-house services, Wi-Fi, proximity to hotels and transportation and other main characteristics are key determinants for choosing meeting facilities.

Moreover, there is a growing interest in self-contained association conventions and congresses precincts or integrated facilities that minimise logistics and travel times.

Subvention and Support

Subvention schemes provided by destinations enable association meeting planners to reduce overall cost of the event, and thus is a determinant to destination selection. Subvention support varies from one destination to another:[27]
–   In-kind or cash subventions from host country, city or main venue;
–   Commissions refunded to association;
–   Hosted welcome receptions or dinners;
–   Interest-free or low interest loans, seed funding;
–   Delegate boosting marketing material and support; and
–   Value add programmes.

The levels of subvention support are normally subject to an economic value assessment of the event. Subvention programmes may be subject to certain performance measures such as the attainment of a set number of delegates. Increasing destinations and governments want to be able to measure the ROI from subvention support provided.

---

27 Ibid.

Accessibility

- **International accessibility:** international association conventions and congresses attract members from different countries worldwide. This makes easy accessibility by air, particularly with direct flights, a desired destination feature for planners. Flight distance and cost for the majority of delegates are often critical factors to consider. The availability of low cost carrier services access to key source destinations make a destination more affordable for a broader range of potential delegates.
  Moreover, visa policies are a concern – will delegates from all countries with association member be able to attend? Thus information availability to delegates is important; and
- **Local accessibility:** additionally, local accessibility, which includes all local transportation systems – such as disability-friendly infrastructure, public transport and distance between main venues, hotels, airport and off-site social venues – are key determinants.[28]

Security

The security of the destination is another important factor. Political instability, terrorist attacks or social unrest will not attract meeting organizers or delegates. This includes economic and political stability, delegates' safety and security against crime, natural disasters and more.

Entertainment/touring for delegates

Accessibility and supply of activities in the city allows delegates to socialise, to access cultural sites – museums and monuments – and to experience local lifestyle, for those desirous of discovering a new city/region. This factor is losing importance due to ROI considerations, but remains significant with some organizations, which still consider it as a key factor, especially when the vote comes from general assembly.

PCOs and support services in the city

It is important that association decision-makers be specific on which local suppliers should be included. Some of them include:
- Professional Congress Organisers (PCOs);
- Destination management companies (DMCs);
- Exhibition services;
- Convention bureau;
- Security personnel providers;
- Volunteer and temporary staff coordinators;
- AV/production/simultaneous interpretation;
- VAT/tax consultants; and
- Government interest and support.

---

28 Ibid.

Hotel stock and facility package

Delegate accommodation is crucial to attendance. Destinations are therefore decided according to hotel availability and quality. This can range from the total amount of bedrooms, within specified distances, star rating, ancillary meeting space, etc. Conference organizers would normally look for a wide range of budget to 5-star hotels within close proximity of the main convention facilities. They also want to minimise the number of hotels they have to deal with so that large-scale hotels that can provide room blocks for larger groups are preferable to small boutique style hotels. Having delegates stay in the same or nearby accommodation is more conducive for networking and logistics.

2.7 Financial and economic models

As of today, international meetings impact beyond-tourism and beyond-direct-expenditure elements. The direct spend and high value of such meetings have been long established, but increasingly the focus has shifted. Indeed, recent trends examine the implications of a strong meeting performance for a destination's inward investment, economic and trade development, knowledge creation and dissemination, high-level education for local university students, business development opportunities for visiting and local delegates, and the delivery of a vast range of healthcare, scientific and environmental objectives. The World Tourism Organization, in its latest *Global Report on the Meetings Industry,*[29] underlines that meetings are both a sub-segment of tourism (related to a proportion of delegate expenditure) and an important part of other broader economic sectors, especially in the increasingly critical knowledge-based economy.

Association conventions and congresses are also important drivers of societal change and opportunities to understand some of the world's most challenging problems. Indeed aside from generating value from foreign visitor expenditure these business events provide a wide range of social and economic benefits to the business community:
– Attracting the world's industry and thought leaders;
– Building brand awareness;
– Creating a world stage for showcasing innovation, products and expertise;
– Generating media attention;
– Providing economic stimulus, foreign exchange and employment;
– Stimulating international markets for goods and services;
– Building business contacts and trade and research links;
– Delivering access to new technologies;
– Strengthening professional expertise through educational programmes and knowledge exchange;
– Inducing development and growth in business services;
– Contributing tax revenues;
– Attracting new customers and investment opportunities;
– Providing direct contact with target markets (exhibitions); and
– Optimising infrastructure and facilities.

---

29 World Tourism Organization (2014a), *AM Reports, Volume seven – Global Report on the Meetings Industry,* UNWTO, Madrid.

2.8   Drivers and barriers of the segment

Drivers	Barriers
– Newer industries such as alternative energy, industrial miniaturisation, and eco-tourism are driving demand for association conventions and congresses; – New market opportunities in developing regions which have been experiencing higher economic growth than traditional markets of Europe and North America; – Regionalisation. Emergence of regional trade agreements, regional associations conventions and congresses; and – Growing access and affordability of destinations with the expansion of low cost carriers, large capacity jetliners (A380), airport and hotel infrastructure developments.	– Increasing competition among associations to attract delegates to their conventions: with increasing number of conventions and congresses organized on similar topics, associations are struggling to meet the target number of delegates; – Market volatility, greater border security. Potential global crisis with increasing conflicts in the Middle East, Ebola outbreak in Eastern Africa; and – Sluggish economic growth in western markets and slower growth in eastern markets.

2.9   Supply chain analysis

The association conventions and congresses segment encompass a large number of fields, service providers and suppliers, which are interacting in a constantly changing environment.

The interest in meetings design is thus clearly a sign of an industry that is growing up. Meetings design plays a role in a natural evolution in the value chain in the industry.[30]

The meetings industry is now growing from a focus on a delivery of goods (participant logistics) to also delivering a service, a partnership; increasing the value added to the product.

The supply chain in the association conventions and congresses segment includes a large number of stakeholders, service providers and decision makers who work together in delivering the best event organization. Service providers include, amongst others, accommodation, transportation or logistic support. Understandably, key consumers are associations, corporates, government bodies, and NGOs. Primarily association management companies, corporate meeting planners and core PCOs influence their decision-making.

Market forces sometimes demand rapid changes from suppliers, logistics providers, destinations, which have significant effects on supply chain infrastructure. Moreover, the specialisation of each player, coupled with diverging characteristics and demand between regions means that the set of partners may change, resulting in variations in the supply chain.

---

30 International Congress and Convention Association (April 2014b).

Figure 2.12 **Supply chain analysis of the association convention and congresses segment**

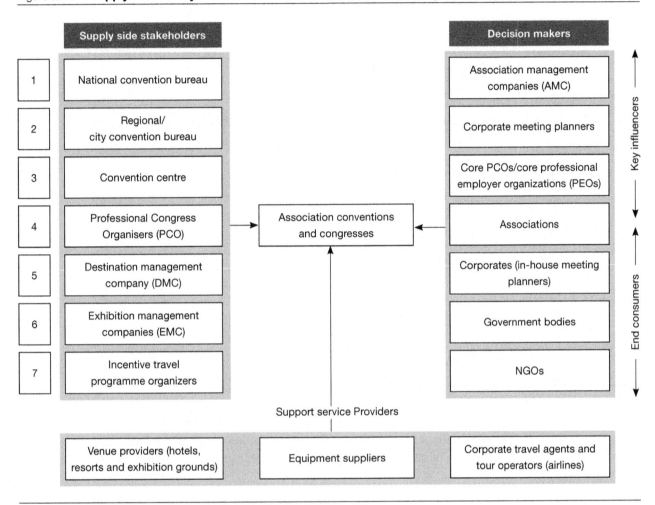

2.10   Destination Europe: characteristics

Europe has been leader in the association conventions and congresses, with an average market share exceeding 54%.[31] Home to leading sectors and companies Europe is an accessible destination, both in terms of transportation and visa.

Figure 2.13   **Global association conventions and congresses in Europe, 2004–2013 (market share, %)**

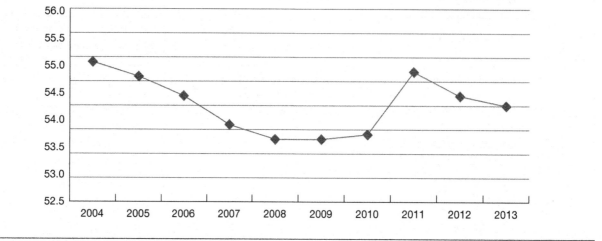

Source: International Congress and Convention Association (2013b).

As a market leader, it is not surprising that rotation areas, length of meetings and main congress venues (meeting facilities in hotels) are following similar trends than at the international level.

Number of meetings per country and city

Germany, Spain and France are currently the top-3 countries to host association conventions and congresses, while Paris, Madrid and Vienna are the most successful cities in 2013.[32]

---

31   International Congress and Convention Association (2013b).

32   International Congress and Convention Association (2013a).

Table 2.8 **Number of conventions and congresses in Europe, 2013**

By country	Number of meetings	Rank	By city	Number of meetings	Rank
Germany	722	1	Paris, France	204	1
Spain	562	2	Madrid, Spain	186	2
France	527	3	Vienna, Austria	182	3
United Kingdom	525	4	Barcelona, Spain	179	4
Italy	447	5	Berlin, Germany	178	5
Netherlands	302	6	London, United Kingdom	166	6
Portugal	249	7	Istanbul, Turkey	146	7
Austria	244	8	Lisbon, Portugal	125	8
Sweden	238	9	Prague, Czech Republic	121	9
Turkey	221	10	Amsterdam, Netherlands	120	10
Belgium	214	11	Dublin, ireland	114	11
Switzerland	205	12	Brussels, Belgium	111	12
Finland	171	13	Copenhagen, Denmark	109	13
Poland	170	14	Budapest, Hungary	106	14
Denmark	161	15	Rome, Italy	99	15
Czech Republic	145	16	Stockholm, Sweden	93	16
Ireland	136	17	Helsinki, Finland	85	17
Norway	136	18	Munich, Germany	82	18
Hungary	132	19	Warsaw, Poland	65	19
Greece	100	20	Oslo, Norway	62	20

Source: International Congress and Convention Association (2013a).

Convention bureaux work locally and regionally to provide the best services and offerings. Improvements in quality, CSR and sustainability parralel the segment's continuous thrive to adapt to new technologies and social media, in order to better promote destinations and target its participants. Although each country promotes its destinations individually, Europe is also promoted as a regional destination for association conventions and congresses.

For Europe destinations, the primary source market is the European continent, followed by North America.

2.11   Destination North America: characteristics

According to the 2014 Meetings Focus Trends Survey,[33] carried out by Meeting Focus, to over 600 meeting planners, 45% of the North American MCCI market (Meeting Focus' definition of North America also includes the Caribbean islands) is dedicated to association planning, 46% to corporate planning, 3% to incentive planning and 7% to government planning. Additionally, growth of the association conventions and congresses has been disrupted by the greater emphasis on ROI (30% of participants), the increased workload due to reduced staffing (30% of participants) as well as the more complicated contract negotiations (24% of participants). The biggest threat for planners, are increasing costs of organizing events and the declining attendance.

Government meetings, which are affected by increasing costs and lower budgets, are also threatened by government regulations (30% of participants). Indeed, more than 41% of respondents claim that their budget has decreased of 10% over the year. Moreover, 77% of respondents from the Meeting Focus Trends Survey have acknowledged that public perception issues regarding meetings affect their choice of destination, a decrease from previous years. Yet meeting planning has changed due to increased workload caused by reduced staffing (37% of participants), fewer days per meeting (30% of participants) and more complicated contract negotiations (26% of participants).

> "Meeting duration is shrinking because of the U.S. Government regulations and downplay of meetings. If they have meetings at all, they are for shorter duration and many fewer services than even 18 months ago".
>
> Patricia Francoise, Senior Associate, PSA, Inc., Watertown

Figure 2.14   **Duration of government meetings in North America, 2013 (%)**

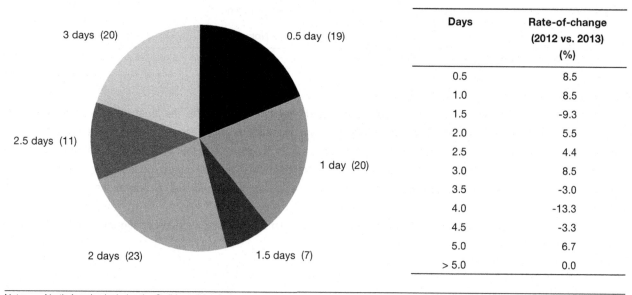

Days	Rate-of-change (2012 vs. 2013) (%)
0.5	8.5
1.0	8.5
1.5	-9.3
2.0	5.5
2.5	4.4
3.0	8.5
3.5	-3.0
4.0	-13.3
4.5	-3.3
5.0	6.7
> 5.0	0.0

Note: North America includes the Caribbean islands.

Source: Davidson, T. (2013).

33   Davidson, T. (2013), '2014 Meetings Focus Trends Survey', *Meetings Focus,* December 2013 (online), available at: www.meetingsfocus.com (08-06-2015).

The United States of America remains the leader in terms of number of international meetings in North America, yet Canada is clearly accelerating to close the gap, increasing from 196 meetings in 2002 to 722 meetings in 2013. Mexico counted 158 meetings in 2013, up from 104 in 2002.

Table 2.9   **Number of meetings in North America by country, 2002, 2006 and 2013**

	Rank	Number of meetings		
		2002	**2006**	**2013**
United States of America	1	599	712	829
Canada	2	196	222	722
Mexico	3	104	149	158

Source: International Congress and Convention Association (2013b).

Interestingly, however, went it comes to city ranking, the three top cities for meetings are Montreal, Toronto and Vancouver, which are all Canadian. The United States market appears to have lost out to Canada because of tighter border security issues.

Table 2.10   **Number of meetings North America by city, 2013**

	Number of meetings	**Rank**
Montreal, Quebec (Canada)	71	1
Toronto, Ontario (Canada)	69	2
Vancouver, British Columbia (Canada)	57	3
Boston, Massachusetts (United States of America)	56	4
Washington, D.C. (United States of America)	53	5
Mexico City (Mexico)	42	6
New York City (United States of America)	36	7
Chicago, Illinois (United States of America)	35	8
San Francisco, California (United States of America)	35	9
Miami, Floria (United States of America)	27	10

Source: International Congress and Convention Association (2013a).

Marketing Challenges International's report on *Trends in International Association Meetings from North America*[34] (excluding Mexico) predicts that the year 2014 for the association conventions and congresses segment, will deliver increasing budgets and event attendance.

---

34 Trends in International Association Meetings from North America 2015 Survey Report (2014).

Moreover, the latest results of the economic significance of meetings to the economy of the United States of America reveal that in 2012:[35]

– The industry's contribution to federal, state and local tax dollars increased by 10%, providing more than USD 28 billion in tax receipts; and

– The industry stimulated growth with an 8% increase, providing jobs for more than 1.7 million Americans.

While North American associations realise that they need to become more international in order to survive in the global marketplace, they are still hesitant to hold their meetings outside of North America. When they do decide to go further abroad, Western Europe is usually their first choice. In a recent PCMA survey,[36] 44% of respondents said that Western Europe would be their choice if they were to hold an international meeting in the future.

2.12   Destination Asia: characteristics

While emerging Asian markets have not been immune to recent world events – weakening global economy, the United States of America and European debt troubles and political unrest in the Middle East and North Africa – the region is anticipated to be one of the MCCI industry's bright spots. Asia is leading the world's growth in numbers of international association conventions and congresses occurring. Its market share of international association conventions and congresses is rising as associations seek to globalize their membership and market delivery. In addition to more meetings, adding Asia to their rotation patterns, more global associations will seek to establish regional offices in Asia, thus driving an increase in Asian regional meetings.

Over the last decade Asian destinations have strengthened their position in the international meetings market with Japan, China, the Republic of Korea, Taiwan Province of China and Singapore in the top-25 in 2013. In 2013, Japan and China are ranked 1st and 2nd – respectively – in Asia, and Singapore is ranked 1st city in the region, holding 175 association conventions and congresses.

---

35 Pricewaterhouse Coopers LLP (2014).

36 Russell, M. (2014).

Table 2.11   **Number of meetings in Asia by country, 2002, 2006 and 2013**

	2002		2006		2013	
	Number of meetings	Rank	Number of meetings	Rank	Number of meetings	Rank
Japan	219	1	264	2	342	1
China	134	2	285	1	340	2
Republic of Korea	118	3	178	3	260	3
Singapore	63	6	131	4	175	4
India	52	8	107	5	142	5
Thailand	74	4	104	6	136	6
Taiwan Province of China	64	5	75	9	122	7
Malaysia	63	7	100	7	117	8
Indonesia	30	10	51	10	106	9
Hong Kong, China	49	9	81	8	89	10

Sources: International Congress and Convention Association (2013a; 2013b).

Table 2.12   **Number of meetings in Asia by city, 2013**

	Number of meetings	Rank
Singapore, Singapore	175	1
Seoul, Republic of Korea	125	2
Beijing, China	105	3
Bangkok, Thailand	93	4
Hong Kong, China	93	5
Tokyo, Japan	89	6
Taipei, Taiwan Province of China	79	7
Shanghai, China	78	8
Kuala Lumpur, Malaysia	72	9
Bali, Indonesia	68	10

Sources: International Congress and Convention Association (2013a; 2013b).

Singapore is a great example of the Asian market's development of the business meeting industry. By developing the appropriate infrastructure, such as hotels, convention centres and attracting a number of sectors, Singapore was able to generate a very successful return. Still today, the nation is investing a lot of money and effort to find innovative ways to develop the segment. The government has been playing a key role in this development, identifying it as strategic for economic growth and diversification.

2.13   Characteristics of other regions

Dominated by Europe and North America, the association conventions and congresses segment is now seeing a shift towards emerging nations, primarily driven by investment in new facilities and technology, investment in events infrastructure and upgrade in tourism.

According to ICCA's latest country rankings,[37] based on the number of international association conventions and congresses held in 2013, six emerging countries made it to the top-25: China, with 340 events, Brazil, with 315 events, Argentina (223), Turkey (221), Mexico (158) and India (142).

ICCA CEO, Martin Sirk (2013) attributes the strength of these newer markets, to increased understanding of how the international association conventions and congresses market works (i.e., by networking, joining industry associations and educating themselves on markets outside their region).

Most associations have noticed increased attendance from emerging economies such as Croatia, Serbia, Slovenia, Azerbaijan, Hungary, Ukraine, Israel, Saudi Arabia, Turkey, United Arab Emirates, China, Africa, etc.; and are opening more offices in these regions.

These changing trends give some insights into future destinations and players in association conventions and congresses.

2.14   Association conventions and congresses segment conclusion

The association conventions and congresses segment is experiencing some changes. Events are becoming smaller in size – less participants, shorter and the number of events being held is increasing. As participants' wants evolve, the quality rather than quantity of events is becoming more important. In general, the rotation of events is mainly driven by two factors: potential for future activity or because current events are held in that particular area.

The segment thrives to enhance its current services by focusing on technology, safety, seeking advice to local community instead of outsourcing, and forging partnerships. Additionally, future trends focus on innovation and engagement and invest in young future leaders, in order to respond to the changing environment and demand, and also aim at better influencing current policies and the regulatory environment.

In order to deliver all services and respond to other technicalities, the association conventions and congresses turn towards international players– international associations – local players – professional conference organizers (PCOs), local hosts, destination management companies (DMCs) – and players who directly serve the association, convention bureaux – in-house meeting planner, association management companies (AMCs), event management companies. Decision-makers vary enormously from association to association. They seek active membership of the association, appropriate meeting facilities, hotel stock and technical services, subventions, accessibility, security, entertainment, PCOs and local support services.

---

37   International Congress and Convention Association (2013a).

Europe has been and is continuing to be the leader in association conventions and congresses, adapting to new technologies and needs. North America is generally affected by increasing costs of organizing events and the declining attendance, but intends to be more international in order to respond to changing trends in the segment. Asia is gaining in competitiveness, threatening Europe and North America, while other emerging countries, with their improved infrastructure and investment, are increasingly targeted for holding association conventions and congresses.

Generally, newer industries are driving demand for conventions and congresses; however, the increased competition amongst associations, to attract delegates is affecting the segment.

Chapter 3

Corporate meetings: analysis and profile

3.1   Characteristics and activity

The corporate meetings segment is characterised by a number of factors that are completely different from the association segment discussed previously. The key characteristics will be described in the sections below.

The decision-making process is particularly complex, due to the fragmented nature of the market and the number of intermediaries who are involved in the value chain. While a few large corporate travel agencies dominate the market, there remain a large number of small agencies that get involved in meetings organization. There is a broad range of companies, on-line sites and other that get involved at different stages of the process, from choosing venues to providing electronic meeting management.

In addition, activity in the corporate meetings (and incentives) segment is closely related to the financial and economic conditions of companies and the economies in which they operate.

3.1.1   Event types

Corporate meetings have high expectations for quality in all aspects of the meeting experience, especially food, service, technology and facilities. Two types of meetings are discernible, internal meetings and external meetings. Corporate meetings can range from very small gatherings to significant groups of people. However, their destination selection criteria tend to focus on destinations in which, or near where they have major operations or a significant commercial interest.

One characteristic of corporate meetings is that meetings are planned with shorter lead times, and represent a very high spending, lucrative end of the market. Major markets, population centres and corporate headquarter cities are the most popular destinations for the corporate meetings.

Destination choice for holding corporate meetings is generally based on any of the following reasons:
–   The company has headquarters in, or near, the city;
–   The company has a major installation in the city;
–   The city is home to a significant number of buyers of the company's products;
–   The city is home to key suppliers to the company; and
–   The company has some other major commercial interest in the city.

Internal focused meetings

Internal corporate meetings are more organizationally focused or "company facing". The internal meetings include activities such as operations, logistics, sales and marketing services. The corporate activities being planned or managed by such meetings include aspects such as firm infrastructure, human resources, technology and procurement. These internal corporate meetings will almost always be held near the location of the corporation and thus have little to do with destination selling.

Internal meetings are:
–   Annual general meetings (AGMs);
–   Planning;
–   Executive retreats;
–   Team building;
–   Sales and management; and
–   Training courses.

Internal corporate business meetings business tend to be smaller groups who are making decisions on relatively short term lead times. Maintaining a quality database is difficult as the influencers and decision makers tend to move frequently to other jobs within the corporation or in other companies. Given that it is mainly a "receptive" market, the hotel community is already covering this market very effectively.

Corporations in the following fields are among the most frequent users in corporate and incentive segments:
–   Pharmaceutical/medical;
–   Financial services/banking;
–   IT/telecommunications/electronics;
–   Chemical/energy/environmental;
–   Media/public relations/advertising;
–   Automotive;
–   Training insurance; and
–   Property/real estate.

External focused meetings

External corporate meetings are more business focused or "market facing". They are about managing supply chain relationships or developing customers. For example, a manufacturing company might have a meeting in a place where it tends to get raw materials as part of its supply chain management activities, or it might have a meeting in a place where assemblers are customers of the components that the manufacturer produces. A large company that is vertically integrated, meaning that it has its own internally owned and operated supply chain might still have meetings up and down the supply chain as more of an internal corporate meeting wherever it has installations.

There is one type of external corporate meeting that can be a destination sell. These are demand-focused meetings that are seeking to engage an audience from a wide geographic area. These are essentially "market promotional meetings". These could be user group meetings or product launches. In these instances, the company is more destination focused, but, with an emphasis on choosing a destination which will meet the company's goals – attracting large number of potential customers to a meeting.

External meetings are:
- Supply chain relationship management;
- Customer relationship management;
- User groups; and
- Product launches.

3.1.2 Venues used

Corporate Meetings use a wide range of conference and convention centres, meeting facilities in hotels, training and conference centres, halls and other spaces within which meetings are held. Meeting venues should provide clear signage, be flexible in terms of space, provide food and beverages, Wi-Fi and other technological services – providing to be optimum and secure for delegates.[1] Thus far, hotels are already covering this market very effectively.

It is important to note that there is pressure from regulatory authorities i.e., PhRMA code, and from corporate governance to limit "extravagant" expenditures during meetings, which has had consequences on the level of venues chosen.

3.1.3 Activity

Number of events

The IAPCO *Annual Survey 2013*[2] shows a slight increase in corporate meetings per region. 2,539 of meetings in 2013 were national, which underlines that corporate meetings are contributing to local destinations rather than international ones. 790 of meetings in 2013 were international. This proves to open opportunities for the development of enhanced services at a national level.

---

1   International Association of Professional Congress Organisers (2014), *Members' Annual Review 2014,* IAPCO, Freshwater.

2   International Association of Professional Congress Organisers (2013).

Figure 3.1   **Number of corporate meetings worldwide, 2008–2013**

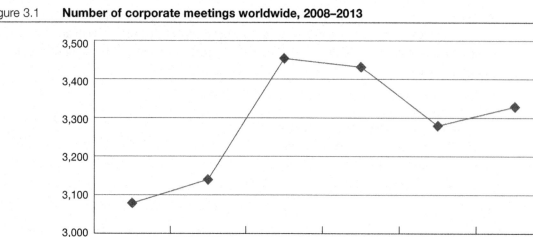

Source: International Association of Professional Congress Organisers (2013).

Number of participants

The corporate meetings segment is seeing a steady increase in the number of participants per event. Increasing corporate budgets and focus on specialising meetings are drivers to this trend. However the trend is forecasted to decrease in the future due to changing needs and demands.

Figure 3.2   **Average number of participants in corporate meetings worldwide, 2008–2013**

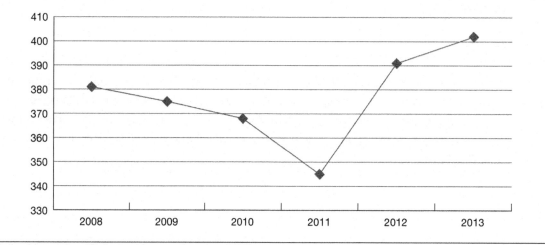

Source: International Association of Professional Congress Organisers (2013).

3.2   Corporate meetings key trends

The post-recession recovery in meetings industry is likely to result in high growth levels, driven by a rise in corporate budgets and number of meetings. On the other side, the duration of meetings is expected to decline, and to become more specialised in nature.

Corporate budget and spending for meetings witnessing post-recession recovery

According to Industry Forecast 2015 by Advito,[3] companies are increasing their meeting budget and spending, which shrunk significantly during the global financial recession. Also, in the IMEX global research,[4] about 41% of meeting professionals reported slights increase in meetings budget in 2014 as compared to 2013, while 14% reported a significant increase.

Additionally, according to a global meeting industry survey, Convention 2020, 74% of respondents expect the investment in meetings, in 2020, to remain the same or increase, compared to the level achieved in 2010.[5]

Increased demand for meetings in 2014

According to the 2014 Advito forecast,[6] demand for meetings in 2013 has improved as compared to 2012. Better business performance has led to growth in demand, which has resulted in shortage of venues in primary destinations, such as London and New York. Demand for meetings in 2014 remained strong, and grew steadily. Yet, while demand stabilises, the 2014 American Express meetings forecast[7] indicates that respondents expect demand to increase mostly within their own region.

Decline in size and duration

As per a survey conducted by American Express,[8] predictions show that there is likely to be some decline in the number of attendees per meeting, while the global average length for all conferences is forecasted to be 2.6 days, a difference from the not-unusual-to-see 4–5-day meetings. Organizations may gain in efficiency.

---

3   Advito (2014).

4   IMEX (2012), 'IMEX Group Issues 2013 Predictions for the Meetings & Events Industry – Participation, Pricing, Political Prowess and Pursuit of Green', IMEX, 03-12-2012 (online), available at: www.imex-frankfurt.com (08-06-2015). Survey respondents included 40–50 senior meetings industry professionals from America, Australia, Argentina and Europe.

5   International Congress and Convention Association, IMEX and FastFuture (2011), *Convention 2020* (online), available at: www.iccaworld.com and www.imex-frankfurt.com (02-10-2015): a global strategic foresight study that is looking at the MICE industry, includes 1,125 participants from 76 countries, the majority being from meetings and events industry.

6   Advito (2013).

7   American Express Meetings & Events (2013).

8   Sherry, Y. (2014). Participants included 200 hotel suppliers and meeting professionals working in North America, Europe, Asia and the Pacific and Latin America.

Reaching to another level, 79% of respondents believe that business events will increase in number, get smaller in size and have a highly specialised content.[9]

The business events industry is witnessing consolidation of meetings with incentives, primarily driven by focus on ROI and managing costs, which are also driving selection of secondary and closer-to-business locations.

ROI of meetings are becoming important

Besides cost curtailment, companies are focusing on assessing the outcome of their investment through measuring ROI of business events. The IMEX global insights survey reveals that for senior management, detailed and comprehensible ROI has emerged as the third-most dominant factor influencing decisions regarding business events.[10]

Emerging demand for secondary and closer-to-business locations

As per the Advito 2014 forecast,[11] with growing demand for meetings, secondary or tertiary destinations are gaining popularity among organizers. Advito reports an increase in demand for meetings in BRIC in 2014, as organizations are trying to expand their local businesses in these emerging markets.

According to the American Express 2015 forecast,[12] hotel suppliers reported that 53% of their clients (primarily meeting planners) are asking for local meetings, in an effort to keep the meeting costs down. Respondents who participated in the survey expect a general increase in demand for local meetings in 2013. European, North American (excluding Mexico) and Latin American (including Mexico) respondents all expect demand for local meetings to increase between 3 and 4% in 2015.

---

9   International Congress and Convention Association, IMEX and FastFuture (2011).

10   IMEX (2012).

11   Advito (2013).

12   Sherry, Y. (2014).

Figure 3.3   **Demand for local meetings, 2013 (%)**

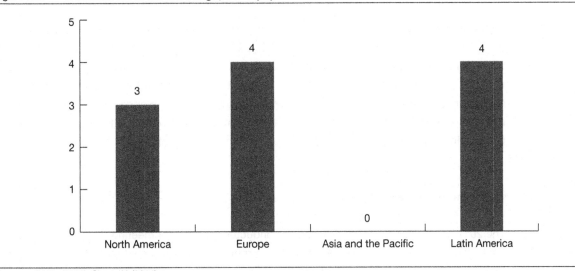

Source: Advito (2013); Sherry, Y. (2014).

Meetings combined with incentives

According to American Express 2015 forecast,[13] suppliers believe that meeting content holds importance for clients in the current scenario, which will result into more incentives getting blended with business meetings. Moreover, the survey reveals that about 47% of the suppliers' customers intend to merge meetings and incentives. Further research from Advito's *Industry Forecast 2015*[14], underlines the growing interest for combining meetings and travel, as key to unlocking additional savings.

Corporate social responsibility (CSR) is becoming an important determinant for decision makers

CSR is becoming an important criterion for selecting a destination, for both decision makers and attendees, with reduction in lead-time and virtual meetings as key challenges for service providers in the meetings industry.

As per IMEX global research,[15] CSR/sustainability has become an influential factor in the decision-making process, particularly for choosing a destination for meetings and conventions. More than half of the respondents in the *IMEX Group Issues* report confirmed their full commitment to CSR. With 24% respondents yet to implement 'Green Initiative', IMEX believes CSR/sustainability is of high priority for business community.

According to the Convention 2020 Survey, 70% of participants believe that CSR/sustainability will become a crucial factor influencing the decision of attending a meeting or not.

---

13   Sherry, Y. (2014).

14   Advito (2014).

15   IMEX (2012).

Increase in the number of virtual meetings

Over the coming 10–15 years, virtual meetings could replace up to 10% of external travel – trips to visit customers, leading to a reduction in corporate travel spending. Moreover, results from a survey by the Professional Convention Management Association, 21% of respondents report that their use of virtual meeting and events increased in the past year and 72% remained the same.[16] On average, the use of virtual meetings went up nearly 2%. The American Express 2015 forecast identifies the most compelling reasons for a virtual meeting in North America, Europe and Asia.[17] Cost savings and reduced travel appear as driving the increase in the use of virtual solutions.

Corporate meetings have shorter planning cycle

The *2012 Meetings Focus Trend Survey,*[18] conducted among 800 meeting planners, reveals that the typical planning cycle for a majority of the corporate and government meetings is 2–6 months. The planning cycle for corporate meetings and association meetings was shorter in 2013, but longer for government meetings.

Figure 3.4   **Typical planning cycle, 2012 (%)**

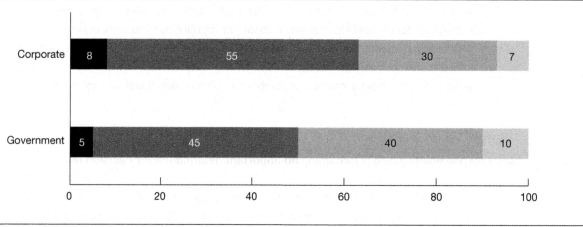

Source: Davidson, T. (2012).

The Advito 2015 Forecast,[19] expects lead times to lengthen as buyers try to avoid high prices and venue sell outs on their preferred dates. However, lead times changes are not expected to be the same across the globe.

16   Russell, M. (2014).

17   Sherry, Y. (2014).

18   Davidson, T. (2012), '2012 Meetings Market Trends Survey', *Meetings Focus,* January 2012 (online), available at: www.meetingsfocus.com (08-06-2015).

19   Advito (2014).

3.3 Decision-making: buying processes

Apart from the infrastructure and cost effectiveness, meeting planners prefer globally renowned (popular) destinations with strong infrastructure (such as Wi-Fi), excellent services and easier accessibility.

The decision-making process for corporate meetings is complex, often involving a large number of intermediaries, and this is becoming more pronounced due to a trend towards a fragmentation of the market.

Key determinants for meetings destination selection

According to a survey conducted in 2013, the most important meeting destination attributes for MPI (Meeting Professionals International) members (includes corporate meeting planners) included:[20]

- Perceived value for money;
- Overall cost;
- Reputation for hosting successful events;
- Desirable destination image;
- Support services for events; and
- Accessibility by air.

Moreover, according to IMEX meetings outlook report 2013,[21] 'Venues with Internet connectivity through Wi-Fi and Broadband' was among the top-5 criteria for the selection of venues.

> "Meeting space is critical. There has to be enough space, right number of breakout rooms, and of course amenities. Everyone wants free Internet. They really complain if it's not there".
>
> Corporate meeting planner in the United States of America, June 2013

Key determinants:
- **Cost effectiveness/ROI:** for meeting planners, return on investment is a key determinant for destination selection. Domestic destinations and cheaper venues/accommodation providing equivalent value are of interest to meeting planners;
- **Reputation/perception of destination:** meeting planners prefer destinations, which offer exceptional services and have a desirable destination image;
- **Perception of security and safety:** meeting planners want low-risk destinations, or destinations that are perceived as being safe places to be and to walk-around;
- **Infrastructure and support services:** the meeting space available and support services (e.g., projectors, laser pointer, and Wi-Fi) provided by venues also influence destination selection. Corporations tend to choose hotels before convention venues especially if there is an accommodation component. They will often have agreements in place with major

---

20 Meeting Professionals International (2014).

21 IMEX (2012).

hotel chains and choose locations where they have properties and appropriate meeting space. Their meetings are normally smaller and do not require numerous break out rooms like associations. They will choose convention venues for larger style events and if there is no accommodation required. Convention centres have started adding smaller more intimate meeting rooms to attract the interest of corporations; and

- **Ease of access:** for corporations, it is important that employees do not spend a lot of time travelling to meeting destinations. Meeting planners prefer destinations with direct and frequent flights.

3.4   Key players: service offerings

Corporate meetings/incentive companies

The corporate market is dominated by a series of large corporate agencies that provide a broad range of travel services. In Europe and North America, some of the larger companies include Carlson, Maritz, American Express, HRG, Meridien, MCI and Kenes among others. In addition, there are a number of smaller companies that work independently, but can be very influential in meeting organization and decision-making. The on-going fragmentation of the corporate meeting and incentive companies makes the market more complicated to influence and to analyse than the association segment.

Importance of on-line tools

The corporate market is also changing radically due to the introduction of on-line tools that enable companies to have access to information and services that improve efficiency and effectiveness. For example, Cvent is an on-line meeting management service. It is being used by many of the large corporate meetings agencies cited above.

Site selection

The decision-making process, when it comes to destinations, is often outsourced to site selection companies, who specialise in proposing appropriate venues, but who also help with negotiations.

3.5   Drivers and barriers for the segment

Drivers	Barriers
- The majority of corporations globally increased their meeting budgets in 2013, over 2012;	- Increasing usage of virtual meeting methods such as video-conferencing is considered as a threat to corporate meetings industry by participants of Meeting Focus' 'Meeting Market Survey'; and
- Globalization is driving many IMCs into emerging regions; and	
- Regional trade agreements are driving B2B meetings between partner countries.	- Tough economic conditions and involvement of procurement departments is creating short haul and shorter duration meetings as well as greater focus on ROI.

3.6 Supply chain analysis

The following two sections individually analyse the internal meetings and external meetings supply chain.

3.6.1 Internal meetings: corporate value chain

Internal corporate meetings involve individuals from the company who organize activities such as operations, logistics, sales and marketing services. Figure 3.5 illustrates the relationship between the various steps of the corporate value chain. For internal meetings, corporations assess the current position of their business, the aims and objectives and decide whether to hold a meeting. To start with, primary activities are closely evaluated and in second step secondary activities, which include all support activities, such as gathering the technology, human resources, infrastructure and other needed services required for the meeting. The final step of the chain is the corporate meeting.

Figure 3.5   **Internal meetings value chain**

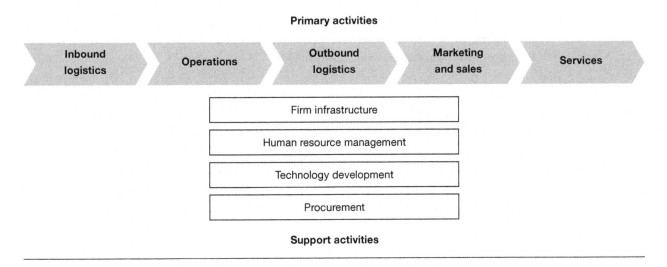

3.6.2 External meetings: supply chain

The supply chain for external meetings follows the traditional supply of commodities, component, sellable products, branding, sales and marketing, shipping, outlets and delivery to the end user. It includes all the preparation from venues to food and beverages, equipment and marketing and communications. Because external corporate meetings are generally much bigger in size and aim to impress, supply chain is an essential part of the success of the event. First the corporation needs to identify what the content of the meeting will be and what resource the corporation has (raw materials), then determine what the event should include (activities, meeting component, etc.), after which the corporation needs to determine which intermediaries and suppliers they need, this allows for the next step, which is the assembly of all the elements before the event takes place (distribution) reaching out to the participants (end user). Figure 3.6 serves to highlight that the end users are an essential part of the success of the external corporate meeting. A large number of external meetings are for demonstrating new product developments, innovations and business developments. Therefore the branding, sales and marketing are an integral part of the supply chain.

Figure 3.6   **External meetings supply chain**

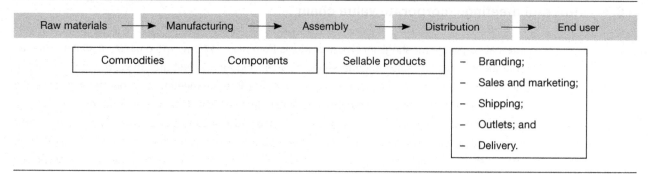

3.7   Destination Europe: characteristics

The absence of new supply amid rising demand has inevitably shifted the meetings market in favour of the seller in 2013. Prices have thus increased, but only of 3 to 5% in Europe.[22] In general, European cities have experienced healthy growth.

Yet across Europe, the region is most likely to see large variations between countries. The American Express 2015 forecast mentions Germany and the United Kingdom are more optimistic than France, Sweden and Spain.[23]

In terms of incoming meeting, PCMA reveals that 44% of respondents are most likely to consider choosing Western Europe, 42% the United Kingdom and 39% Eastern Europe for holding their meetings.[24] Demand for meetings outside Europe, are however, expected to remain flat or decline slightly.

Moreover, according to Advito's 2014 forecast, demand to Asia rose by 6.1% and travel between Europe and the Middle East reached 12.2%. This reflects the low demand for long-haul destinations and the increasing focus for short-haul destinations.[25]

Due to budget challenges, time considerations and as a means of public support for the local community, the region is increasing its local meetings,[26] in turn generating valuable internal and external support.

22   Advito (2013).

23   Sherry, Y. (2014).

24   Russell, M. (2014).

25   Advito (2013).

26   Sherry, Y. (2014).

3.8   Destination North America: characteristics

According to the *2014 Meetings Focus Trends Survey,*[27] carried out by Meeting Focus, 45.5% of the North American[28] MCCI market is dedicated to corporate planning.

Table 3.1   **Duration of corporate meetings in North America, 2013**

Number of days	Rate-of-change 2012 vs. 2013 (%)
0.5	2.4
1.0	3.3
1.5	-1.8
2.0	-2.9
2.5	-1.9
3.0	1.6
3.5	1.5
4.0	-0.5
4.5	-1.1
5.0	-2.1
> 5.0	1.3

Note: Here North America refers to the United States of America, Canada, Mexico and the Caribbean islands.

Source: Davidson, T. (2013).

Increased workload due to reduced staffing, more complicated contract negotiations, fewer meetings and less entertainment are the main changes seen by the corporate meetings planners in the United States of America and Canada.[29] The duration of corporate meetings is generally decreasing.

Similarly to Europe there has been rising demands yet a shortage of new supply. The shortfall in meeting space led to shorter lead times. In the United States of America, hotels have responded by reducing the time they will hold provisionally booked space and the time to sign the contract.

27 Davidson, T. (2013).

28 Meeting Focus defines North America as the United States of America, Canada, Mexico and the Caribbean islands.

29 Davidson, T. (2013).

3.9   Destination Asia: characteristics

While Asia's corporate meeting segment predicted strong growth for 2013 (+6.4%), it was expected to see a slight decline in 2014 (-1.2%) although no data was available yet. This is largely driven by heightened scrutiny and formalised approval processes.

Asia is leading in a number of industries, having headquarters in key industries. As the industry develops in this region, and globalization increases the need for trade and local demands, Asia is experiencing growth in corporate meetings. However, demand versus supply varies greatly across the region, given significant hotel investment in countries such as India and China.

As more meeting space is becoming available in markets such as China, India, Malaysia and Indonesia, the increased capacity is leading to softer rates.

3.10   Characteristics of other regions

According to American Express 2015 forecast,[30] Central/South America respondents expect meeting demand from the region to remain the same and demand from other regions to Central and South America to increase. Currently increasing local meetings, the region is expecting to become more open over the years as it invests in more hotel developments and infrastructure building.

The majority of the corporate meetings held in South Africa are domestic meetings. International corporate meetings, mostly take place at short-haul locations; hence, companies from Europe and the United States of America, generally do not prefer South Africa for corporate meetings. As corporate meetings generally have a small number of attendees (less than 100), these meetings usually take place in hotels meeting rooms.

In South Africa, Johannesburg hosts majority of the corporate meetings, due to the presence of headquarters of majority of the companies operating in the country. The country's meeting industry is also witnessing mergers and partnerships among PCOs and DMCs, in an order to provide wider breadth of services to corporates holding meetings in South Africa.

> "What we are seeing is that PCOs and DMCs are merging to become one-stop destination for corporates, and this is expected to continue going forward, as the competition increases".
>
> General Manager of a convention bureau, February 2012

Key industry sectors are typically from the medical, or pharmaceutical sectors, mining, agriculture and engineering or African Unions.

---

30 Sherry, Y. (2014).

3.11   Corporate meetings segment: conclusion

The corporate meetings segment varies greatly from association conventions and congresses. Two types exist: internal meetings, which are organizationally orientated, and external meetings, which are focused on business, and markets. This segment represents a very high spending, lucrative end of the market, targeting headquarters cities, population centres and major markets. It uses a wide range of conference and convention centres, meeting facilities in hotels, training and conference centres, halls and other spaces. A recent increase in corporate budgets was illustrated by an increasing number of corporate meetings and participants per event.

The segment is witnessing post-recession recovery, with corporate budget and spending growing and demand for meetings increasing. Nonetheless, there is emerging demand for secondary and closer-to-business locations or combining incentives. ROI of meetings is therefore becoming important, especially as CSR, shorter planning cycles, decline in size and duration of meetings and the increased number of virtual meetings, are reshaping the organization of corporate meetings.

In response to the changing environment, decision-makers increasingly focus on financial aspects: perceived value for money, overall cost; the destination: reputation for hosting successful events, desirable destination image; and services and accessibility: supportive service for events, ease of access. And, while procurement departments have a greater role in the decision-making process, decisions are generally made at a higher level of management. Nonetheless, corporates are also doing direct contracting with major hotel chains for global/regional meetings. In emerging markets corporate travel agencies dominate the market.

In Europe, cities have experienced healthy growth in the corporate meetings segments. And, while some variations between countries, means that some countries are doing better than others, there is an increased focus for short-haul destinations. Overall, budget constraints, time considerations, and the will to support local communities increase local meetings. That said, North America stays an important destination for the segment. However the recent trend shows fewer meetings, less entertainment and increased workload due to reduced staffing. Asia, on the other hand, is generally experiencing growth, as it has many headquarters in key industries, and increased infrastructure is leading to softer rates. Nonetheless, the region needs to focus in significant hotel investment. Other regions are also investing to become more attractive, developing new infrastructure and becoming more open.

Overall, while the general increase in budgets is a driving force of the segment, the increased usage of virtual meeting methods presents a threat.

Chapter 4

Incentives: analysis and profile

Incentive travel has grown even faster than regular meetings over the past year, as companies increasingly recognise the importance of motivating their best salespeople.[1]

Organizations are becoming more virtual in structure, and have become hungrier for new ways to build trust, teamwork and camaraderie. This creates an opportunity for executives to increase employees' engagement, which in turn result in revenue-related outcomes. CEOs need to attract and retain talent, especially as demographics change and different ways of thinking are reshaping the industry. Incentives offer the opportunity to engage their workforce.

4.1 Characteristics and activity

Many companies offer incentive programmes for their employees, distributors or customers. The programme usually represents some type of reward for levels of sales or productivity achieved. These incentives can take the form of cash rewards or gifts of some kind. The key is to offer some form of reward as a means to motivate employees, agents and customers. Many companies offer travel incentives because they are highly motivational. These events are in some instances mostly recreational, but, in recent years, increasingly, they include a formal meeting component. This is because having a meeting may provide corporate tax benefits and offer additional value in terms of networking, communication, education and team building. In general, incentive programmes are meant to be highly entertaining. Therefore, incentive planners are looking for destinations that offer an exciting range of entertainment options in hotels and facilities that offer high levels of service.

Table 4.1   **Meeting content added to incentive trips, 2014–2015 (%)**

	North America	**Europe**	**Central and South America**	**Asia**
Adding meeting component to incentive trips	1.2 ↑	1.2 ↑	2.3 ↑	2.4 ↑

Note: North America excludes Mexico; Central and South America includes Mexico.

Source: Sherry, Y. (2014).

In the final annual SITE Index survey in 2013,[2] 80% of respondents agreed that the effectiveness of various motivational tools varies depending on the generation of those to be motivated. This

---

1   Advito (2014).

2   Society for Incentive Travel Excellence (2013).

is a call for programme designers to be able to offer an array of options in incentive programmes so that different generations are given the choice to find the right reward/activity for themselves. Interestingly, in terms of destination marketing approaches, email news, familiarisation trips and direct mail were rated as the most effective tools, followed by trade shows participation. Internet destination websites and telephone calls were rated as the less effective ways to promote incentive destinations. Moreover, incentive trips are increasingly adding meeting content.

4.1.1   Venues used

High quality hotels, four or five stars are characteristic of incentive travel. These venues generally offer a wide range of activities such as golf or other group activities in order to provide the best holiday-type travel and an opportunity for team building. But with the recent trend of including formal meeting components, chosen venues should have the ability to offer the necessary facilities to accommodate meetings, thus hotels and resorts with meeting facilities are increasingly being targeted.

According to the 2013 SITE annual survey[3] a majority of respondents believe that the use of all-inclusive hotels show minor changes – mostly decreases – while cruise products show somewhat greater variation from prior years. Service levels of local destination management companies, such as hotels, venues and facilities are key destination differentiators. If these are poor, the destination will suffer.

4.1.2   Activity

Top destinations

North America, the Caribbean and Europe are still the top destinations for outbound incentive travel – a third of planners use these destinations. Other destinations include Central America, South America and Asia. Emerging countries are becoming increasingly popular, with China, Bali, Vietnam and Peru as common choices for planners. Luxury hotels, continuously improving infrastructure and guaranteed cultural and authentic experiences are the main factors attracting organizers.[4]

---

3   Society for Incentive Travel Excellence (2013).

4   van Dyke, M. (2014), *2014 Trends in Engagement, Incentives, and Recognition'*, International Research Foundation, 30-01-2014 (online), available at: http://theirf.org/research/2014-trends-in-engagement-incentives-and-recognition/102/ (05-10-2015).

Figure 4.1   **Destinations for incentive travel, 2014 (market share, %)**

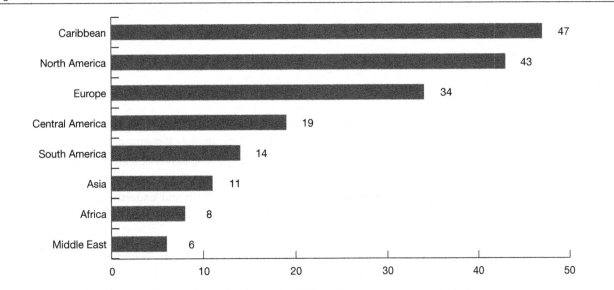

Source: QRA Analytics (2015), *IRF Fall Pulse Survey – Fall 2014,* International Research Foundation, 07-02-2015 (online), available at:
http://theirf.org/research/irf-full-pulse-survey---fall-2014/152/ (08-06-2015).

The recession had pushed planners to move their programmes from international to domestic destinations. Today, planners are now returning to longer-haul international destinations.[5]

Size and duration of events

There have been very stark decreases in the number of planners who were previously cutting their programme's size and duration. The IRF last four Pulse Surveys has shown that only an average of 7% of planners are increasing the duration of their programmes and 9% are increasing their programme's size (measured in room nights).

4.1.3   Budget spend

IRF Fall Pulse Study shows that incentive travel budgets are finally stabilising, with more planners increasing their budgets. On average, 47% of planners expect a slight increase of their budgets for 2015 with only 15% expecting a decrease. This trend is expected to continue and will lead to emerging growth in the segment.

Moreover, the research shows that many planners are continuing their investment in the additional non-meal components of their programmes such as including all airline fees, offsite excursions, transfers, gifts, etc.

---

5   van Dyke, M. (2015).

In sum, planners are targeting quality over quantity, allowing for programme contraction to dissipate, planners to continue investing in more robust programmes and the development of slight programme expansions.

4.2   Key trends

Corporates are increasingly adopting cost-cutting measures as a result of the past economic conditions. As per-person incentive expenditure is moderately increasing, more value-for-money offerings and the rise of emerging destinations are expecting to reshape the segment. Additionally, executives are finding it difficult to attract and retain top talent employees – who would benefit from the incentive – and who are those who possess the skills and leadership potential companies need to grow.[6]

Per-person incentive expenditure is moderately increasing: according to an IRF survey,[7] 43% of participants said that their budget for the incentive travel programmes, in 2012, remained the same than what it had been for the year 2011. Furthermore, 49% of participants expect it to remain the same in 2015. However, the average budget, per person, reduced from USD 3,100 in 2010 to USD 2,603 in 2012. Today, as the industry recovers from the recession, per-person expenditure is moderately increasing, with an average spend per-person of USD 3,000–4,000.[8]

Increasing focus on value for money, clients seek 'more for less': the IRF/CMI survey[9] reported that corporates are adopting several measures to adjust per-person expenditure and fit more within their budgets. The top-5 steps companies were planning to take in 2013, in order to reduce the expense of their incentive travel programme, are presented in the following figure.

Figure 4.2   **Focus on value for money for incentives**

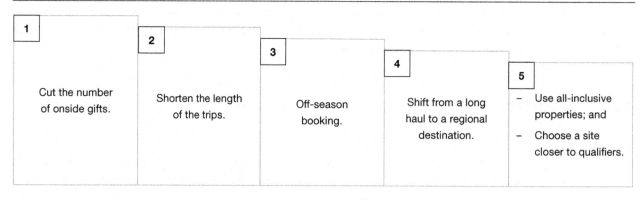

Note: Heights of the boxes indicate the greater affinity of steps taken for cost cutting.

Source: van Dyke, M. (2012).

---

6   Ibid.

7   van Dyke, M. (2012), *2013 MeetingsNet IRF Annual Incentive Travel Trends Survey,* International Research Foundation, 31-12-2012 (online), available at: http://theirf.org/research/2013-meetingsnet-irf-annual-incentive-travel-trends-survey/278/ (08-06-2015).

8   van Dyke, M. (2014).

9   van Dyke, M. (2012).

The incentive industry is encountering a shift as the increase in usage of social media for promotion of incentives, the preference for smaller group size, and the change from group travel programmes to individual awards, drives the need for customised, 'self-defining experiences' and unique packages/offerings.[10]

Shift from group to individual awards: in a pulse study, conducted by IRF in 2014,[11] 29% of incentive professionals, who were surveyed, were considering a shift, either temporarily or permanently, from group travel programmes to individual awards. In the 2012 IRF/CMI survey, 40% of respondents reported using individual travel incentives with an average per person budget of USD 2,105.

Decreasing focus on CSR aspects: as per the 2014 *IRF Fall Pulse Survey,* only 37% of companies included CSR in their incentive programmes in 2013, compared to 40% in 2010.[12] However, according to industry experts the incentive travel programmes now also include a 'corporate giving' element, such as a team-building project organized for supporting a local charity or community.

Social media becoming an important tool to promote incentive programmes: many organizers are now using social media tools, such as Tripadvisor, to seek feedback, from the attendees, on destinations for incentive travel programmes.

Social media use is growing at high speed, attracting a large number of new users, every year, who understand the benefits of acquiring the new communication devices. When asked, which social media platforms they are using for marketing their company or clients' incentive programmes, Linkedin and Facebook appeared to be the most popular.[13]

Yet the 2014 IRF Pulse Survey identifies a number of other enhancements tools used by planners in order to enhance their incentive programme. The proliferation of mobile devices has also given rise to 'apps for everything'. On the positive side these apps provide needed data on-demand, but, on a more negative side, allow attendees to take more control of their experience, without necessarily turning towards the help of planners.[14]

---

10 van Dyke, M. (2015).

11 QRA Analytics (2015).

12 Ibid.

13 Society for Incentive Travel Excellence (2013).

14 van Dyke, M. (2015).

Figure 4.3   **Enhancement tools used for incentives, 2014 (%)**

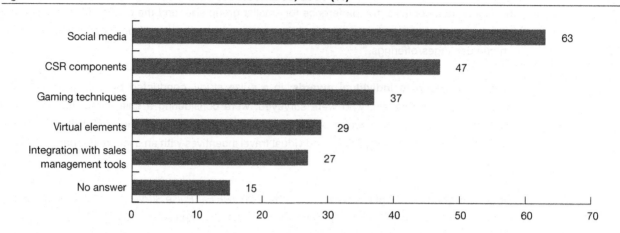

Source: QRA Analytics (2015).

Increasing demand for unique experience: companies increasingly prefer easier-to-manage, smaller sized groups, in order to provide a more personalised experience to the attendees.

> "Attendees of incentive programmes prefer to have an exotic experience, and want to experience unique culture during the travel".
>
> President, an association of events and exhibitions, February 2012

Wellness incentives: wellness has experienced some recent interest among incentive planners.[15] In IRF's last survey, 62% of respondents were interested about wellness as part of their programmes and are thus reviewing how to incorporate it. The wellness incentive is becoming bigger, with 38% of companies already offering the incentive in 2012 and 21% planning to within 12 and 18 months. The primary goal of wellness programmes is generally to improve employee health/fitness.[16]

4.3   Key players

Incentive travel programme organizers: depending on the corporation's needs and requirements, Incentive Travel Programme organizers may offer the following services to bring support to planners organizing incentive programmes:
–   Preparation of budget;
–   Exclusive off-site dinner venues and dine-around programmes;
–   Pre and post-touring activities;
–   Providing gifts;
–   Team-building;
–   Assistance for visa, accommodation at hotels and transportation; and
–   Providing travel insurance.

---

15   Ibid.

16   '2014 Incentive Safety and Wellness IQ Survey' (2014), *Incentive What Motivates,* 26-03-2014 (online), available at: www.incentivemag.com (29-09-2015).

Corporation: a corporation may engage the services of an incentive house, travel fulfilment company or corporate travel agent to create their incentive travel programme. The purpose of the incentive programmes is to motivate and reward employees and/or distributors that achieve exceptional results.

Incentive agencies: an incentive agency will develop motivational programmes for corporations, which may include incentive travel, bonuses and/or merchandise. Incentive agencies are more common in western markets whereas corporate travel agents are used in Asia to create incentive travel programmes. They employ the services of a local DMC to provide itineraries using local products and services.

Travel fulfilment company: travel fulfilment companies specialise in the development of incentive travel programmes for corporations. They do not undertake the same range of services as an incentive house. The term travel fulfilment company is more common in the United States of America.

Corporate travel agents: corporate travel agents specialise in making business travel arrangements for corporations, which may or may not include incentive travel programmes. Corporate travel agents are commonly engaged in Asia to manage and coordinate incentive travel programmes.

Destination management companies (DMCs): a DMC provides ground support for the corporation and/or incentive house and/or travel fulfilment company and/or corporate travel agent. They manage and coordinate transfers, transport, accommodation, themed events and tour programmes specifically for the conference and incentive programmes. Some PCOs offer DMC services and vice versa.

Event management companies (EMCs): event Management Companies are responsible for organizing a specific event for an incentive programme. These events may be themed, awards nights or gala dinners. The EMC will coordinate all aspects of an event such as invitation design, venue selection and management, decor/theming, catering, staging and audio visual, entertainment and on site management of the event.

4.4 Decision-making: buying processes – key determinants for incentive destination selection

The President of the Society of Incentive and Travel Executives (SITE) listed the following points as main characteristics and trends influencing the incentive's segment competitive environment:
– Economy is driving decisions;
– There is a negative perception about luxury incentive travel, with luxury segments hurting (using 4- instead of 5-star hotels, "cheaper is chicer");
– Lead times are shorter with protracted negotiations;
– Transparency is a priority;
– There is a need to prove financial viability (ROI measurement);
– Including CSR elements in programmes is important; and
– Sales incentive programmes will rebound with a major focus on ROI.

When selecting destination for incentive programmes, most important factors include a unique/ exotic experience, along with participants' safety and security. Expanding on the above-mentioned points, the following part identifies key determinants for incentive destination selection.

According to the SITE, "a fashionable or new destination/holiday type that gives winners something to boast about to friends" was the most important factor for respondents while selecting destinations.[17] Other important factors were:

–   Safety and security;
–   An expensive-sounding programme at a good value price;
–   Ease of access (direct air access) – participants can often come from one source market (versus those attending association conventions and congresses), which places a greater emphasis on direct air services;
–   Local knowledge and expertise;
–   High quality hotels and service levels; and
–   Unique and exclusive experiences (beyond that of the average traveller).

"Incentive destination selection is primarily being driven by provision of unique, exotic experience to employees".

President of an association of events and exhibitions

The following determinants have thus been selected as key for incentive destination selection.

Unique experience: in order to motivate employees, incentive planners prefer destinations, which offer distinct features and would provide a memorable experience to the participants. Often referred to as the "wow" factor, it is experiential rather that "touristic" sighting seeing tours.

Safety and security – risk assessment: incentive planners prefer destination where participants would feel safe and secure, i.e., a stable political and labour environment, no transportation disruption, no medical emergencies (such as Pandemic (H1N1) 2009), no acts of terrorism and violence, no natural disasters, etc.

The incentive segment bears a degree of responsibility; ethical and legal, to provide care in a programme. Being preventive rather than curative is thus necessary. Risk management is an especially important consideration for destination-centred suppliers, particularly for such eventualities as natural or man-made disasters.[18] Planners must also assess the risks involved in the activities that are included in a programme. It is therefore important to know and qualify supplier partners. Sources of information include:

–   Government travel advisories;
–   Destination experts – qualified DMCs, hotel management and tourist offices or convention and visitor bureaux;
–   Insurance companies – know what your insurance policies covers including those of your suppliers;
–   Airline companies;

17   Society for Incentive Travel Excellence (2013).

18   Ibid.

- Legal departments;
- Private security companies; and
- Financial advisors.

Ease of access: to minimise the time away from work, Incentive planners prefer destinations that are easily accessible and provide desirable experience to the participants. Incentive participants often come from one market unlike association conventions and congresses where delegates come from multiple destinations. Having high frequency, high capacity direct services to a destination from the source market is a key consideration especially for larger groups. In some situations incentive programmes have been known to charter air services for their participants.

Value for money: planners also consider the value of the programme as perceived by the participants before selecting the destination. ROI/ROO (return on investment/return on objective) considerations continue to surface. The primary reason for choosing a destination is financially driven, which is no surprise in this economy. But quality service is an extremely close second. 93% of planners said they would use a destination again if it measured up on both counts. Therefore, future business from a planner is almost certain if programme value and quality service are evident and measureable. The correlation between delivering value and providing exceptional experiences is critical given the economic environment.

4.5   Financial and economic variables

Incentive travel is a very important segment in destinations tourism statistics stimulating the markets' economic and social sectors. David Sand, former president of the SITE mentions a number of other ways in which this segment develops local economies:
- Visitors usually return with family and friends on a second more regular visit;
- They usually spend up to three times what regular visitors spend since they do not have travel bills;
- They spend their money on all the extras, (shopping, art, local crafts and restaurants) – creating jobs; and
- Guests experiences the destination and become important ambassadors.

"This is a multibillion-dollar annual marketplace that is growing as developing economies understand the power of using structures incentive schemes to drive company performance".

David Sand, president of SITE, April 2013

4.6   Drivers and barriers of the segment

Drivers	Barriers
Corporates are increasingly using incentive travel as a reward for high performing employees (particularly sales employees).	Expenditure per head has seen a declining trend over the last few years as corporates aim to attract more value from their constrained budgets. They want to reduce cost without compromising on quality.

4.7   Supply chain analysis

The incentive segment can be separated between inbound and outbound activity. An Inbound incentive programme is defined as any incentive programme held fully or partly in the given country for which the primary client is an international corporate, society or association. On the other hand, an outbound incentive programme is defined as any incentive programme held in an international destination for which the primary client is a given country corporate, society or association.

Because incentive programmes are targeted for best performing employees, the main decision maker is the corporation – buyer, sales, planner, human resources, etc. With the help of governmental travel advisories, insurance companies, legal entities and Incentive Travel Programme organizers, the corporation is able to assess risk and opportunities before taking the appropriate decision when choosing incentive destinations.

The main components of the incentive programme include the following services: hotels, air transportation, merchandise, awards nights, gala/themed dinners, CSR, team building, experiential tours, adventure programmes – increasingly combined with meetings – etc., which are delivered through Incentive House, Travel Fulfilment Company, Corporate Travel Agents, DMCs, Event Management Companies, and Incentive Travel Programme organizers. Additional providers such as consultants, tour operators or travel agents are mostly important for the delivery of the service at the moment of the incentive programme.[19]

Increasingly however, corporations and agencies are cutting out DMCs, EMCs and going direct to hotels and suppliers.

---

19   QRA Analytics (2015).

Figure 4.4   **Supply chain incentives**

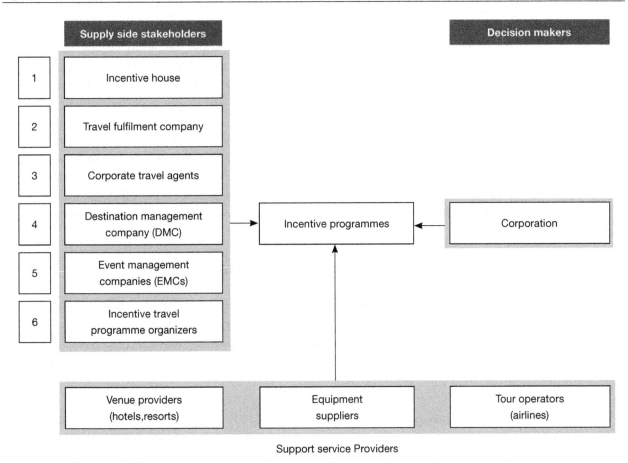

Support service Providers

4.8   Destination Europe: characteristics

Europe is very diverse in nature, with over 45 countries, distinguishable cultures, languages, traditions and customs. Although most share a common currency – the euro (EUR) – legislation, taxation, business etiquettes and service infrastructure vary greatly across the region. The Global Incentive Council and IMA Europe (2013)[20] consider the complexity of the European market in incentive programmes.

> "The desirability of real-time rewards differs from country to country […]. Choice is the key when providing incentive and recognition rewards throughout Europe".
>
> Sheila Sheldon, Senior Vice President EMEA, 2013

The frequency of incentive and recognition varies across countries, with the United Kingdom generally considered to be amongst the most advanced. According to IRF's *Fall Pulse Survey*,[21]

---

20   Global Incentive Council and Incentive Marketing Association Europe (2013), *Recognition and Incentives in Europe,* White Paper (online), available at: www.incentivemarketing.org (29-09-2015).

21   QRA Analytics (2015).

Europe represents 37% of chosen destination for Incentive Travel programmes, decreasing from past pulse surveys.

The variety of experiences afforded in Europe ensures that the region will continue to be an extremely popular incentive destination for groups. Europe encompasses a variety of activities – historical, cultural, luxurious, adventurous, epicurean – making the region very enticing for incentive programmes.[22]

The region is also making use of new technologies to incorporate in incentive programmes. A meeting expert, explains in the American Express 2014 meeting forecast,[23] how he witnessed a unique use of mobile app at an incentive event: "It incorporated a walking tour of Paris. In teams, attendees were asked to take a picture of the most beautiful part of Paris they saw during the tour and then share it with the entire group after the tour, which resulted in much discussion."

4.9   Destination North America: characteristics

According to the *2014 Meetings Focus Trends Survey*,[24] 3.3% of the North American MCCI market (excluding Mexico) is dedicated to incentive planning. Currently, the United States of America and Canada are the leading destinations for incentive programmes; with 43% of respondents from the IRF Fall Pulse Survey[25] indicating that North America (excluding Mexico) was their chosen region for Incentive Travel Programmes.

The United States of America itself held in 2012 67,700 incentive meetings, which hosted altogether a total of 9,172,000 participants, 4% of all participants in the business events industry.[26]

Canada is also seen as a popular destination, combining nature with contemporary charms.[27]

In the past, companies from the United States of America were more likely to choose the Caribbean for incentive travel. Today they are increasingly venturing to Europe or South America as destinations. Outbound incentive travel from the United States of America, is experience a growing trend to stage incentives in cities rather than resorts, especially in Rome, Paris, London and Prague.[28]

Findings confirm that the incentives market is very large and thriving – 74% of United States business using incentive travel merchandise, and gift cards spend USD 76.9 billion annually in this category. The market is largely driven by smaller businesses (those between

---

22   Ting, D. (2013), 'The Top Incentive Travel Destinations of 2013', Incentive What Motivates, 24-09-2013, (online), available at: www.incentivemag.com (08-06-2015).

23   American Express Meetings & Events (2013).

24   Davidson, T. (2013).

25   QRA Analytics (2015).

26   Pricewaterhouse Coopers LLP (2014).

27   Ting, D. (2013).

28   'EIBTM Trend Watch Report Indicates Growth for 2014' (2014).

   Davidson, R. (2013), *EIBTM 2013 Trends Watch Report*, The Global Meetings & Events Expo, Read Travel Exhibitions, Elsevir.

USD 1–10 million in annual revenue), whose budgets are considerably smaller, but the huge number of these businesses creates a USD 39 billion market.

4.10 Destination Asia: characteristics

The 2014 *IRF Fall Pulse Survey* indicates that Asia was chosen by 11% of respondents as destination for incentive programmes.[29]

Inbound incentive travel is successful in Asia since the region offers a set of unique experiences. These are important differentiators, which encourage a number of companies to bring their top employees to the destination.

Outbound incentive business from Asia to the world is in maturing phase; with very high growth it offers hope and opportunity for regional and world destinations to boost their economies.

The region is growing in popularity, attracting incentive programmes that seek out unique cultural experiences.[30] However, incentive travel remains a very new concept, especially in China, and only a limited number of incentive companies offer the same level as Europe and the United States of America. Incentives exist, but they are organized by corporates through local travel agents. In Asia and emerging regions, planners mainly use corporate travel agents, as incentive houses are not as well known. Nonetheless, the China outbound incentive market is growing rapidly and travelling further as it matures. It is also a source of some of the world's largest incentive group movements, with some groups attracting thousands of participants.

Asia is still in a developing phase, and as corporate clients' requirements become more sophisticated, company specialisation will emerge to meet the needs. There are some exceptions, such as Thailand, which has become a popular destination over the last few years. Other popular destinations have included Hong Kong, China; Singapore and Bali.

Nonetheless, some drawbacks are still at stake, such as pollution in major cities or Internet restrictions in China. Government needs to take action to ensure better development creating in turn more opportunities for the incentive segment.

4.11 Characteristics of other regions

Emerging markets are becoming more popular in the incentive segment. While the first tier of top destinations remains North America and Europe, the second tier includes Central and South America, which are destinations full of authentic experiences, with rich cultures and traditions, attractive to planners. On the other hand, while South Africa is widely used, less than 10% of planners choose Africa and the Middle East as destinations for incentive travel.[31]

---

29 QRA Analytics (2015).

30 Ting, D. (2013).

31 *Meetings and Conventions* (2014), website: www.meetings-conventions.com/magazine/.

SITE's biggest expansion has come from India, China, South America and Africa, all of which are expected to produce double-digit increase in membership over the next few years.

> "All of these countries are growing their infrastructure – hotels, entertainment venues and facilities, airports, trains, rail and road infrastructure, convention and meeting spaces, creative product and incentive experiences – at a rapid rate".
>
> David Sands, SITE President, 2013

Emerging markets increase outbound destination – as is seen by the increasing membership in international associations – but they also increase inbound destination appeal by developing their own market.

Planners are constantly looking for latest trends. Authentic destinations with rich culture and traditions, guarantee new discoveries and experiences, a great selling point for the segment. Latin America, India, Africa and the Middle East offer these advantages. In Latin America, Mexico has always been a top incentive destination.

In an interview for MeetingsNet in 2014,[32] Ron Officer, CEO and President of Creative Group in Chicago, is always on the lookout for 'the next great thing'. Yet he underlines that some destinations are not for every group. In emerging regions, countries are reaching out to increase their level of attractiveness as an incentive destination, by developing better infrastructure and making efforts to improve safety issues such as drug trafficking or violence.

South Africa, particularly Cape Town, is among the most preferred destination in the world for international incentive travel. And, unique experiences such as safaris increase the motivational value tremendously.

> "Safaris are very unique and there's a thirst among incentive travel participants to experience new and different destinations like South Africa".
>
> Jim Ruszala, Senior Director of marketing for Maritz Travel Company

4.12   Incentives segment conclusion

The incentives segment is growing steadily as companies recognise the importance of motivation and well-being. Highly entertaining, incentive programmes use high quality hotels, generally located in North America, the Caribbean and Europe. The size and duration can vary, but is remaining relatively stable, and occasionally, increasing; which is reflected in stabilising and sometimes increasing budgets.

The segment is experiencing a number of changes as per-person incentive expenditure declined but is now increasing again, demands for 'more for less' increase and as meeting elements are being added to the programmes. In order to respond to new demands, many incentive programmes shifted from group to individual awards, decrease focus on CSR aspects, and use social media

---

32 MeetingsNet (2014), *Top 5 Emerging Incentive Destinations in 2014,* 12-02-2014 (online), available at: www.meetingsnet.com (08-06-2015).

to promote incentive programmes. Moreover, demand for wellness incentives and for unique experience, are reshaping the segment.

Key players include corporate players: corporate travel agents, corporation and incentive players: incentive travel programme organizers, incentive agencies, travel fulfilment company, destination management companies (DMCs) and event management companies (EMCs). Decision-makers seek unique experience, safety and security, ease of access, high quality products and services and value for money as key determinants for incentive programmes.

The diversity of the European destination ensures its popularity. However the frequency and recognition varies greatly across countries. The region is increasingly using technology to respond to changing needs. North America is also a leading destination for incentive programmes. Companies from the United States of America are gradually venturing outbound incentive travel to Europe or South America. In general, there is a growing trend targeting cities rather than resorts for incentive programmes. Asia is successful in attracting incentive travel, and outbound incentive travel is in maturing phase, with very high growth.

While incentive travel remains very new in the region, the destination is attracting those who seek unique cultural experiences. Some drawbacks include Internet restrictions, in China and pollution. Emerging markets are becoming more popular, offering authentic experiences, rich cultures and traditions. While South Africa is widely chosen, India, China and South America are expanding this segment and Africa and the Middle East are not as popular. In general, emerging markets are expanding their outbound destinations.

Although there is an increased use of incentives to reward high performance employees, there is a general decline of expenditure per head.

Phase 2

Analysis of the decision-making processes of MCCI organizers

Chapter 5

The decision-making process of MCCI organizers

To bring further support to the first section of this study, phase 2 captures relevant insights concerning the decision-making process of MCCI decision makers.

The section offers a clear overview of typologies of decision-making processes for each segment, and an inventory of planners' needs and expectations with respect to the choice of destination and venues. The research results are presented by segment, comparing the three regions of Europe, North America and Asia.

As the MCCI continues to grow, reflecting on these results can offer additional valuable information for the development of strategies for European destinations.

Key messages:
- A meeting, convention or incentive is an integral part of the overall strategy of the organization;
- Association meeting planners: most associations require a competitive bidding process, and the decision about choice of destination, is most often made by a Board or event committee. The key criteria that influence the decisions tend to be related to cost and size of meeting facilities. Results reveal that issues such as advocacy, membership recruitment and local presence are the most important. Planners prefer to choose destinations that fit with their objectives, which ensures that the event is attended by a larger and interested audience, and also choose destinations that allow freedom to discuss topics that may be political in nature;
- Corporate meeting planners: the decision-making process is very different and can be characterised by the desire to provide quality and high profile events and are largely dependent on the nature of the meeting – internal or external. In most cases final decisions are taken by top management or event committee. Destination appeal and access are considered as being the most influential criteria affecting decision-making. The second phase of the research shows that corporate planners reinforced the necessity for accessibility and cost considerations when making final decisions, yet added that destinations with local presence are preferred;
- Incentive planners: needs and expectations are largely dependent on the destination and the desire to offer the additional 'wow factor', and final decisions are mostly taken by top management or event committee. Key decision-making criteria go hand in hand with the aims of the corporation's communication strategy;
- CBs are largely used across regions, with some noticeable differences. Convention planners use CBs the most. For all segments and regions, the most commonly used services include site visits, bid support, impartial advice and marketing material; and
- Survey results also show that since the industry developed differently across countries, there are varying decision-making processes across regions: CBs are solicited differently, intermediaries are different, key influencing criteria and final decision makers may vary. As North America and Europe find innovative ways to enhance their mature markets, Asia invests extra efforts to continue growing its MCCI industry.

5.1   Methodology

In order to provide a comprehensive picture of the decision-making process in the area of meetings, congresses, convention and incentives, secondary and primary research were conducted focusing on the European market and with comparison from the North American and Asian markets. This research was conducted with the help of Marketing Challenges Intl that focused on the North American region, comprised of the United States of America and Canada but excluding Mexico.

The analysis aimed at capturing relevant insights concerning the decision-making process of MCCI decision makers. The primary research was organized in two phases. In total 300 people were contacted. For the first phase of the research, conducted during the months of October and November 2014, an online survey was sent to meeting planners, corporations and associations in Europe, North America (excluding Mexico) and Asia. The online-survey questions intended to gather more information with less in-depth content, to which 120 responses were received, 45% from Europe, 35% from North America and 20% from Asia. For the second phase of the primary research, conducted during the months of December 2014 and January 2015, two sets of phone interviews were conducted. The first set of phone interviews aimed at gathering a more in depth understanding of planners' decision-making processes. For this 25 phone calls were conducted in Europe, the United States and Canada and Asia. The second set of phone interviews aimed at gathering more in depth information regarding planners' decision-making once basic criteria are met to understand which 'added value' criteria influence their final decisions the most. For this, and additional 15 phone calls were conducted in Europe, North America (the United States and Canada) and Asia. Phone interviews questions remained for the most part open-ended questions in order to encourage 'full disclosure', qualitative rather than quantitative.

The sample of participants was drawn from GainingEdge's and Marketing Challenges International's lists of contacts, including convention, corporate and incentive planners and suppliers, in the European, North American and Asian regions. This was a representative sample, which included international, regional and national clients (AMCs, core PCOs, corporate and in-house planners, amongst others) and suppliers. Participants from the sample either take final decisions, research, recommend, plan/organize events, or a combination of the above. Moreover, this includes participants organizing events of 1–250 people, 250–500, 500–1,000 and more than 1,000 participants. An anonymous survey tool was used to conduct the survey, therefore the exact respondents are not known, nonetheless the representative sample allows for responses to be significant and provide a comprehensive depiction of organizers' needs and expectations.

5.2 Typologies of decision-making processes

5.2.1 Association conventions and congresses

Given the diversity of the association segment, decision-makers vary greatly from association to association, which has important influence on the overall decision-making method. Moreover, the process can be extremely complex and generally happens over a long period of time.[1] Generally speaking, an association convention or congress is part of associations' overall strategy, particularly the marketing strategy. This element dictates the decision-making process. Based on secondary research, the following figure presents the general decision-making process followed by associations.

There is a current gap in the literature covering the area of decision-making typologies. However, based on the primary research and on some secondary research it was possible to determine four main patterns of decision-making for association conventions and congresses.[2] Depending on the association, final decisions can be taken very differently, either through the board of directors, the association meeting planner, the convention organizing committee or the general assembly. This supports UIA's findings from their annual survey, where respondents' answers show that final decisions are made either by committee (38.6%), executive officer (29.4%), general assembly (26.3%) and others (5.7%).[3]

---

1   International Congress and Convention Association (April 2014b).

2   Smith, E. (2014), 'Helping Hands for Meeting Planners', *MEET*, 02-10-2014, Associations Now (online), available at: www.associationsnow.com (08-06-2015).

   Mair, J. (2014), *Conferences and Conventions: A Research Perspective*, Routledge.

   Rogers, T. (2013), *Conferences and Conventions – A Global Industry*, 3rd edition, Routledge, Abingdon – New York.

3   Union of International Associations (2013).

Figure 5.1   **The decision-making process for association conventions and congresses**

Objective of the association

Determine the objectives of the congress:

- To grow membership in specific regions;
- To spread knowledge;
- To highlight social/health issues;
- To expose members to new markets;

- Advocacy;
- Continuing education;
- New market opportunities; and
- Others.

Review past conventions:

- Financial results;
- Attendance;

- Venues and destinations; and
- Analyse feedback of participating members.

Identify potential markets or regions:

- Global;
- Domestic; and
- Local.

Pre-selected specific destinations and venues:

- Research on the web;
- Past experiences;
- Obtain information from informal network of colleagues or through industry association database;

- Trade show and events;
- Interest shown from regional member; and
- CB and/or convention venue.

Send detailed RFPs to pre-selected destinations and venues.

Plan site selection.

Review and compare proposals:

- Determine costing;
- Potential attendance;

- Set a preliminary budget; and
- Negotiate.

Present choices to Board or final decision makers.

Final decision:

- Finalise contracts (venues, hotels, PCOs, etc.); and
- Announcements to the members and the press.

Congress takes place.

Post-congress evaluation:

- Financials;
- Attendance; and
- Feedback from members.

Table 5.1   **Final decision-makers for association conventions and congresses**

Board of Directors	Takes final decision from a selection of locations recommended by committee or meeting planner and can also act to: – Assist in lining up venues; – Connecting planners with key contacts; – Want to vote on site selection; and – Help build buy-in on the selection with association members.
Association meeting planner	Given authority to: – Research; – Recommend; – Organize; and – Make the final decision for site location.
Convention Organizing Committee	Make the site selection and other decisions related to the organization of the conventions and congresses, and will typically receive the help from intermediaries.
General Assembly	Destination is chosen by vote amongst various members of the association.

A first pattern illustrates that final decisions are taken by the board of directors, whose decisions are based on recommendations and pre-selections from the association meeting planner or convention committee. In this case, the board of directors can assist, for instance, by connecting planners through their networks of key contacts.[4] A second pattern of decision-making suggests that some associations may have an association meeting planner, usually responsible for planning conventions and taking final decisions. In this context, association meeting planners are given the authority to research, recommend, organize and take final decisions with regard to conventions. Yet a third pattern, which is for some considered to be the most common, identifies that some associations have a convention organizing committee in charge of taking final decisions, such as site selection.[5] A final decision-making pattern is the general assembly, whereby final decisions are taken by member vote.

Gathering from the findings, it appears as though, in many instances, staff members involved in the organization of association conventions and congresses do not have an 'event organizer' title in their job title, and are likely to work in administration, sales and marketing, public relations or human resources.[6] Moreover, within some associations – omitting the larger ones – volunteers play a substantial role in the organization of conventions and congresses, which adds to the difficulty of identifying clear decision-making processes.

---

4   Smith, E. (2014).

5   Mair, J. (2014).

6   Ibid.

The bidding process

Most associations require a bidding process, although a growing minority is no longer including an official bidding process,[7] This step enables associations to identify – through a set of presentations – which entity – destination or supplier – is best qualified and enthusiast for holding the conventions and congresses, this associations are required to communicate the appropriate information necessary for receiving intelligently thought-out proposals to then proceed with the general bidding process.[8]

Figure 5.2   **The bidding process**

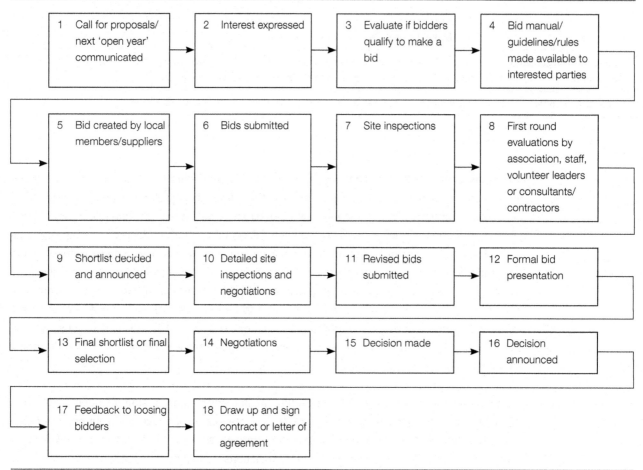

1 Call for proposals/ next 'open year' communicated	2 Interest expressed	3 Evaluate if bidders qualify to make a bid	4 Bid manual/ guidelines/rules made available to interested parties
5 Bid created by local members/suppliers	6 Bids submitted	7 Site inspections	8 First round evaluations by association, staff, volunteer leaders or consultants/ contractors
9 Shortlist decided and announced	10 Detailed site inspections and negotiations	11 Revised bids submitted	12 Formal bid presentation
13 Final shortlist or final selection	14 Negotiations	15 Decision made	16 Decision announced
17 Feedback to loosing bidders	18 Draw up and sign contract or letter of agreement		

Source: International Congress and Convention Association (April 2014b).

Despite the general use of bidding process for electing the destination, recent trends indicate that 25–30% of the decision-making processes have a central initiator, selecting location and venues based on strict pre-determined criteria, which replaces the formal bidding procedure.[9]

---

7   Rogers, T. (2013).

8   International Congress and Convention Association (April 2014b).

      Mair, J. (2014).

9   Rogers, T. (2013).

Lead times

Because of the scale of associations' conventions and congresses, accompanied by the increasing competition and high number of players, associations have the longest lead times for planning their events. Meetings that last longer, generally have a longer lead-time.[10] On average, lead times for association conventions and congresses ranges between 3–6 years. Yet it is not unusual for the largest conventions and congresses that are restricted to very few cities, to have lead times of 10 years or more[11]. Associations which want to hold conventions and congresses with more than 1,000 delegates, usually face very long lead times, due to the limited choice of venue accommodating such a large number of participants[12]. Moreover, lead times can vary based on association membership and rotation. Indeed, regional conventions and congresses have a tendency to have shorter lead times, while international conventions and congresses, often bigger in size and with long bidding processes, can have much longer lead times.

Figure 5.3   **Average association conventions and congresses lead times (%)**

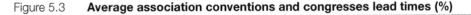

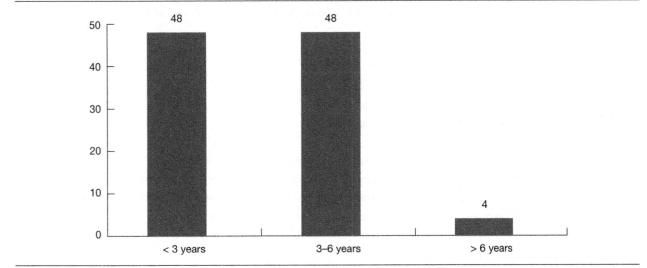

Intermediaries

The role of intermediaries is to assist and/or advise associations through the various steps of the decision-making process. This can range from destination to site selection, and other key areas needed for association conventions and congresses. They provide local knowledge and offer contacts and expertise in order to ensure the event is organized successfully. This is further developed in part 6.10.

Associations generally organize conventions and congresses with in-house management. Some however, engage in alternative approaches to decision-making, either by outsourcing the

---

10 International Congress and Convention Association (2013b).

11 Chon, K.S. and Weber, K. (2002), Convention Tourism: International Research and Industry Perspective, Haworth Press, New York.

12 Rogers, T. (2013).

organization of its congresses to a PCO for a certain period of time, or by asking AMCs who provide full service management.[13] Generally speaking, the main intermediaries for associations are:

– Professional conference organizers (PCOs);
– Destination management companies (DMCs);
– Local chapter assistance/ambassadors;
– Third party planners;
– Online meeting management tools;
– Hotel national sales offices; and
– Site selection providers.

Key determinants

Decisions are based on a number of criteria, which are key to the planning of conventions and congresses. Once again, because of the diverse nature of associations, criteria can vary greatly. However the following categories identify some of the determining factors influencing planners' decision-making:[14]

– Logistical criteria;
– Financial criteria;
– Internal association objectives;
– Political/emotional criteria; and
– Business links/market issues.

The description of key criteria for the association conventions and congresses segment is developed in phase 1. This second phase presents the results gathered from the primary research, which identify association meeting planners' needs and expectations with respect to destinations and venues, in order to respond to the association's objectives.

5.2.2   Corporate meetings

Corporate meetings are high profile, and a communicating vehicle for conveying important messages about the company. For this reason, meeting planning should be well organized to meet objectives. Strategic meetings management is a concept, which has recently come forward, describing the necessity for a strategic approach to meeting planning and the management of relationships between internal and external stakeholders.[15] Similarly to conventions and congresses, corporate meetings are an integral part of the corporation's marketing strategy, thus clearly influencing the decision-making process. Therefore, planners do not only plan a meeting, but also develop a communication strategy that will include (or not) meetings.

---

13 International Congress and Convention Association (April 2014b).

14 Ibid.

15 Cvent (2014), Strategic Meetings Management Software (online), available at:
    www.cvent.com/uk/strategic-meetings-management/ (08-06-2015).
    Rogers, T. (2013).

The process

Typically, the decision-making process for corporate meetings follows a conventional path. Once corporations recognise the need for a meeting to be held, and choose the type and objectives of the event, meeting planners need to make of a set of logistical, strategic and operational decisions with regard to the event management.

Figure 5.4   **The decision-making process for corporate meetings**

Decision to have a corporate meeting.

Decide what type of meeting to hold:

- Internal; or

- External.

Discuss the objectives of the meeting, to decide:

- Virtual vs. face-to-face meeting;   - hort haul vs. long haul;

- Number of participants;   - Add incentive; and

- In-house or external;   - Entertainment/activities (e.g., golf).

Pick an organizing committee.

Site selection analysis.

Site selection.

Meeting is held.

Post-meeting evaluation/measuring ROI.

Despite the limitations of the literature with regard to corporate meetings decision-making processes, the primary research enables us to present four main patterns of final decision-makers. Depending on the corporation, final decision can be taken by the CEO/board of directors, corporate, sales, marketing and management, the corporate planner or a third party agency.

Table 5.2   **Final decision makers for corporate meetings**

Board of Directors	Take final decision from recommendation and selections from influencers or corporate planners.
Corporate sales, marketing and management	Recommend and take the final decisions for corporate meetings.
Corporate planner	Given authority to: – Organize; – Research; and – Recommend.
Third party agencies	Advise and given the authority to take final decision.

A first typology for corporate meeting decision-making is one where the CEO of the company or board of directors take all final decisions – generally based on a set of recommendations and pre-selections from influencers and corporate planners. Yet in some corporations, final decisions are taken by corporate, sales, marketing and management, who are given the authority to conduct the necessary research for corporate meeting organization. A third pattern shows that in some instances, the corporation will have a corporate planner within the corporation in charge of organizing, researching, recommending and taking final decisions. Finally, other corporations give full responsibility to a third party/independent agency, responsible for advising and taking final decisions when organizing corporate meetings. Depending on the nature of the meeting – internal or external – the objectives, and the corporation, final decision makers can vary greatly.

Lead times

Corporate meetings have reasonably short lead times, which is reflected by the lower number of delegates. These can generally be organized within just a few months, and, although the typical planning cycle being between 2 to 6 months,[16] survey results show that, on average corporate lead times can be between 6 and 12 months. As meetings become smaller and shorter, lead times are likely to remain the same.

---

16   Davidson, T. (2013).

Figure 5.5   **Average corporate meeting lead times (%)**

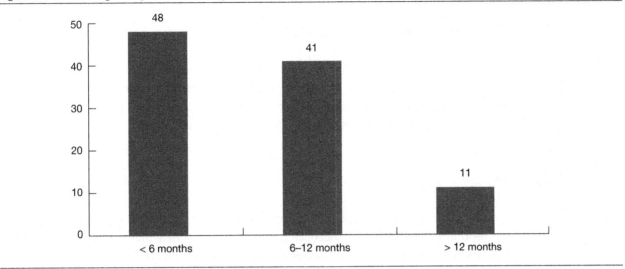

Intermediaries

Corporate meeting planning can be complex, engaging a large number of intermediaries. These can help with bringing local knowledge, expertise, contacts and support. The main intermediaries included in corporate meeting planning includes:

- Corporate travel agencies;
- Meeting and event management companies;
- Destination management companies (DMCs);
- Third party planners;
- Hotel national sales offices;
- Site selection firms; and
- Corporate meetings and incentive companies.

Key determinants

Decision makers are influenced by a certain number of factors when selecting destination, venue, activities and other key aspects of the event. Because internal and external focused meetings have different objectives, the criteria, for each type of meeting, is also different. Internal meetings, which are generally organizationally oriented, require planners to focus on the following criteria:

- Internal corporate objectives;
- Site selection;
- Logistical criteria; and
- Financial criteria.

On the other hand, while organizing external meetings, which are more business focused, planners must pay attention to the following key determinants:

- Business links;
- Market issues;
- Potential for future;

- Logistical criteria;
- Financial criteria; and
- External environment (political, social, economic stability).

The description of key criteria for the corporate meetings segment was developed in phase 1, chapter 3. In this second phase, chapter 7 presents the results gathered from the primary research regarding corporate meeting planners' needs and expectations with respect to destinations and venues. These closely follow the objectives of both internal and external focused meetings.

5.2.3 Incentives

The planning of incentive programmes is mainly driven by destination selection. Corporations first need to decide to have an incentive programme, before determining the objectives of this programme and selecting the employees who will benefit from it. While planners need to focus on some logistical and operational issues, the focus of decision-making lies in destination selection and activity programmes. Nonetheless, just like conventions and congresses and corporate meetings, the decision-making of incentives is largely dependent on the corporation's communication strategy. Once the incentive is held, post-event evaluation is necessary in order to measure its success.

Figure 5.6 **Incentive programmes decision-making process**

Decision to have an incentive programme.

Discuss the objectives of the programme, to decide:
- Group vs. individual reward;
- Number of participants;
- Type of the reward (trip, cash, other);
- Short-haul vs. long haul;
- Add meeting content; and
- Entertainment/activities (e.g., golf).

Target the employees to reward.

Select a third party to organize the incentive.

Site and activities selection.

The incentive programme is held.

Post-incentive evaluation/measuring of success.

Similarly to corporate meetings, final decision makers can vary greatly depending on the corporation or incentive programme. Final decisions are usually either made by the incentive planner, the board of directors, the committee, the corporate management, the corporate travel agency or the events/production agency.

Table 5.3   **Final decision makers for incentive programmes**

Incentive planner	Research, recommend, organize and are given the authority to take final decision.
Board of directors	Takes final decision from a selection of locations recommended by committee or incentive planner.
Committee	Make site selection and other decisions related to incentive planning; will typically receive help from intermediaries.
Corporate management/ director of sales	Advise and take final decision at different stages of the incentive programme planning.
Corporate travel agency	Given the responsibility to do the necessary research and make the final decision.
Events/production agency	Research, advise and organize incentives.

Final decision makers are often directly related to the company. A first pattern emerges, where the corporate travel agency is given full responsibility to research, advise, connect and take final decisions with regard to the incentive programme. In the same way, other corporations, which may not have a dedicated corporate travel agency, can give full authority to their events/production agency, fulfilling the same role of researching, recommending and taking final decisions. To continue, as part of a third pattern, incentive programmes' final decision-maker can in some instances be given to the incentive planner. Moreover, because incentive programmes are a corporation-based event, final decision can, in some cases, depend on the board of directors, who take final decisions based on recommendations from the incentive planner or committee, or in a different pattern, can depend on a committee, who takes final decisions related to the incentive programme. A final pattern of decision-making goes through corporate management/ director of sales, who recommend and take final decisions throughout the process of organization.

Lead times

Similarly to corporate meetings, the incentive segment has relatively short planning cycle. Survey results indicate that incentive lead times run on average between 6 and 12 months.

Figure 5.7   **Average incentive lead times (%)**

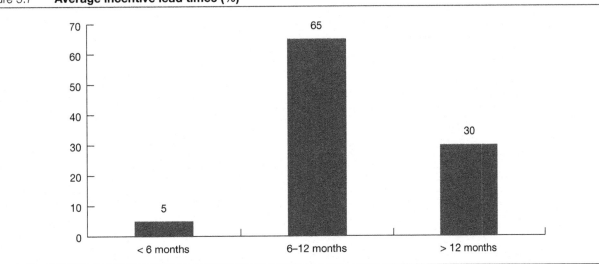

Key determinants

The nature of incentive programmes is mainly to reward employees, but also suppliers in order to enhance employee satisfaction and performance. The decision-making process is therefore influenced by a number of factors, which directly influence the success of the programme. These include:

– Logistical criteria;
– Financial criteria; and
– Emotional criteria (the 'wow' factor).

The description of key criteria for the incentive segment is developed in phase 1, chapter 4. In this second phase, chapter 8 presents the results gathered from the primary research, identifying planners' needs and expectations with regard to the organization of incentive programmes.

Chapter 6

Association conventions and congresses: needs and expectations

6.1 What association meeting planners want

Association conventions and congresses are designed for discussions and information sharing. Because the segment includes a wide variety of industries, meeting planners may expect different outcomes from the events. In general however, association meeting planners coordinate the strategic, operational and logistical activities of the event in order to raise participants' awareness, interest and knowledge. As delegates get together to discuss the latest issues of the industry, meeting planners need to ensure that the event goes smoothly. Association meeting planners design an event in order to engage delegates, and make it a platform to support ideas and communication within the industry.

6.2 Description and evaluation of key criteria

Association meeting planners make their final decisions based on a number of criteria. While phase 1, chapter 2, identified some relevant factors influencing planners' decision-making process; following is a selection of key criteria, selected by participants of this survey, including planners and the supply-side players. Clearly, advocacy for subject matter is the least influencing factor for destination choice, yet it is nonetheless considered as determinant added value criteria once basic factors have been met. Cost and size of meeting facilities figure on average as most important. Variations exist between regions.

Figure 6.1   **Summary of key criteria of planners' destination choice for conventions and congresses**

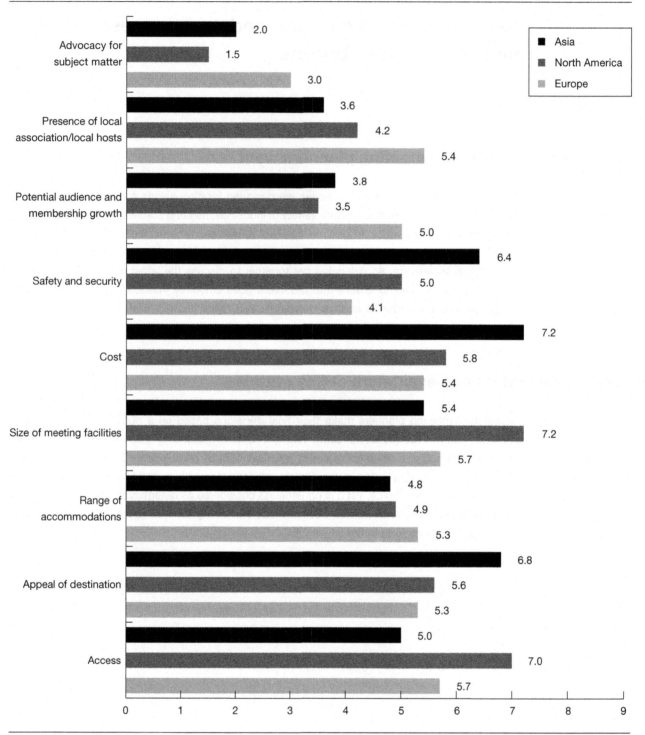

Notes: Average order of importance: 1 = least important, 9 = most important.

North America excludes Mexico.

6.2.1   Financial considerations

Holding association conventions and congresses can present some financial risk. It is therefore important for associations to clearly determine their financial requirements in order for events to be planned accordingly. There are a number of financial considerations to keep in mind, with PCOs/DMCs/AMCs, transport costs, delegate accommodation, visas and other general financial issues.[1]

On average, financial considerations are ranked third by European and North American planners. On the other hand, it is a top criterion for Asian planners who rank cost as their most important criteria influencing destination choice. Nonetheless, a planner further advised us that the budget is determined once and only once they have received proposals from venues.

Figure 6.2   **Key association convention and congresses criteria: cost**

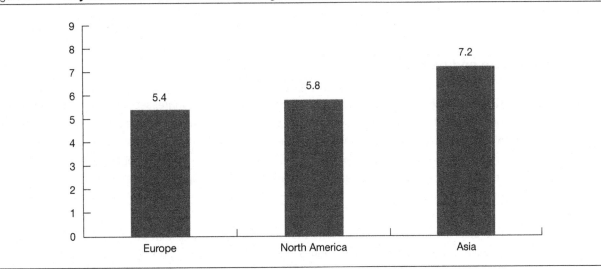

Notes: Average order of importance: 1 = least important, 9 = most important.

North America excludes Mexico.

Furthermore, association meeting planners may receive support from destinations through subvention schemes, reducing the overall cost of the event, and can thus be a determinant factor for destination selection. On average, 54% of respondents from this research say they require subvention for their events. European planners are the most interested and Asian planners are the least concerned about subvention.

1   International Congress and Convention Association (April 2014b).

Figure 6.3   **Subvention required by association meeting planners, in Asia, Europe and North America (%)**

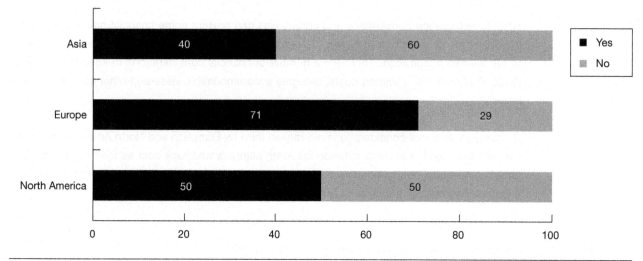

Note: North America excludes Mexico.

6.2.2   Venue size and configuration

Because of their large size, association conventions and congresses are generally held in large purpose-built conference or convention centres. Depending on the size of the event, hotels are also popular, or other facilities, which can accommodate such events, such as universities or multipurpose venues. While some hotels may offer cheaper rates, combining accommodation and meeting space, convention centres offer expertise and support services depending on the needs of the association.

It is clear from these survey results that, on average, convention centres and university-based facilities are the most popular venues used for conventions and congresses. There is a trend towards hotels with meeting space, with an increasing number of larger meeting space that can accommodate association conventions and congresses, such as integrated resorts. These facilities provide all in one packages including meeting space and accommodation, which help reduce cost and minimise need for logistics.

Figure 6.4   **Venues used for association conventions and congresses (%)**

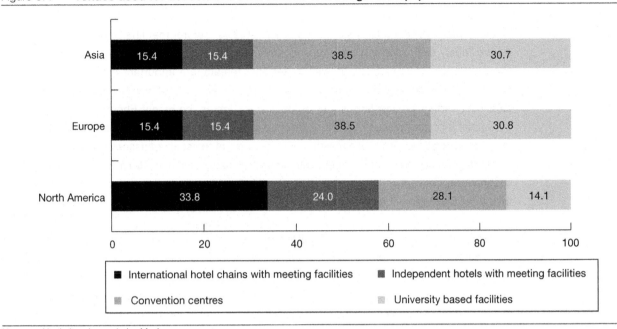

Note: North America excludes Mexico.

More importantly, the choice of venue is based on venue size, venue flexibility, venue services – audio-visual equipment, Wi-Fi, catering, security, and many more.

Participants to this research rank the size of meeting facilities as a top criteria influencing destination choice. In Europe, planners rank size of meeting facilities as the second most influential criteria for destination choice. North America planners rank it as the most influential criterion for decision-making, while Asian planners only rank venue size as the fourth most influential criteria. Overall, venue size and infrastructure are crucial considerations for selecting the best option to hold the association convention or congress.

Figure 6.5   **Key association convention and congresses criteria: size of meeting facilities**

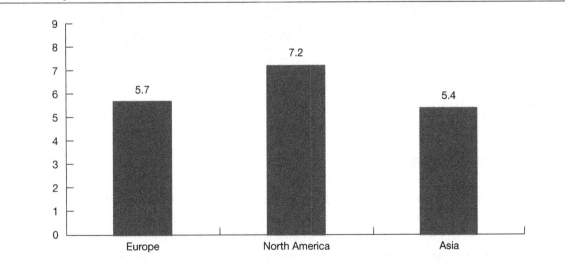

Notes: Average order of importance: 1 = least important, 9 = most important.

North America excludes Mexico.

6.2.3   Risk adversity and safety

Meeting planners conduct risk management studies before the final destination selection. As previously discussed in phase 1, concerns of safety and security towards health, political, social and economic stability, as well as terrorist threats, are important considerations for the success of the conventions and congresses. Moreover, risks of natural disasters – such as tsunamis, earthquakes or floods – or epidemics – such as the recent Ebola – means that some conventions or congresses may be postponed or cancelled, which results in important financial loss for associations. For these reasons, and because of the scale of association events, meeting planners generally prefer destinations considered as 'safe', which can be a disadvantage to some destinations. convention bureaux can therefore play an important role in educating and promoting their destinations to act against the negative image and misinformation that may exist.

Overall, planners surveyed ranked safety and security as a significant criteria influencing destination choice. European planners are the exception, as safety issues are their second to the last influential criteria. That said the recent terrorist attacks might have a changing effect on European planners' consideration of safety and security issues. North American planners on the other hand rank safety as the 5th most influential criteria and Asian planners are particularly concerned with safety and security issues, ranking it as the third most important factor influencing destination choice.

Figure 6.6   **Key association convention and congresses criteria: safety and security**

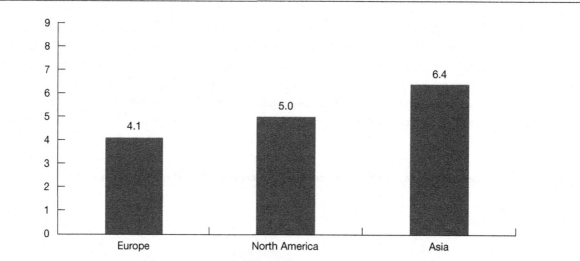

Notes: Average order of importance: 1 = least important, 9 = most important.

North America excludes Mexico.

6.2.4   Appeal of destination

Destination appeal includes all the characteristics that make a destination attractive to both the planner and the delegate. It is a range of activities, entertainment, cultural or historical heritage, pre- and post-touring activities, a general awareness of the destination, which play an influential role in planners' final decision of destination choice. Because annual associations' conventions and congresses are a major source of revenue for associations, planners are influenced by the appeal of the destination. Destinations with more appeal generally increase participation rate, and thus revenue generation.

Participants to this survey have, on average, ranked this as a major influencer. Fourth most important criteria for European and North American planners, it is the second most influential criteria for Asian planners.

Figure 6.7   **Key association convention and congresses criteria: appeal of destination**

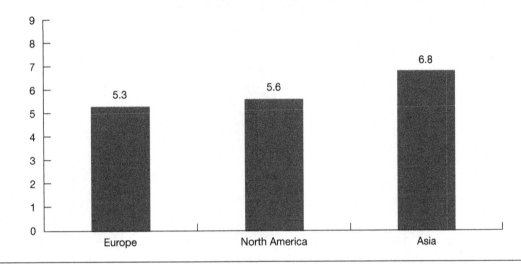

Notes: Average order of importance: 1 = least important, 9 = most important.

North America excludes Mexico.

6.2.5   Access

Meeting planners consider both local and international accessibility when evaluating destinations. The accessibility of the destination is important to ensure that delegates do not lose time in transportation. Moreover, because associations attract delegates from around the world, accessibility by air, particularly direct flights, is a decisive, yet challenging one. Visa policies are an important factor to consider when choosing destination – delegates should, for instance, be made aware of visa requirements. Associations meeting planners consider access as a key factor for determining destination choice. In this context, access for association conventions and congresses is considered as being the international accessibility of the destination. Because this segment attracts a large number of delegates, from many countries, the destination should be accessible to as many participants as possible.

As previously discussed in phase 1 local accessibility is also important. This includes transportation between accommodations to convention or conference centres, as much as transportation to the city or other entertainment activities. Information on public transport, disability-friendly infrastructure, and distance between venues is therefore important for decision-makers.[2]

2   International Congress and Convention Association (April 2014b).

Results from the survey reveal that access is another factor in choosing destination. European planners ranked it as the most influential criteria for destination choice. Similarly North American planners ranked access as the second most influential criteria. However, based on a scale from 1 to 9, 9 being the most important, North American planners consider accessibility to be more valuable, evaluated it as a 7, than for European and Asian planners who evaluate it as a 6. Asian planners on the other hand, consider accessibility to be the 5th most influential criteria. These findings underline the importance of access for selecting destination.

Figure 6.8   **Key association convention and congresses criteria: access**

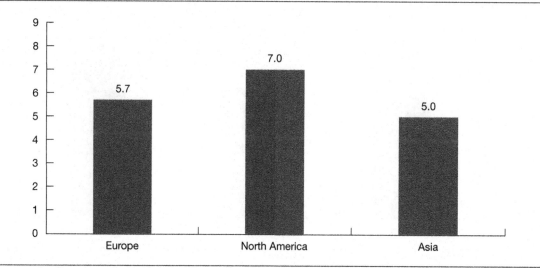

Notes: Average order of importance: 1 = least important, 9 = most important.

North America excludes Mexico.

6.2.6   Accommodation

Delegate accommodation is another aspect of decision-making. Destinations are heavily investing in infrastructure and increasing the number of high standard hotels in order to attract conventions and congresses. Destinations must deliver both quality and quantity for such events. Hotel stock is evaluated in terms of the amount of bedrooms, distance to convention centre, stars rating, meeting space and other key characteristics.

Planners participating in this research said range of accommodation to be another criterion affecting their choice. Associations require a full range of accommodation options from budget to luxury, within close proximity of the venue. On average, this criterion has the same influence on planners across the continents, but is not the most influential.

Figure 6.9 **Key association convention and congresses criteria: accommodation**

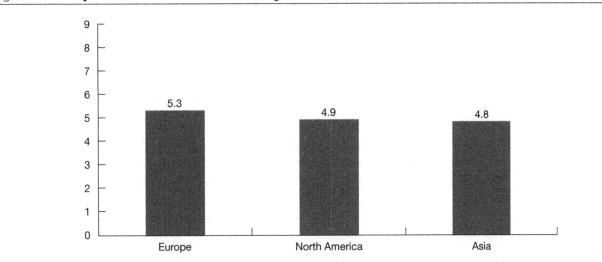

Notes: Average order of importance: 1 = least important, 9 = most important.

North America excludes Mexico.

6.2.7 Other key criteria influencing association meeting planners

Other influential criteria include, in average order of importance, presence of local association, potential audience and advocacy for subject matter. Local host/member can often be a mandatory criterion. The association may also consider the strength, profile, activity level and experience of the local host. How active the local member is at a regional and international level of the association may often be of importance.

Figure 6.10 **Key association convention and congresses criteria**

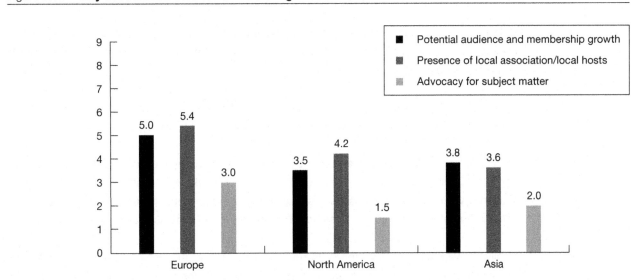

Notes: Average order of importance: 1 = least important, 9 = most important.

North America excludes Mexico.

Basic criteria, such as access, accommodation, costs and logistics are one part of the decision-making. In order to differentiate destinations, planners also evaluate the 'value added' criteria, which include potential audience and membership growth, advocacy for subject matter and presence of local association. These criteria enable planners to take final decisions on destination choice. When asked what criteria come into play when basic factors have been met, the responses fall into three main categories.

First, planners will choose a destination based on the presence of potential audience and the potential to increase membership growth. Association planners look for destinations that fit with their objectives and those of their members, so there is inevitable topic focus and a desire for lasting legacy. This also ensures higher interest and bigger audience.

Secondly, there is advocacy. This is often political in nature. Some associations need to be in destinations where one can speak freely about taboo topics, ensuring academic freedom. These associations will not choose destinations that need to approve the content of the conference. Examples cited include, sustainability, gay rights, human rights, and more.

Thirdly, presence of local association is another criteria. Some planners issue call for bids for their international conference directly to their member organizations, who bid as hosts rather than requesting bids from destinations.

6.3   Decision-makers vs. -influencers (roles of intermediaries)

Associations usually organize their conventions and congresses within their own organizations – volunteer members, committee or in-house event management teams, while others may content themselves with support from professional conference organizers (PCOs).[3] Generally speaking, the meeting-planning department of an association is part of the "knowledge department" that includes marketing, public relations and more.

Results from this survey indicate that, on average, final decisions with regard to destination choice, are made by an executive (33%), by the board (24%), a committee (23%), membership vote (9%) or other (11%).

In Europe, the Board (40%) most commonly takes the final decisions, while it can also be taken by a committee (30%), the executive (20%), or by membership vote (10%).

In North America, the final decision of the destination is made by the Board (33%), an Executive (28%), a Committee (24%), or other (15%). 'Other' final decision-making processes may be situations where the general assembly selects one out of two viable finalists by secret ballot, or a combination of all of the above, based on the meetings team professional input.

Finally, in Asia, the final decision of the destination is either made by the executive (50%), by membership vote (17%), or a by committee (16%). In other instances, for 17% of planners, the secretariat makes the final decision.

---

3   Union of International Associations (2013).

Figure 6.11   **Association conventions and congresses final decision-makers (%)**

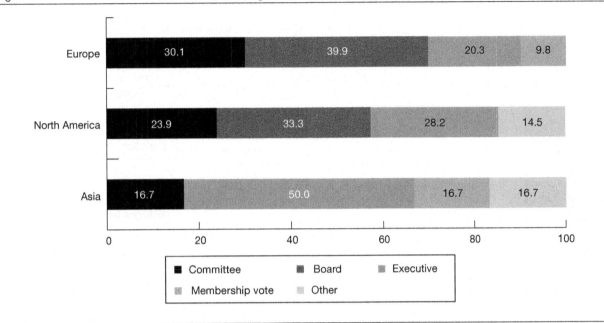

Note: North America excludes Mexico.

Moreover, the financial and time constraints which are affecting the association segment push some associations to directly contact local support to ensure that events run smoothly, particularly convention bureaux and PCOs. Generally speaking, association conventions and congresses planning can involve a large number of partakers; an example is presented in figure 6.12.

Intermediaries for Association conventions and congresses planning include local chapter assistance, PCOs, DMCs, third party planners, hotel national sales office, site selection firms and online meeting management. Only 2% of total participants say they do not require additional services to manage their events.

Figure 6.12   **The relationship between key association convention and congresses players**

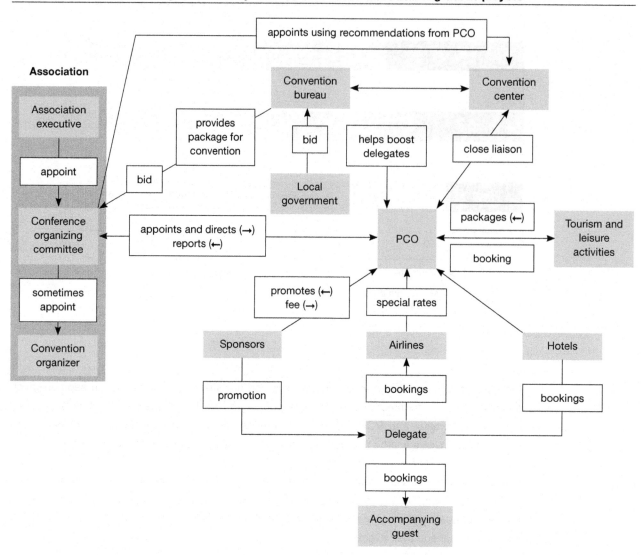

Source: Jago, L. K. and Deery, M. (2005), 'Relationship and Factors Influencing Convention Decision-Making', *Journal of Convention & Event Tourism*,
          Vol. 7 (1), pp. 23–41, published online: 23-09-2008.

Figure 6.13 **Intermediaries for association convention and congresses planners by region (%)**

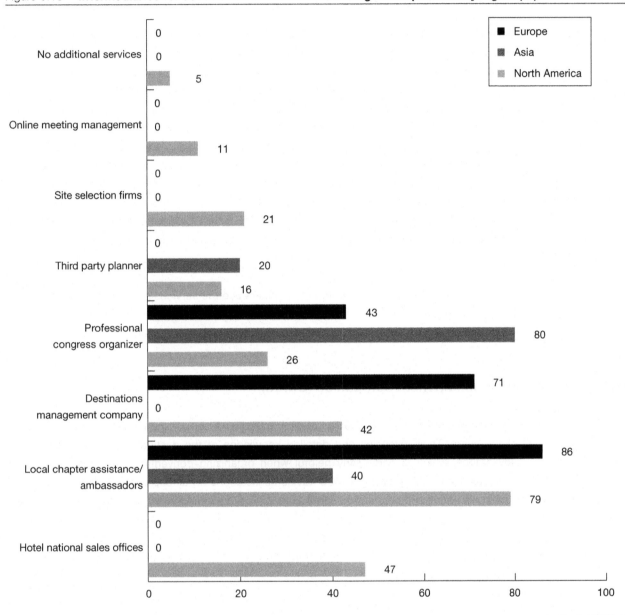

Note: North America excludes Mexico.

6.3.1 Local chapter assistance/ambassadors

Local chapter assistance provides associations the guarantee of having the local member/ chapter of the international association to become the local host organization. Their role is key in contacting local providers and assist in involving the local community.

For both European and North American planners services of local chapter assistance/ambassadors are the most commonly used – 86% of planners in Europe and 79% of planners in North America. 40% of Asian planners also use the services of local chapter assistance.

6.3.2   Professional conference organizers (PCOs)

Professional conference organizers act as association meeting planners, by providing their experience and knowledge in order to make events successful. PCOs remain very flexible in terms of their services, and, since associations generally organize events with in-house management, PCOs may only play a specific role. For this reason, associations need to have clearly defined objectives and requirements in order for PCOs to respond most efficiently. Because association conventions and congresses attract a large number of delegates, and because lead times are long and financial expenditure high, associations prefer high quality and experienced PCOs. While some associations may not understand the need for PCOs, many regard them as essential to convention planning, as they bring extensive support on local venues, transport, restaurants, accommodation and provide other key local information – logistical or financial – essential to conventions and congresses' success. Even though core PCOs were described in phase 1 as another type of PCO helping with international associations' events, they were however, not mentioned by participants to this survey.

This survey reveals that 43% of European planners use the services of PCOs to receive support for the planning of their conventions and congresses, against 26% of North American planners. PCOs are, moreover, the most common intermediary used by Asian planners (80%).

6.3.3   Destination management companies (DMCs)

Destination management companies are key intermediaries, generally based at the destination of the event. Their extensive and detailed knowledge of the destination is one of their main advantages, which is particularly helpful when organizing conventions and congresses from overseas. Generally speaking, DMCs advise associations on all social and logistical aspects of their conventions and congresses – transport, dining, accommodation, entertainment and more.

71% of European planners use the services from DMCs – making them the second most used intermediary in Europe, while 42% of North American planners solicit their support – their third most used intermediary.

6.3.4   Online meeting management tool

Associations are now benefiting from the increasing use of online tools. These offer associations a direct and efficient access to information and services that are necessary for the preparation of their meetings. This new tool is a platform, which covers all areas of planning from budgeting, to contacting, app development and so forth. Recently added to the range of intermediaries, online meeting management tools are for now, according to this research, only used by North American planners, and still, only 11% of them. Participants have mentioned CVent and Etouches as popular online meeting management tools.

6.4 Key trends affecting decision-making and lead times

Organizing conventions and congresses depends greatly on the current environment of the industry. Some key trends particularly affect the decision-making process and lead times, yet this can vary from region to region.

6.4.1 Organizational resources and characteristics

Organizational resources and characteristics influence planners' perception of value as well as the final content of conventions and congresses. In other words, the association's final decision and lead-time are dependent on internal factors such as knowledge, experience, budget and other key resources proper to the association. These characteristics and resources directly affect channel choice and the overall organization of the event.[4]

Moreover meeting planners for association conventions and congresses need to ensure that the decision follows the vision and mission of the association. Some associations may rely on experience from members or previous events when making decisions.

Budgets can play a major role in affecting the decision-making process of association meeting planners. According to this survey results, budgets are an important trend affecting planners' decision-making. Budgets had a tendency to remain the same between 2013 and 2014 (59%) and are expected to follow the same trend for upcoming international events (77%). Yet planners are looking for quality over quantity and good value for money deals, which can help maximise their investments. The fluctuating economy has pushed them to be more vigilant and take precautious decisions with regard to the organization of conventions and congresses.

In Europe, 14% of respondents saw their 2014 budgets decrease, from that of 2013, 14% experienced an increase and 71% of respondents' budgets remained the same. The increase in budgets experienced in Europe is largely dependent on the destination. Association meeting planners are generally expecting their budgets to remain the same for their next international events (71%) while the rest (29%) expect an increase in their budgets.

In North America, 44% of planners saw their 2014 budgets increase, while the rest saw no changes in their budgets from that of 2013. Of those planners who saw their budgets increase, 40% experienced an increase of 30%, 20% an increase of 10% and 40% an increase of 5%. Similarly to European planners, North American respondents highlight that budgets change depending on destination as well as local foreign currency. 59% of association meeting planners are expecting their budgets to remain the same for their next international events, 35% expect an increase and 6% expect them to decrease.

In Asia, half of planners saw a decrease of their 2014 budget while the other half saw no change. Moreover, all planners expect their budgets to remain the same for their next international events.

---

4   Alexander, A. C.; Kim D. Y. and Groves, J. (2012), 'Individual and Organizational Characteristics Influencing Event Planners' Perceptions of Information Content and Channel Choice', *Journal of Convention & Event Tourism*, volume 13 (1), 22-02-2012, Routledge, pp. 16–38 (online), available at: www.tandfonline.com (15-09-28).

Figure 6.14   **Budget changes for associations' international events (%)**

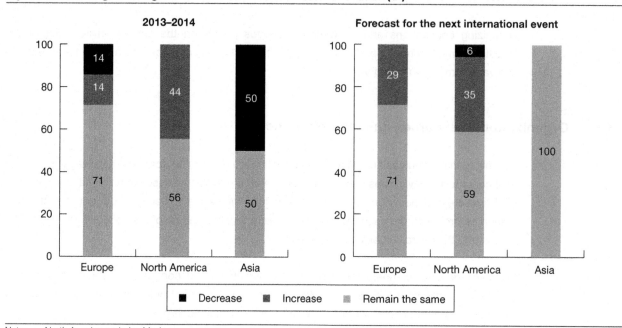

Note: North America excludes Mexico.

The weak economic growth experienced in western countries, coupled with the slow growth in eastern countries is affecting associations' budgets, and thus planners' decision-making. Yet the Asian segment is presenting some opportunities as it generally experiences a better growth than western countries.

Moreover, as presented in figure 6.3, more than half of planners interviewed are reliant on subventions for the planning of conventions or congresses. In other words, decision-making can be highly dependent on the planner's capacity to acquire such financial support.

6.4.2   Information channels

The quality of the content gathered through information channels is important to decision-making and lead times. Information should be found efficiently, should be up-to-date, straightforward and easily understandable by planners. This ensures that the decision-making is made in the best conditions as possible. Information channels can include both formal and informal influences:[5]
–   Formal: magazines, brochures, websites, social media, expos, networking, etc.; and
–   Informal: family, friends, personal interactions, etc.

Information channels can be influential in the way they raise awareness, knowledge and interest. Today, more and more organizations underline the advantages of Big Data, which aims at facilitating decision-making and information sharing. However, the collection of data is getting very large and complex, making it difficult to process meanings or find connections.[6] Big Data, illustrates

5   Alexander, A. C.; Kim D. Y. and Groves, J. (2012).

6   van Dyke, M. (2014).

the role new technologies has in shaping the way one accesses information, communicate and make decisions. Strategically using 'big data' can have cost-saving effects, reduce risk and create operational efficiencies.[7]

The survey reveals that association meeting planners use various sources of information to help them with their decision-making:
–   Destination/hotel/convention bureaux' websites (39%);
–   Local associations/ambassadors (31%);
–   Online meeting management (10%);
–   Social networking sites (5%); and/or
–   Travel blogs (2%). That said, 13% of planners do not use any additional services.

In Europe, planners use the following tools to help them in their decision-making process:
–   Destination/hotel/convention bureaux' websites (46%);
–   Local associations/ambassadors (46%); and
–   Online meeting management tools (8%) such as international firms.

In North America, 2% of planners do not use any particular information source to research international destinations. Those who do, seek information through:
–   Destination/hotel/convention bureaux' websites (45%);
–   Local associations/ambassadors (35%);
–   Online meeting management (10%), such as CVent, Conference Direct, and InLine Meetings;
–   Travel blogs (5%); and/or
–   Social networking sites (3%).

In Asia, 37% of planners do not use any particular information source to research international destinations. Those who do, seek information through:
–   Destination/hotel/convention bureaux websites (25%);
–   Social networking sites (13%);
–   Online meeting management tools (13%); and/or
–   Local associations/ambassadors (12%).

---

7   Iwamoto, K. (2014), *Demystifying the Big Data Buzz*, MeetingsNet, 06-10-2014 (online), available at: http://meetingsnet.com/strategic-meetings-management/demystifying-big-data-buzz.

Figure 6.15   **Sources of information used to research international destinations (%)**

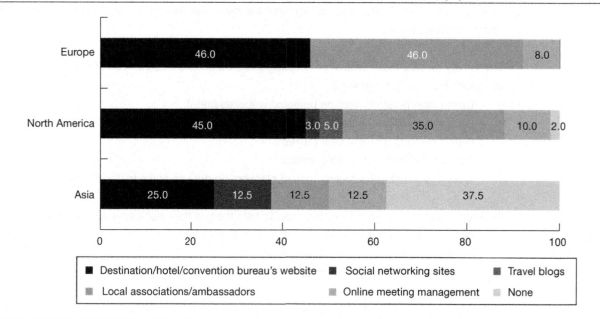

6.5   Role of convention bureau in bidding and decision-making

Convention bureaux encourage and support associations for the bidding process. They are an important vector to propose their destination for hosting conventions and congresses. The bureaux generally help associations throughout the process, from compilation of the bid to recommending service providers, and organizing site inspections. 69% of planners participating in this survey follow a formal bidding process. However, planners mentioned that this depends greatly on the purpose of the event and the association.

Figure 6.16   **Association conventions and congresses requiring a formal bidding process (%)**

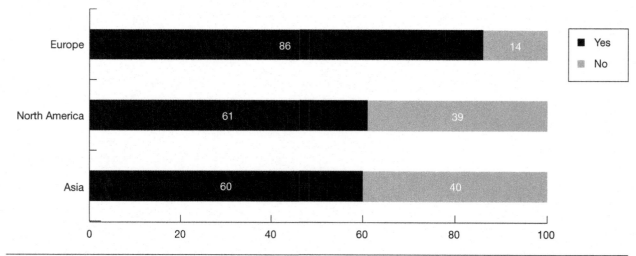

Note: North America excludes Mexico.

Because of the competitive nature of organizing associations' conventions and congresses, ambassadors can greatly influence the bidding process and overall decision-making. Consequently, convention bureaux generally develop ambassador programmes in order to attract associations' conventions and congresses by partnering with local 'ambassadors' from various industries.[8]

6.6 Value of ambassador programmes

The value of the ambassador programmes can be summarized as follows:[9]
– Contest a higher volume of bids;
– Win a higher proportion of bids;
– Reduce "no-hoper" bids and wasted marketing spend;
– Build political support for the activities of meetings professionals;
– Improve the professionalism of the events which the destination hosts;
– Create great PR opportunities;
– Contribute towards civic pride in a destination;
– Low cost/high return strategy; and
– Align meetings priorities to the destination's economic educational and social priorities.

The goal of an ambassador programme is to identify and secure an increasing share of regularly occurring international association conventions and congresses that call for competitive bids from a local chapter of the association.

The aims of the ambassador programme are to:
– Reinforce economic development around strategic priorities for growth;
– Establish partnerships and relationships with large associations;
– Reinforce bid effectiveness for targeted events; and
– Establish a city-wide government engagement around the MCCI industry.

It is the role of a convention bureau to drive the bidding process for its destination. They need to prepare the adequate tools and resources in order to be successful in securing international convention bids.

Table 6.1 **Bidding process**

Driving bidding process	**Management event support**
– Bid Materials;	– Subvention;
– Letters of Support from Government;	– Delegate boosting;
– Lobbying and Promotional support;	– Airport meet and greets/hospitality suites;
– Presentations to show government support;	– Coordination of tour desks and visitor information centers;
– Local contacts; and	– Welcome ceremonies; and
– Site inspections.	– Conference planning advice and assistance.

8   International Congress and Convention Association (April 2014a), *Congress Ambassador Programmes,* ICCA, Amsterdam.

9   Ibid.

More generally, convention bureaux assist planners in the logistical, operational and strategic activities of the event, particularly in the following areas:

–   Sales and promotions;
–   Bid preparation;
–   Liaison services;
–   Promotional material and support;
–   Technical visits;
–   Conference planning advice and assistance;
–   Attendance promotion; and
–   On site services.

Convention bureaux are also in great positions to assist local/regional associations in establishing partnerships or connections with other relevant local government agencies that are relevant to their trade and industry for the purpose of boosting businesses and intellectual exchanges.

The positioning of local associations as thought-leaders in the region has become ever more important in face of global competition as other international associations and destinations strive to be the authoritative voice of their industry or sector.

Associations are challenged to constantly stay innovative and anticipate various expectations of its members and stakeholders. They are also required to adopt good practices (CSR, safety measurement, new technology tools, etc.) to stay ahead of competition. Convention bureaux can therefore be advocates of such good practices, for associations and in order to position the city.

Nonetheless, the role of CBs in assisting meeting planners is considerably evolving. Developing concepts of 'synchronicities' and informal alliances between CBs are emerging. Both concepts are designed to optimise CBs' services and enhance their competitiveness. Synchronicities, or informal alliances, are a way to offer partner CBs and meeting professionals, competitive prices and enhanced services such as knowledge transfer or customer services.[10] Informal alliances between several European national convention bureaux, is another example illustrating the changing environment of the industry. Such alliances enable a stronger promotion of the regional destination, strengthen connection with associations and assist in establishing partnerships.[11] An example is the BestCities alliance, the first in its kind, which has now a BestCities global network, including cities such as Singapore, Berlin, Bogota, Edinburgh and many more, which allows members to conduct and share research and know-how.

Results from this survey show that 80% of participants use the services of a convention bureau or tourist board.

---

10   Bair, B. (2014), *New Tri-City Alliance Offers Rotating Association Meetings Value Pricing, Added Services,* MeetingsNet, 18-08-2014 (online), available at: www.meetingsnet.com (09-06-2015).

11   Harwood, S. (2014), 'European Convention Bureaux Create Strategic Alliance', *Conference & Incentive Travel,* 16-10-2014 (online), available at: www.citmagazine.com (08-06-2015).

'European National Convention Bureaux Form Strategic Alliance' (2014), *International Meetings Review,* 16-10-2014 (online), available at: www.internationalmeetingsreview.com (08-06-2015).

Figure 6.17 **Association meeting planners who use convention bureaux (CBs) (%)**

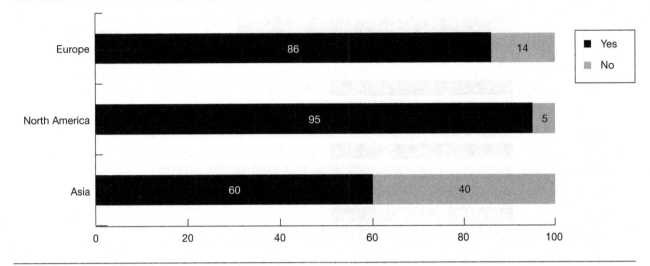

Note: North America excludes Mexico.

Participants were asked which convention bureau services they use the most.

In Europe, planners use in majority bid support (80%) and site visits (80%), but also enjoy their marketing material (60%) and impartial advice (60%), with the venue finding service being the least used (40%).

In North America, convention bureaux are largely solicited by planners for site visits (84%), marketing material (79%), and impartial advice (79%), but also for venue finding services (63%) and bid support (47%). 26% of planners mention using other services from convention bureaux, particularly financial support – such as finding the availability of local grants or subventions to support bringing the meeting to the destination – organization support – such as with the organization of tours that may be of interest, finding local event staffing, hotel reservation, transportation and vendor sourcing assistance – and for a general in-kind support.

Asian planners extensively use the services of convention bureaux for impartial advice (40%), venue finding services (40%), bid support (40%) and the marketing material (40%), but also enjoy site visits (20%) and other services such as support with accommodation (60%) – for example identifying which range of accommodation is best suited for the association.

Clearly, CBs are solicited differently depending on the region, Asian planners being the least inclined to use their services.

Figure 6.18   **Summary of convention bureau services used by association meeting planners by region (%)**

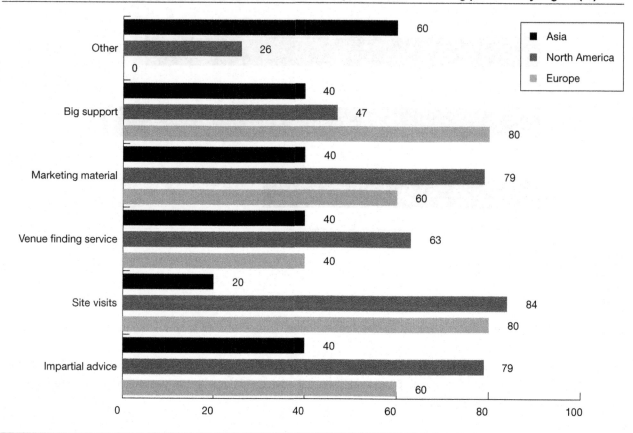

Note: North America excludes Mexico.

6.7 Conclusions

A summary of survey results concerning association meeting planners' needs and expectations with regard to destination and venues is available in the table below.

Table 6.2 **Summary of association meeting planners' needs and expectations**

	European planners	North American planners	Asian planners
Key criteria (five most important, in order of importance)	1. Access; 2. Size of meeting facilities; 3. Financial considerations; 4. Appeal of destination; and 5. Range of accommodations.	1. Size of meeting facilities; 2. Access; 3. Financial considerations; 4. Appeal of destination; and 5. Safety and security.	1. Financial considerations; 2. Appeal of destination; 3. Safety and security; 4. Size of meeting facilities; and 5. Access.
Final decision maker (in order of popularity)	– Board; – Committee; – Executive; and – Membership vote.	– Board; – Executive; and – Committee.	– Executive; – Membership vote; – Secretariat; and – Committee.
Intermediaries (in order of popularity)	– Local chapter assistance/ ambassadors; – DMCs; and – PCOs.	– Local chapter assistance/ ambassadors; – Hotel national sales office; – DMCs; and – PCOs.	– PCOs; – Local chapter assistance/ ambassadors; and – Third party planners.
Average use of CBs	86%	95%	60%
CB services used (in order of popularity)	– Site visits; – Bid support; – Impartial advice; – Marketing material; and – Venue finding service.	– Site visits; – Impartial advice; – Marketing material; – Venue finding service; – Bid support; – Organization support; and – In-kind support.	– Support with accommodation; – Impartial advice; – Venue finding service; – Marketing material; – Bid support; and – Site visits.

To conclude, because association conventions and congresses are a main source of revenue for associations, planners serve as key players in the organization of these events. Based on the survey findings, association meeting planners' choice of destination is primarily influenced by cost and size of meeting facilities. The scale of association conventions and congresses mainly drives this trend. Moreover, with some variations across regions, an executive or the board generally take final decisions. And, although planners have been affected by weak economic growth, especially in western countries – bringing them to be more vigilant thus affecting decision-making – budget forecast for next international events are optimistic, with some planners even expecting their budgets to increase. Most planners use the services of convention bureaux, yet these are solicited differently across regions, Asian planners being the least active in using their services. This may come from the fact that the industry is still in a developing phase in this region, compared to the other two mature regions.

Chapter 7

Corporate meetings: needs and expectations

7.1   What corporate meeting planners want

Depending on the nature of the corporate meeting, planners may have varying expectations. For internal events, where participants are employees of the company, focus may be to increase awareness, CSR, corporate culture, changes in the company or other issues proper to the functioning of the entity. Planners therefore need to organize the meeting according to the aims of the gathering. Similarly, external meetings, which are a vital part of Customer Relationship Management (CRM) strategies generally, intend to build strong relationships with clients and suppliers.[1] Therefore meeting planners need to fully understand the nature of the meeting in order to deliver appropriate returns such as:

–   Increased loyalty;
–   Better relationships;
–   Product launches;
–   Educational meetings; and
–   ROI.

In other words, while planners aim at enhancing employee satisfaction and participation through the organization of internal meetings, they also look for real-time feedback and opportunities to measure ROI. In general, meeting planners look to impress through the meetings they organize, in order to give participants a positive image of the corporation.

7.2   Description and evaluation of key criteria

While corporate meeting planners may be influenced by a number of criteria, destination appeal is the most influential, whereas reputation and infrastructure have the least influential role.

---

1   Rogers, T. (2013).

Figure 7.1   **Summary of key criteria influencing European, North American and Asian planners' destination choice for corporate meetings**

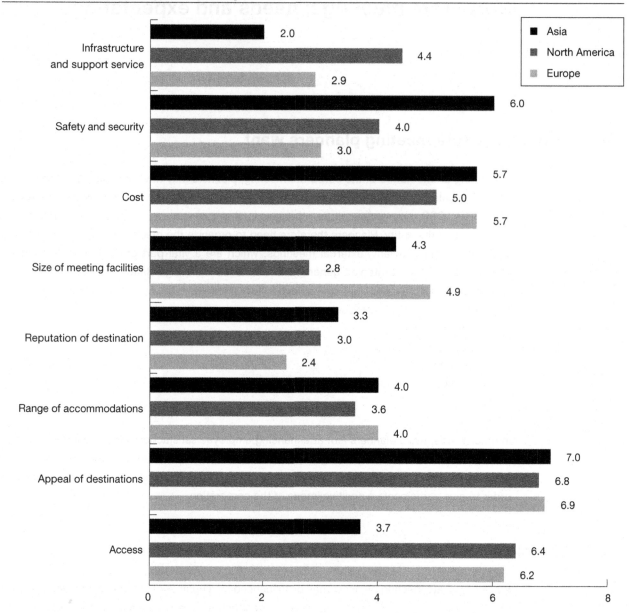

Notes: Average order of importance: 1 = least important, 8 = most important.

North America excludes Mexico.

7.2.1   Appeal of destination

When organizing corporate events meeting planners expect exceptional service quality. Because these events attract suppliers, clients and employees, corporations are putting their image forward and thus need to offer the highest standard. Destination appeal is therefore a determining factor in corporate meeting planning. Moreover, meeting planners may be influenced by the location of headquarters, suppliers, clients or the possibility for future expansion. 73% of planners participating in this research indicate that local presence is a major factor in choosing the destination for the event.

Figure 7.2   **Is local presence a major factor in choosing destination? (%)**

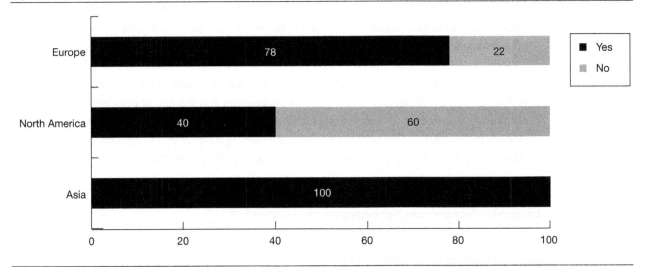

Note: North America excludes Mexico.

Moreover, destination appeal is on average, ranked as the top factor, for all three European, North American and Asian planners, influencing their choice of destination for corporate meeting planners.

Figure 7.3   **Key corporate meeting criteria: appeal of destination**

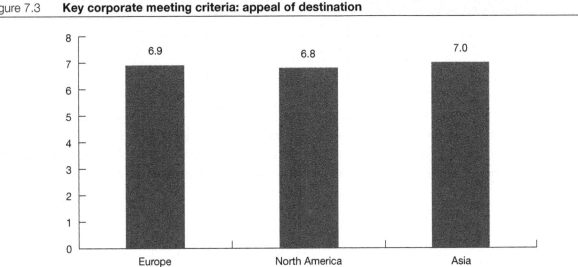

Notes: Average order of importance: 1 = least important, 8 = most important.

North America excludes Mexico.

From the corporate standpoint, planners indicate that once basic criteria are met, they would choose the most attractive destination. The reason is that there is always a motivational factor when choosing destination. If a company chooses a 'high end' destination, then they are flattering their employees, sending them a message that they are important to the company.

Nonetheless, there is growing interest in planning meetings in emerging countries. Many of these countries, notably China or Brazil, are becoming important destinations for business or investment. Meeting planners must focus on some aspects, which are imperative to ensure meetings go well. These include security, political and economic stability, health security, social stability and more.

On average, 39% of participants would consider an emerging destination to hold their corporate meetings. While this depends greatly on the corporation and the aim of the event, planners also showed their concerns for security issues. European planners mentioned Africa – Kenya, Nigeria, Morocco – and Asia – Indonesia – as potential emerging destinations to hold their events. On the other hand, North America planners mentioned Latin America and Asia.

Figure 7.4   **Do corporate planners consider emerging destinations? (%)**

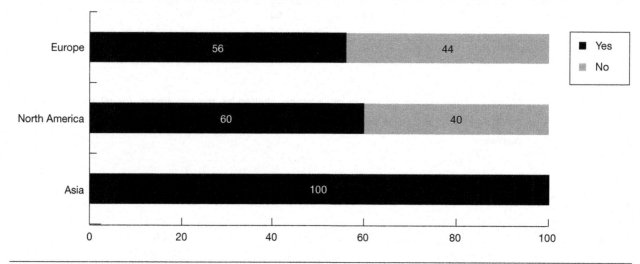

Note: North America excludes Mexico.

Moreover, there is a general trend for planners to go for seaside and mountain resorts, especially in Asia (67%) and Europe (57%), however agencies are trying to push city destinations more and more. Overall, capital cities are a main destination choice for corporate meeting planners.

Figure 7.5   **Destination type for corporate meetings (%)**

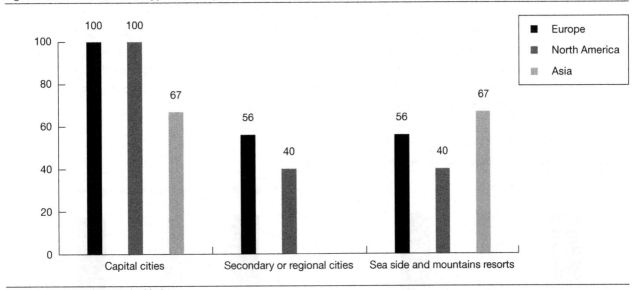

Note: North America excludes Mexico.

7.2.2   Financial considerations

General financial considerations are evaluated by meeting planners, such as accommodation, flights, venue, transportation, and other necessary expenditure. Because corporate meetings are very important for strengthening client, supplier and employee relationships, spending can be relatively important.

Survey results further support this. Cost is the third most important criteria for both European and North American planners, while it is Asian planners' second most important factor.

Figure 7.6   **Key corporate meeting criteria: cost**

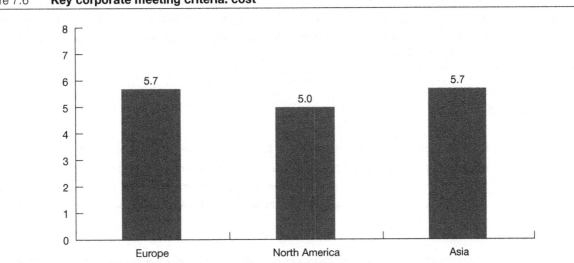

Notes: Average order of importance: 1 = least important, 8 = most important.

North America excludes Mexico.

Moreover, while budgets generally remained the same across regions, European planners experienced for the most part (56%) a decrease in budgets. They are also more sceptical about the future, with only 11% of European planners expecting an increase in their budget for the next international event, against 60% of North American planners. Even more sceptic than European planners are Asian planners who do not expect any increase in their budgets. This may reflect the recent slowdown in economic growth in the region. This underlines that depending on the region, there is a clear difference in spending amongst planners.

Figure 7.7   **Budget changes for corporate meetings (%)**

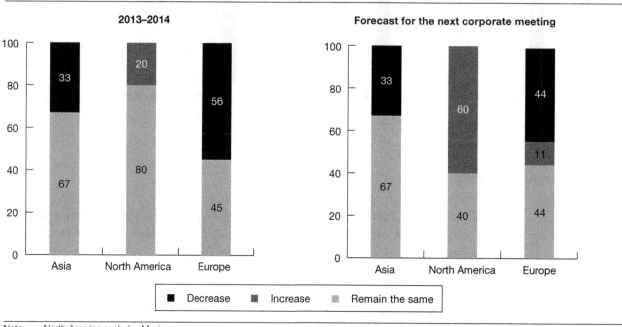

Note: North America excludes Mexico.

Nonetheless, most meeting planners are now looking for cost effectiveness. For this reason measuring ROI is important to meeting planners when selecting destinations. Organizers prefer cheaper venues and accommodation, focusing more on quality and value and thus turning to domestic destinations.

7.2.3   Access

Ease of access is another determinant for final destination selection. In general, corporations do not want employees to spend too much time away from work and understand that clients or suppliers may have only short time frames available for such events. For this reason, appealing destinations for corporate meetings are those, which are easily accessible by direct and frequent flights.

As meetings become shorter, planners do their best in choosing destinations with shorter travel time – including transfers and transportation. Ease of access is therefore a major criterion in choosing destination. European planners mentioned Brussels, Amsterdam and Berlin a number of times, as examples of accessible destinations. Access is ranked second most important for both European and North American planners, scoring on average a high 6 – on a scale from 1 to 8, 8 being the most important. However access is only ranked sixth by Asian planners, with low average weight of 4.

Figure 7.8   **Key corporate meeting criteria: access**

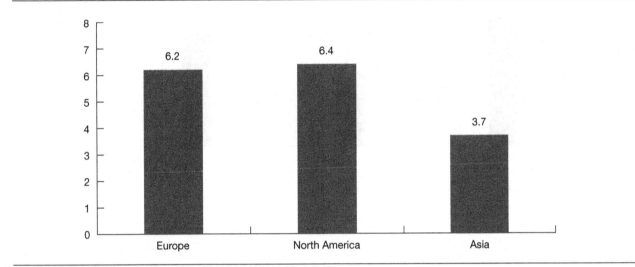

Note: Average order of importance: 1 = least important, 8 = most important.

North America excludes Mexico.

7.2.4   Venue size and configuration: facility package

Although recent trends underlined that there may be a shift towards virtual meetings, the latest facts show that these cannot replace real face-to-face meetings, which remain essential for, amongst others, networking.[2]

Destination selection is also influenced by the meeting space and services available. Meeting planners often outsource the decision process for destination and venue selection to intermediaries, who are specialised in finding appropriate venues and help with negotiations. Corporate meetings require both high-end accommodation and quality meeting space, which are flexible to the needs of the corporation. Procurement is playing a much larger role in venue and destination choice. Corporations are contracting with global hotel chains to secure better deals for their meetings and business travel arrangements.

Corporate meeting planners do consider the size of meeting facilities and the infrastructure and support services when choosing the destination, yet their importance varies across regions. For European and Asian planners, size of meeting facilities is fourth most important criteria, while it is the least important in North America (eighth). Reversely, infrastructure is fourth most influential for North American planners, yet seventh most influential for European planners and least important for Asian planners.

2   Fox, J.T. (2014), 'Why Virtual Conferences will not Replace Face-to-Face Meetings', *International Meetings Review*, 08-10-2014 (online), available at: www.internationalmeetingsreview.com (08-06-2015).

Figure 7.9   **Key corporate meeting criteria: size of meeting facilities and infrastructure**

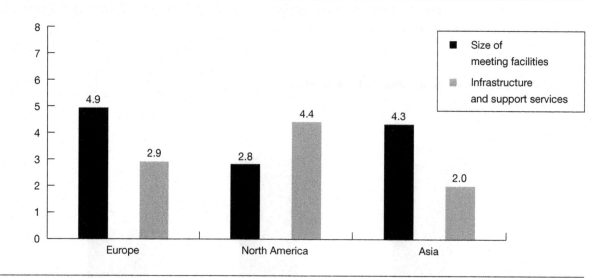

Notes: Average order of importance: 1 = least important, 8 = most important.

North America excludes Mexico.

Recent trends have shown the growing role of mobile apps, virtual/hybrid meeting tools and other new technologies. Corporate meeting planners need to be aware of these options when organizing events, and consider if technology is appropriate for the meeting and/or can be used as an innovative tool for conducting meetings.[3] With emerging technologies and digital solutions growing, meeting planners have the possibility to rethink or redesign meetings in order to engage the audience in a different and interactive way. Some new digital event possibilities include social media, mobile applications and hybrid solutions.

However, only 36% of participants use hybrid technology for the benefit of those attendees prevented from attending an international meeting. Leading are Asian planners, as 67% of them are active in using hybrid technology. This shows that despite the many benefits of technology, incorporating it has yet to become a standard practice. Planners have nonetheless expressed the necessity and desire to incorporate new technologies in event planning. Having the appropriate infrastructure and support services could therefore be increasingly important for influencing destination choice.

3   'American Express Forecasts "Return to Business Fundamentals" for 2015' (2014), *International Meetings Review*, 13-10-2014 (online), available at: www.internationalmeetingsreview.com (08-06-2015).

Figure 7.10   **Use of hybrid technology for corporate meetings (%)**

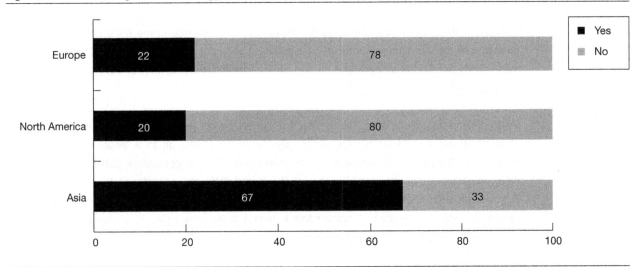

Note: North America excludes Mexico.

7.2.5   Other key criteria influencing final decisions

Additional criteria influence final decision-making. Safety/security, is particularly influencing for Asian planners who rank it, on average, as second most important. Yet it is amongst the least influencing for both European and North American planners. Once again, however, because of the recent terrorist attacks in Europe, and general rising concern over safety, this factor may become more important across all regions. Range of accommodation is another criteria influencing destination choice. As corporate planners enjoy higher quality accommodation, it is important to consider for final destination choice. However it is not amongst top influential criteria.

Figure 7.11   **Key corporate criteria: range of accommodations and safety and security**

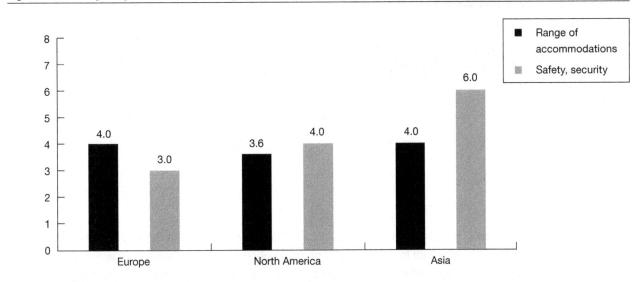

Notes: Average order of importance: 1 = least important, 8 = most important.

North America excludes Mexico.

7.3   Decision-makers vs. -influencers

Decisions about corporate meetings are taken by the corporate conference organizer or a line manager or the managing director, or by a group of such people in consultation. Decision-making has initially been fairly straightforward, yet procurement departments may sometimes extend the time before a decision is made.[4]

According to the results from this survey, final decisions are generally made by top management (63%) but also by the committee (17%), by the board (14%) or, to a lesser extent, by other decision makers (7%). In Europe, top management (62%) or a committee (30%) commonly take final decisions for destination choice, yet the board (8%) can sometimes take final decisions. Some planners further specified that the final decision maker is changing. Before it used to be one designated person deciding, however this is less and less the case. Final decision makers can vary a lot depending on the corporation.

Similarly, in North America, final decisions are taken by top management (60%), a committee (20%) or by other decision makers, which include the executive (20%).

In Asia, top management is also the most common final decision maker for destination choice (67%), while other decisions are taken by the Board (33%).

Figure 7.12   **Corporate meetings final decision makers (%)**

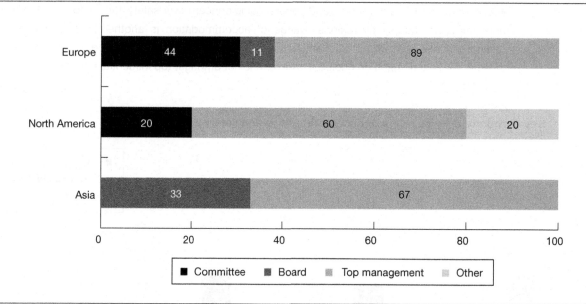

Note: North America excludes Mexico.

As presented in phase 1 chapter 3, corporate planners may solicit the services of intermediaries in order to help with the organization of the meeting. While procurement departments are having a much stronger influence on site selection, many corporations and/or corporate agents are by

---

4   Rogers, T. (2013).

passing DMCs and dealing directly with hotels, venues and suppliers. Results from the survey and interviews show that the most popular intermediaries are destination management companies (69%) and hotel national sales offices (47%). Nonetheless, 22% of European planners do not require support from additional intermediaries.

Figure 7.13   **Intermediaries for corporate planners, by region (%)**

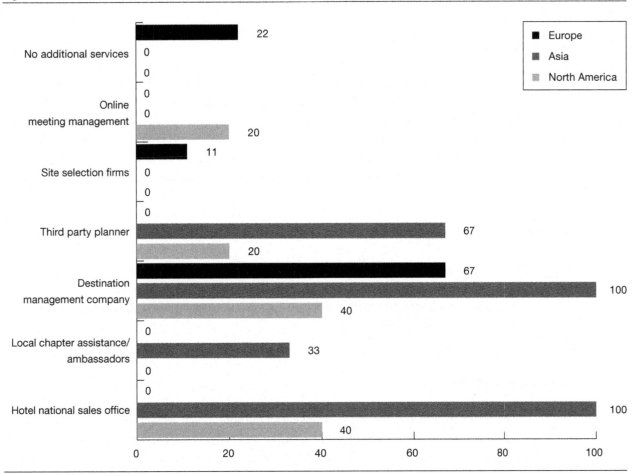

Note: North America excludes Mexico.

7.3.1   Destination management companies (DMCs)

Similarly to conventions and congresses planning, DMCs offer valuable support to corporate planners. According to this research, in Europe, DMCs are the second most popular intermediary, with 67% of planners benefiting from their services. In North America, they are also popular intermediaries, with 40% of planners asking for their support. But it is Asian planners who use DMCs the most, as all planners claim to use their services.

7.3.2   Hotel national sales office

Hotel national sales offices, through their expertise, offer planners support in finding the appropriate fit for their meeting experience. They are often across the country and allow planners the convenience to work with someone locally. According to the survey, 40% of North American planners use the services of Hotel national sales offices, along with an average majority of Asian planners.

7.3.3   Third party planners

As the industry grows, third party planners, such as HelmsBriscoe, have been increasingly solicited for support in event planning. Their multitasking and assistance in all areas of the organization of the event are attracting a lot of corporations to take on their services. These planners, who have extensive buying power and client reach, are real competitors to hotels and CBs.[5] Nonetheless, third party planners have yet to expand to other regions since, according to the survey, 20% of North American planners and a high 67% of Asian planners use their services.

7.3.4   Online meeting management tools

Similarly to associations, Corporations are also benefiting from the increasing use of online tools. According to the research, these were only used by North American planners, where the industry is more mature. 20% of meeting planners use online meeting management tools, CVent was mentioned a number of times.

7.3.5   Site selection firms

Site selection firms are specialised in looking for the appropriate venues and infrastructure needed for corporations. These are particularly useful for negotiations and meeting the needs of the event. The survey results indicate that European planners are the only ones to solicit such intermediaries. 11% of them enjoy these services for support in the organization of their meetings. However the United States of America is also big on using site selection firms.

7.4   Role of convention bureau in decision-making

Convention bureaux are able to create the first contact between corporations and a dedicated events company to help organize the event, or can directly assist with venue recommendations, activities and more. The convention bureau helps decision makers by delivering information and standing as the intermediary between local services. It can also help corporations with price negotiation, which is key to decision-making.

---

5   Grimaldi, L.A. (2015), 'Third-Parties: Big Small or None at All?', *Meetings and Conventions,* 01-01-2015 (online), available at: www.meetings-conventions.com (08-06-2015).

Nonetheless, not all planners use the services of convention bureaux. 25% of participants of the survey say they do not turn to convention bureaux to plan their meetings.

Figure 7.14 **Corporate planners who use CBs**

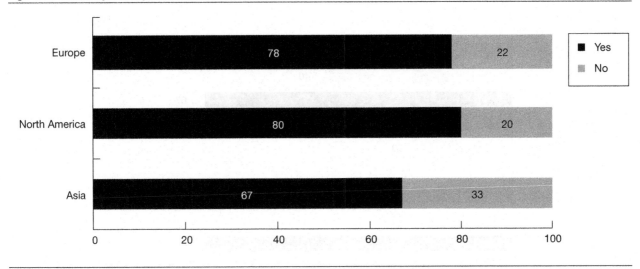

Note: North America excludes Mexico.

Amongst those who do, site visits and bid support are the most demanded services.

In Europe, 78% of planners use the services of a CB. They value the following services – in order of preference: (1) site visits, (2) bid support, (3) impartial advice, (4) venue finding service and (5) marketing material. Planners specify that they use the services of convention bureaux on a varying basis, depending on, for instance, the destination. However this segment does not think about using convention bureaux and prefers relying on local contacts. Those who might use the services of a CB at times say they value the – free – marketing and collateral image that can be provided, the advice service being the least important.

North American planners appear to be using the services of CBs more extensively than European planners. 80% of planners, which value the services of CBs, particularly enjoy, in order, the (1) impartial advice, (2) site visits, (3) venue finding services, (4) marketing material and (5) bid support.

Asian planners are those who use CBs the least, with 67% of planners benefiting from (1) marketing material and (2) site visits.

Figure 7.15   **Summary of convention bureau services used by corporate planners by region (%)**

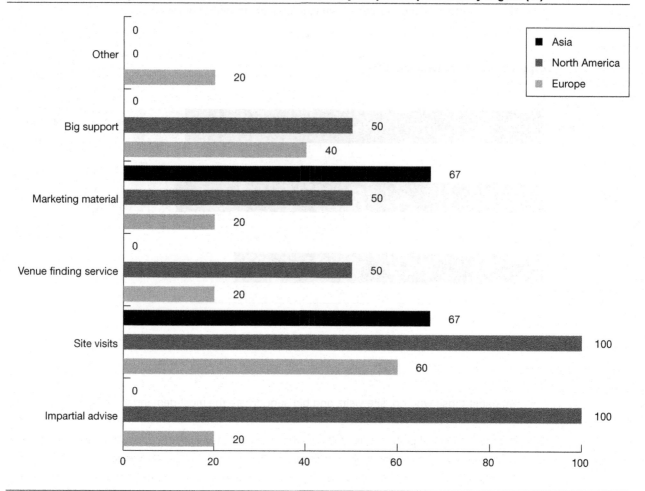

Note: North America excludes Mexico.

7.5   Conclusions

A summary of survey results concerning incentive organizers' needs and expectations with regard to destination and venues is available in the table below.

Table 7.1   **Summary of corporate organizers' needs and expectations**

	European planners	**North American planners**	**Asian planners**
Key criteria (five most important, in order of importance)	1. Appeal of destination; 2. Access; 3. Cost; 4. Size of meeting facilities; and 5. Range of accommodations.	1. Appeal of destination; 2. Access; 3. Cost; 4. Infrastructure and support services; and 5. Safety and security.	1. Appeal of destination; 2. Safety and security; 3. Cost; 4. Size of meeting facilities; and 5. Range of accommodations.
Final decision maker (in order of popularity)	– Top management; – Committee; and – Board.	– Top management; – Committee; and – Executive.	– Top management; and – Board.
Intermediaries (in order of popularity)	– DMCs; and – Site selection firms.	– DMCs; – Hotel national sales office; – Third party planners; and – Online meeting management.	– Hotel national sales office; – DMCs; – Third party planners; and – Local chapter assistance/ ambassadors.
Average use of CBs	78%	80%	67%
CB services used (in order of popularity)	– Site visits; – Bid support; – Impartial advice; – Marketing material; and – Venue finding service.	– Impartial advice; – Site visits; – Marketing material; – Venue finding service; and – Bid support.	– Site visits; and – Marketing material.

Note: North America excludes Mexico.

To conclude, corporate planners' needs and expectations are highly dependent on the nature of the meeting – internal or external. Nonetheless, because corporate meetings are aimed at impressing participants – employees or suppliers – and because delegates have less time available, appeal of destination and access are the most important criteria affecting planners' decision-making. Incorporating hybrid technology has yet to become more popular. Although the results of the survey show that hybrid is not well used, it is definitely growing, and still expecting to grow. Amongst planners surveyed who still do not use new technologies, all show great interest and the urge to incorporate them into their corporate meetings. But, as corporate planners were still affected by the weak economic growth, this segment is more sceptical about their budget forecast for their next meetings. This also underlines the latest trend in planners focusing on cost effectiveness and ROI.

Chapter 8

Incentives: needs and expectations

8.1   What incentive meeting planners want

The increasing number of studies demonstrating the benefits of incentive programmes has triggered corporations to engage more and more into rewarding their employees, especially among their sales forces. Incentive decision makers are particularly engaging in incentives for stimulating sales, employee satisfaction, and the overall morale of the company, amongst others.[1]

1. Recognise performance;
2. Increase sales;
3. Build morale;
4. Improve employee loyalty;
5. Build customer loyalty;
6. Foster teamwork;
7. Improve customer service;
8. Increase market share;
9. Sell new accounts; and
10. Introduce new products.

However the rush towards incentive and recognition programmes has led to many misdirected and poorly designed programmes, and thus unintended consequences.[2] It is therefore important for incentives to be well designed and to reflect the culture of the company.

8.2   Description and evaluation of key criteria

The criteria influencing destination choice vary, as planners appear to have differing priorities depending on the region. On average though, destination appeal, unique experience and the 'wow' are considered most influential, while access is the least determining factor influencing final decisions.

---

1   'Incentive Travel Buyer's Focus – Program Design Structures' (2012), *Successful Meetings,* December 2012, Northstar Travel Media, pp 49–60 (online), available at: www.incentivemag.com/uploadedFiles/Travel/Travel_Buyers_Guide/incentive_buyers_handbook_1212.pdf (08-06-2015).

2   van Dyke, M. (2014).

Figure 8.1   **Summary of key criteria influencing European, North American and Asian planners' destination choice for incentive programmes**

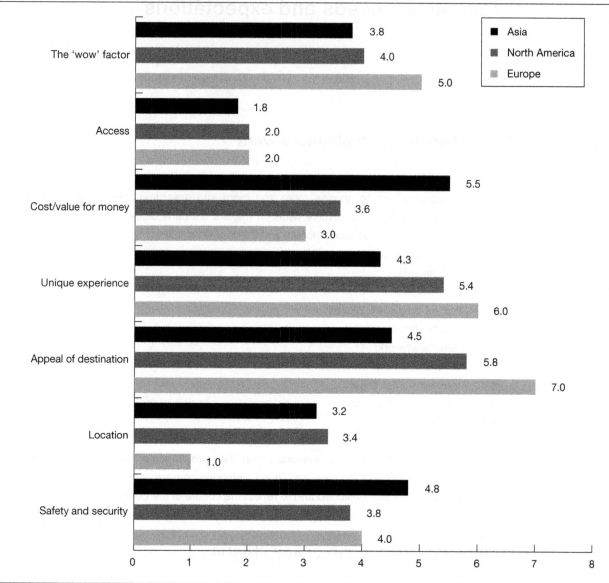

Notes: Average order of importance: 1 = least important, 7 = most important.

North America excludes Mexico.

8.2.1   The 'wow' factor

Creativity can sometimes be affected by practical factors such as flight times; nonetheless, incentive planners constantly strive to provide a 'wow' factor to their programmes, or 'the next great thing'.[3] The 'wow' factor provides a unique experience, which employees remember and it triggers emotional appeal. Incentive planners therefore choose destinations which offer distinct features and which provide memorable experiences.

---

3   Bair, B. (2014).

The 'wow' factor is a combination of a unique experience, the appeal of the destination and the extra bit that makes it 'wow'. European and North American planners rank appeal of destination as the most influential factor, followed by unique experience and the 'wow' factor. While Asian planners, rank the destination as third most influential, followed by unique experience and the 'wow' factor.

Figure 8.2 **Key incentive criteria: the 'wow' factor, appeal of destination and unique experience**

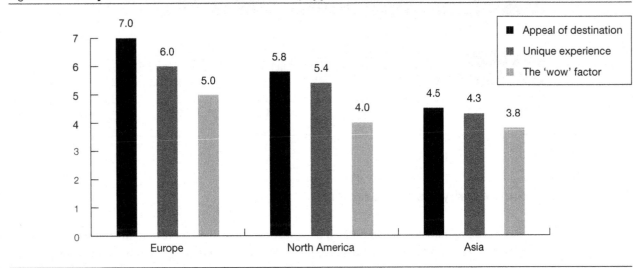

Notes: Average order of importance: 1 = least important, 7 = most important.

North America excludes Mexico.

Where the Caribbean used to be an all-time favourite, emerging market destinations such as China, or South America, rich in culture and traditions, as well as exotic experiences are increasingly chosen as incentive destinations.[4]

66% of planners would consider an emerging destination for incentive programmes. Although this largely depends on the corporation, European planners mentioned Africa, Latin America and Asia as attractive destinations, while North American planners thought of Latin America – i.e., Colombia – and Asia – i.e., Myanmar. Surprisingly, only 17% Asian planners would consider emerging destinations. This may be explained by the fact that the industry is still maturing in this region.

---

4   van Dyke, M. (2014).

Meetings and Conventions (2014), website: www.meetings-conventions.com/magazine/.

Figure 8.3   **Incentive planners use of emerging destinations (%)**

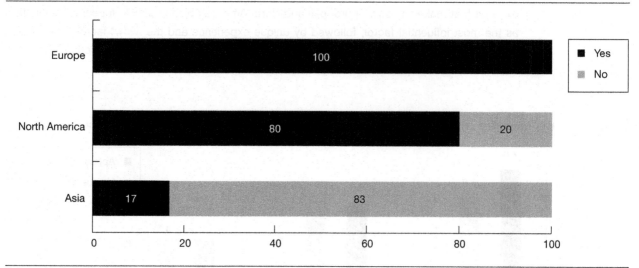

Note: North America excludes Mexico.

8.2.2   Safety and security: risk assessment

Incentive programmes aim at offering an agreeable experience for rewarded employees. Planners therefore prefer safe and secure destinations. Evaluation of external factors is critical, such as:
–   Political stability;
–   Labour (i.e., no strikes);
–   Health (i.e., epidemics);
–   Natural disasters (i.e., risk of tsunami, flooding); and
–   Terrorism and violence.

Additionally planners must perform proper risk assessment for the activities of the programme, followed by risk management. For this, planners can gather the required knowledge through various sources such as:
–   Government travel advisories;
–   Destination experts;
–   Insurance companies;
–   Legal departments; and
–   Financial advisories.

Overall, there is a certain degree of responsibility to provide care for the participants.

Results from this survey show that European and North American planners rank, on average, safety and security as the 4th most important factor influencing destination choice, while Asian planners rank it, on average, second most important. However, because of increasing terrorist threats and extreme weather conditions, such as storms, the safety and security factor may become more influential in the future.

Figure 8.4   **Key incentive criteria: safety and security**

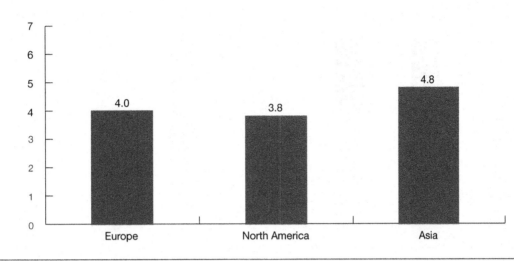

Notes: Average order of importance: 1 = least important, 7 = most important.

North America excludes Mexico.

8.2.3   Financial considerations

Incentive planners consider a number of financial features when organizing programmes, ranging from changing corporate budgets, to value for money for participants.

Corporate budgets have fluctuated a lot over the past few years, pushing planners to adopt cost-cutting measures. Because of this, planners have reduced per-person incentive expenditure.[5] Today, as budgets increase steadily and planners work in a more stable financial environment, investments are going to non-meal components.

The survey reveals that planners' budgets for incentive programmes generally remained the same between 2013 and 2014 and the trend is likely to continue for upcoming incentive programmes. Decreasing budgets between 2013 and 2014 were only experienced in Europe, by 33% of planners, while a 5% increase in budget was experienced by 20% of North American planners. While European and North American planners do not expect to see any change, 50% Asian planners expect their budgets to increase for their next incentive programme.

5   van Dyke, M. (2014).

Figure 8.5   **Budget changes for incentive programmes (%)**

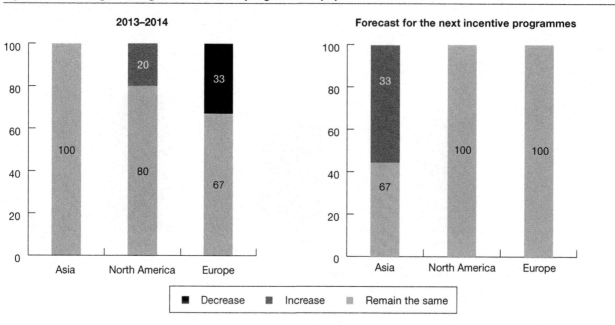

Note: North America excludes Mexico.

This survey results further seem to confirm the trend identified by the IRF Pulse study that incentive programmes are increasingly transferring from group awards to individual awards. In Europe, only 23% of programmes are group awards, against 41% North America and 45% Asia.

Nonetheless, the changing environment coupled with increased considerations for ROI/ROO (return on investment/return on objective) have led to a greater focus on quality over quantity.[6] Value of the programme, as perceived by participants, is an important criterion for decision-making, driving the need for customised and unique packages/offerings. Participants not only look for reduced costs, but also for quality services. Given the current economic environment, it is crucial for planners to offer exceptional experiences and value.

European and North American planners rank cost as the 5th most important factor influencing destination choice. Asian planners, on the other hand, consider cost to be the most important factor influencing destination choice. This further reflects differences experienced across regions.

6   Ibid.

Figure 8.6   **Key incentive criteria: cost/value for money**

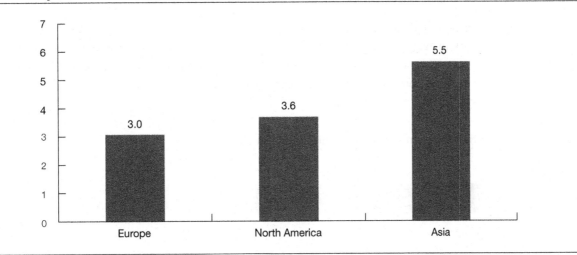

Notes: Average order of importance: 1 = least important, 7 = most important.

North America excludes Mexico.

8.2.4   Access

Incentive planners have a preference for closer to home, easily accessible destinations, in order to minimise the time away from work. Issues of visa requirements are also considered which influences the choice of destination. While this is an influencing criterion, it is not amongst the most important ones. Incentive participants are usually sourced from one country, therefore direct air linkages from the source country to the proposed destination can be critical, especially for large-scale groups within Asia.

Participants to the survey agree that access is a criterion influencing their destination choice, however it is not amongst the most important. For both Asian and North American planners, access is the least influencing factor, and for European planners it is the second least influential factor for destination choice.

Figure 8.7   **Key incentive criteria: access**

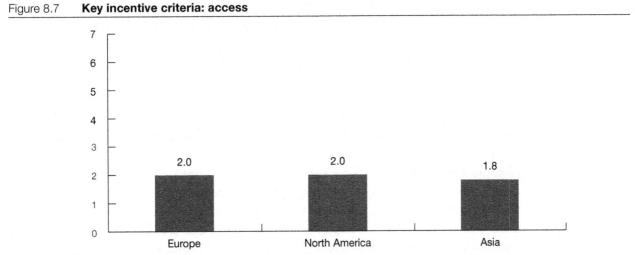

Notes: Average order of importance: 1 = least important, 7 = most important.

North America excludes Mexico.

8.3   Decision-makers vs. -influencers (roles of intermediaries)

Incentive travel planners have many roles, ranging from motivators, negotiators, event designers, risk managers and travel trend expert. Because incentive programmes are part of corporations, the decision-making process is similar to that of corporate meeting planners. The most common final decision makers are top management (38%).

Figure 8.8   **Incentive programmes final decision-makers (%)**

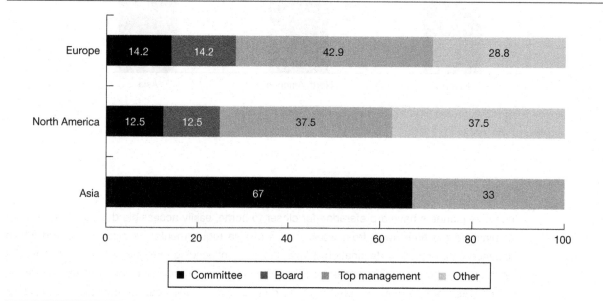

Note: North America excludes Mexico.

Some European participants (29%) explained that the final decision maker for incentive programmes could vary depending on the corporation and the programme; this includes either top management, board or event committee. Yet top management is often the final decision maker (43%), followed by the board (14%) and the committee (14%).

North American planners also underline that final decision makers vary depending on the programme and corporation. Therefore, some planners (38%) experience situations when the final decision maker can be either option – top management, board, or event committee. Nonetheless, top management is a popular option (38%), while board and committee can also be the final decision makers (12% respectively).

As a slight contrast, Asian planners expressed that the committee is, on average, the most common final decision maker (67%) while top management can sometimes take that role (33%).

While procurement departments are also playing a more influential role for incentive organization, common intermediaries include incentive houses, travel fulfilment companies, corporate travel agencies and DMCs. According to this survey, incentive planners appear to be using similar intermediaries than for corporate planning. While Asian planners use a larger variety of intermediaries, European planners turn to only two types of intermediaries.

Figure 8.9   **Intermediaries for incentive planners by region (%)**

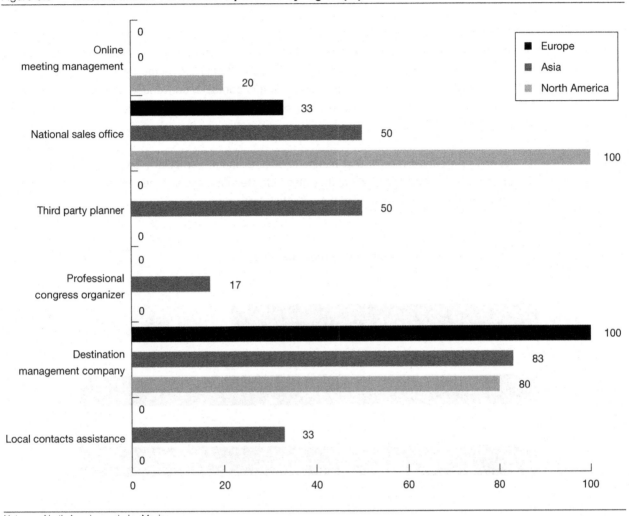

Note: North America excludes Mexico.

8.3.1   DMCs, hotel national sales offices, third party planners, local chapter assistance, online meeting management tools and PCOs

In Europe, planners enjoy the services of hotel national sales offices (33%), destination management companies (100%).

In North America, planners turn to hotel national sales offices (100%), DMCs (80%) as well as online meeting management (20%), such as CVent.

Finally in Asia, DMCs are the most commonly used (83%) yet intermediaries such as hotel national sales offices (50%), third party planners (50%), local contacts assistance (33%) and PCOs (17%) are also popular.

8.4   Role of convention bureau in decision-making

Convention bureaux assist incentive planners by offering guidance in choosing local suppliers and intermediaries. Their services can be as broad as suggesting activities for the programme, helping with accommodation, recommending DMCs, and offering brochures for participants, amongst others. With their elaborated local knowledge and contacts, convention bureaux are particularly helpful in assisting incentive planners in finding unique, original experiences and activities for their programmes.

Overall, this survey reveals that planners, 89% of them, particularly enjoy the impartial advice given by convention bureaux. Yet they also indicate that these services will be used according to the needs of the corporation and the potential destination.

Figure 8.10   **Incentive planners who use convention bureaux (CBs)**

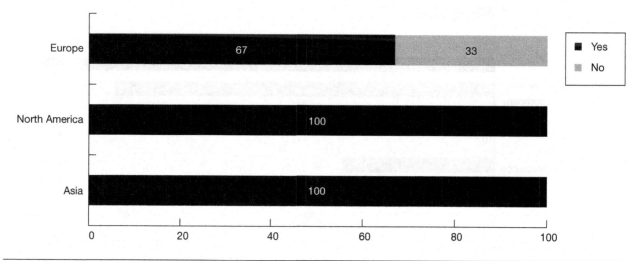

Note: North America excludes Mexico.

In Europe, planners were the least likely to use the services of convention bureaux, only 67% of participants. All planners appreciate the impartial advice provided by the convention bureaux and 67% like to benefit from marketing material provided.

North American (USA and Canada) planners on the other hand are quite active in using convention bureaux' services, with all participants claiming to use their services. The most appreciated are once again the impartial advice (80%) and marketing material (80%), yet site visits (60%) and venue finding services (20%) are often used. Another small portion of planners (20%) like to benefit from information available from convention bureaux' websites.

Asian planners also turn towards convention bureaux to assist them in decision-making. 17% of planners enjoy the impartial advice, venue finding service and marketing material, and with high majority 83% of planners use the site visits service from CBs.

Figure 8.11   **Summary of convention bureau services used by incentive planners, by region (%)**

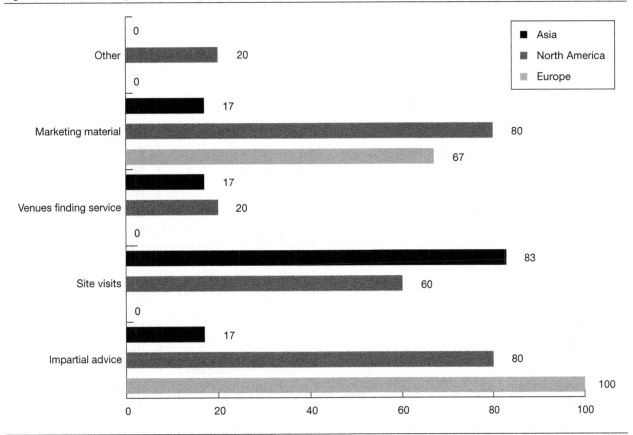

Note: North America excludes Mexico.

8.5   Conclusions

A summary of survey results concerning incentive organizers' needs and expectations with regard to destination and venues is available in table 7.3.

Table 8.1   **Summary of incentive organizers' needs and expectations**

	European planners	**North American planners**	**Asian planners**
Key criteria (five most important, in order of importance)	1. Appeal of destination; 2. Unique experience; 3. The 'wow' factor; 4. Safety and security; and 5. Cost/value for money.	1. Appeal of destination; 2. Unique experience; 3. The 'wow' factor; 4. Safety and security; and 5. Cost/value for money.	1. Cost/value for money; 2. Safety and security; 3. Appeal of destination; 4. Unique experience; and 5. The 'wow' factor.
Final decision maker (in order of popularity)	– Top management; – Committee; and – Board.	– Top management; – Committee; and – Executive.	– Committee; and – Top management.
Intermediaries (in order of popularity)	– DMCs; and – Hotel national sales office.	– Hotel national sales office; – DMCs; and – Online meeting management.	– DMCs; – Hotel national sales office; – Third party planners; and – Local chapter assistance/ ambassadors.
Average use of CBs	67%	100%	100%
CB services used (in order of popularity)	– Impartial advice; and – Marketing material.	– Impartial advice; – Marketing material; – Site visits; – Venue finding service; and – Website information.	– Site visits; – Impartial advice; – Venue finding service; and – Marketing material.

Note: North America excludes Mexico.

To conclude, incentive organizers' needs and expectations are mainly dependent on the destination, yet are also driven by the desire to offer a quality experience to employees, with the additional 'wow' experience. Planners' attention to detail also requires a good sense of creativity and innovation. As the segment develops, driven by stabilising and rising budgets, organizers are optimistic for the future.

Phase 3

Best practices: convention bureaux in Europe, America and Asia

Chapter 9

Best practices: convention bureaux in Europe, America and Asia

As the industry sees solid recovery from the recent global financial crisis, many destinations around the world are looking to the MCCI industry as a means to move forward their economic development agendas. In this context, convention and visitor bureaux (CVBs) have grown into major actors in helping cities, regions and countries around the world to meet their strategic objectives in areas of economic priority.

The survey conducted in phase 2 included questions on planners' use of convention bureaux (CB). From this it was discovered that association planners use CBs the most. Many expressed the important role bureaux play in helping them choose destinations for their events (often including a bid process). They also value the help CBs can provide in the organization of their events. CB services are solicited differently depending on the region, the event type and according to the needs of the organization. However, within each region, there are models of 'best practices' that stand out, and it is useful to describe the characteristics of the outstanding CB from different parts of the world. The experience as a consultancy agency acted as a guide to look at specific criteria that were used to decide who was a best practices CB. Convention bureaux were evaluated on their:

1. Performance;
2. Governance, particularly the level of government and industry partnerships;
3. Resources available, especially government and/or ministries support;
4. Strategic planning;
5. Level of research and development, innovation and business development;
6. Marketing, promotional and brand management; and
7. Bidding support.

Best practices CBs were chosen based on being generally recognised leaders in their regions of the world.

Convention bureaux work differently on local (city), regional (provincial) and national levels, but share fundamental roles. Variations usually occur on the level of structure, size and/or funding. Within Europe itself, CBs have been established differently and at different moments; this coupled with varying policies and governments results in more than one CB model.

This is also the case in the Americas, where major differences exist between North American (United States of America and Canada) and Latin American CBs. Furthermore, Asia, which is steadily expanding its industry, has a different landscape as well.

Regional CBs are mainly seen in Europe, but still only represent a very small portion of the industry. These do not play such an important role in attracting MCCI events to a destination.

Destination's economic, social and political environments influence the extent to which the MCCI industry is developed in their region and how CBs are structured and developed.

Evaluating CB best practices is a way to apply the know-how to develop new convention bureaux and also helps already implemented bureaux to enhance performances and acquire a better understanding of the evolving industry. Properly understanding the roles and best practices of convention bureaux can provide useful for maximising the return on staffing, budget allocation and more. The benchmarking can also be used to support decision-making.

For the purpose of this best practices analysis, a closer look has been taken at national and city convention bureaux, in mature and developing markets, in Europe, the Americas and Asia. The results are included in the following section.

Key messages:
- Differences exist across bureaux, on local, regional and national levels, especially between mature markets and developing destinations;
- The European landscape is very diverse and also has the most regional CBs. Local/city CBs are the most important;
- The North American market (United States of America and Canada) is very well established and has the largest number of CBs and important budgets. Latin America, on the other hand is overcoming difficult security and economic conditions, is today trying to promote another image;
- Asia includes a large number of developing countries. For this reason the landscape remains relatively diverse. Some dominating CBs, such as MyCEB and SECB are becoming quality examples for future CBs to follow;
- Governments provide important financial support and policy developments, which are essential for the implementation of strong CBs; and
- Despite the regional and cultural differences, there are a number of 'best practices' characteristics that characterise the convention bureaux mentioned below:
  1. Clearly defined business development strategy;
  2. Strong support from government institutions;
  3. Close working relationships with MCCI partners;
  4. Strong marketing/branding strategy;
  5. Presence in global markets; and
  6. Investment in research and development, and innovation.

9.1   European landscape

As a leading region for MCCI events, Europe has a large number of national, regional and local/city convention bureaux. The European MCCI landscape can be divided between mature markets and developing markets. As the industry continues to grow, and national, regional and local destinations understand the importance of developing a strong MCCI industry, more and more convention bureaux are being created.

The recently launched European National Convention Bureaux Alliance is an example of this ongoing activity. It aims at boosting partnerships and encouraging knowledge sharing amongst European convention bureaux to reinforce Europe's position as the leading destinations for MCCI events.[1] The alliance currently has 22 members including: Germany (co-founder), Austria, The Czech Republic, Denmark, Estonia, Finland, Holland (a co-founder), Hungry, Iceland, Montenegro, Norway, Poland, Serbia, Slovenia, Spain, Switzerland, Italy, Ireland, France, Portugal and Latvia.[2]

National convention bureaux: Europe has 22 formal national convention bureaux, with varying models and main activities. Staff numbers range between two and 19 employees, with an average of five employees. Germany, the oldest and most successful national convention bureau, has 19 employees, making it the largest bureau. Public funding is the main source of income for European national CBs, either through direct contributions from the regional or central government, ministries or national tourism organizations or as income from taxes and membership fees. In mature markets, national CBs are not very popular, whereas developing markets (i.e., Serbia) extensively refer to national CBs as they are a main source of contact and resources for planning MCCI events. Most national CBs assist event planners with bidding, support services and advice, and a large number of them have developed membership/partnership programmes, with an average of 60 members.

Regional convention bureaux: regional convention bureaux are mainly found in Europe's mature markets, particularly in countries such as Belgium, Holland or Germany, to name a few. They are responsible for promoting the region as a destination for MCCI events and generally cooperate in joint projects with both local/city CBs and national CBs as well as other regional CBs. As regional authorities recognise the importance of business tourism, and develop relevant policies for the development of regional tourism, they also support regional CBs financially. However, in this survey, it was discovered that the regional convention bureaux play a marginal role in the MCCI landscape and decision-making process, and therefore were not included in the best practices analysis.

Local convention bureaux: local convention bureaux are the most common and developed bureaux in Europe. In total, Europe has more than 250 local convention bureaux.[3] The bureaux are, for the most part not-for-profit organizations and generally provide financial support, such as subventions, to bring conventions to the destination. Local bureaux promote the city and sometimes region as MCCI destination, and provide support in all activities of event organization, including bid preparation, promotion and advice. Moreover, local convention bureaux have major industry partners and are more and more developing ambassador programmes to engage local leaders.

Following is a description of best practices for two national CBs: Germany and Serbia and for two local/city CBs: Prague and Vienna.

---

1   Meetpie.com (2015), *New Members Bolster European National Bureaux Alliance,* 05-02-2015 (online), available at: www.meetpie.com/Modules/NewsModule/NewsDetails.aspx?newsid=20363 (09-06-2015).

2   German Convention Bureau (2015), *Recently Launched European National Convention Bureaux Alliance Experiencing New Growth & Strong Interest,* newsblog, 03-03-2015, GCB, Frankfurt (online), available at: www.gcb.de/article/newsroom/newsblog/recently-launched-european-national-convention-bureaux-alliance-experiencing-new-growth-strong-interest (29-09-2015).

3   Cvent (2015), *Europe CVB Directory* (online), available at: www.cvent.com/rfp/europe-cvb-directory-18129d1549184b9a8117deee791ae01a.aspx (08-06-2015).

German Convention Bureau (GCB): 'Germany as a travel destination for fairs and congresses'

History

The German Convention Bureau (GCB) was established in 1973, as an independent association founded by the German National Tourist Board (GNTO), Lufthansa and German Railways, which remain strategic partners of GCB.[4]

Performance

Germany is the leading destination for business meetings and events in Europe. For the last 10 years it has held second place in the world – after the United States of America – and is first in Europe for hosting international association conventions and congresses.[5] The ICCA statistics revealed that Germany hosted 722 international association conventions and congresses in 2013, 11.2% more than in 2012. More than 30 cities contributed to this result, with the most important players being Berlin, Munich and Hamburg.

One of the main reasons for Germany's outstanding position as a MCCI destination is the high service standards and clear profile: Germany presents itself as a sustainable and innova¬tive destination as well as a location with expertise in important sectors of science and the economy.

Governance

GCB's Board of Directors has 12 members (3 permanent members from strategic partner institutions and 9 elected by General Assembly). It is connected with the Federal Government through the German National Tourist Board (GNTB). GCB also has a close collaboration with the European Association of Event Centres, the main objective being to increase the media and politicians awareness of the MCCI industry. They are also partners when organizing "Green meetings and events" conferences and MEXCON (Meeting Experts Conference). MEXCON, which is a platform for intensive dialogue with governmental bodies and politicians, allows the exchange of knowledge and ideas within the MCCI industry in Germany.

---

4   German Convention Bureau (2015), official website: www.gcb.de/en.

5   International Congress and Convention Association (2013b).

Local support/resources

- **Funding:** GCB's annual budget is not disclosed. Around one third of the budget comes from the Federal Government through its strategic relation with GNTB. The rest of the budget comes from annual membership fees and joint marketing activities. In addition, some projects are supported from other governmental resources. These activities are supported as part of the Foreign Trade Fair Participation Programme financed by the German Federal Ministry for Economic Affairs and Energy. Compared to other European national convention bureaux, GCB is one of the most resourced bureaux;
- **Subvention:** GCB does not have a developed "Subvention Programme" on a national level to attract MCCI organizers to hold their meetings in Germany. Strategically, the GCB is more focused on offering strong service and specific benefits, having contact with key experts in different areas;
- **Staff:** the bureau has 15 employees. The marketing sector has five employees, engaged in activities related to trade fairs and events, media and communication and database marketing. The international business sector has four employees, covering international business, customer relations and market research. Other employees are involved in the business development sector and PR. Another office is located in the United States of America; and
- **Membership/partnership:** there are over 200 industry members and over 400 partners under GCB's umbrella. This includes 31 cities and local destinations, convention and exhibition venues, hotels, event agencies (PCO, DMC, EMC), service providers, transportation companies, but also universities, trade press, publishers.

  GCB has developed a network of individual members, which includes board members, General Managers (GM), CEOs, Director of Sales (DOS) of leading convention centres, hotels, agencies, and municipalities. Other co-operative members include the European Association of Event Centres and the Association of German Event Organizers. As influential industry associations, they are involved in some strategically important projects, studies and statistics reports.

  In addition to membership, the GCB offers companies and institutions further opportunities for co-operation and participation in marketing campaigns, depending on their needs.

Strategy

GCB gets strategic direction through strong and very developed communication and discussion with major stakeholders from public and private sectors. The GNTB and the GCB work together to secure and develop Germany's market position as a leading international meeting destination. Focus is put on the country's superior infrastructure, economic and scientific achievements and its high level of professionalism and quality of services.

Research and development/innovation

One of its most important activities is to conduct in-depth market research for the business events industry. GCB is very active in providing research and studies and every year, in cooperation with industry associations, academic and business sector and other stakeholders, conducts and publishes statistic data, studies and publications: *Meeting & Event Barometer: B2B source market studies* (China, United States of America, the United Kingdom, Brazil and the Russian Federation)[6], *Meetings and Conventions in the Future* (2013)[7], *Position Paper: Germany's future international competitiveness*[8], and the *German Meetings and Conventions Sector in the course of transformation, discussions, thoughts, stories*[9].

Marketing/promotion/brand

GCB is currently promoting Germany as a meeting destination and organizes destination promotion in trade shows, sales missions, educational trips and site visits. The bureau also provides promotional materials (print and web) for all planners and is active in organizing educational and networking events.

GCB's marketing strategy in the next five years (2015–2020) will be focused on three key subjects:
1.   Expert Field Strategy: Germany's key sectors of expertise will be put at the heart of the destination's marketing activities, with a goal to profit its strong expertise;
2.   Innovation: develop Germany's innovative potential as a meeting destination; and
3.   Sustainability: GCB is active in the area of sustainability, for the benefit of the environment and society as well as to achieve competitive advantage.

With these three key points Germany will try to differentiate itself from competitors and will try to enhance presence in China as a future market, alongside with other traditional markets such as the United States of America, Europe and national markets.

Bidding/bid support

While GCB is not active in the bidding process – the job being left to local convention bureaux – it helps with coordination and collaboration between German cities and local destinations.

Useful information:

German Convention Bureau official website: www.gcb.de.

---

6   original German title: *USA (UK, China Brasilien) als Quellmarkt für die deutsche MICE Branche – Eine B2B Marktstudie mit Branchenfokus.*

7   original German title: *Tagung und Kongress der Zukunft.*

8   original German title: *Positionspapier für den Veranstaltungsstandort Deutschland.*

9   original German title: *Die Tagungs- und Kongressbranche im Wandel der Zeit. Gespräche, Gedanken, Geschichten.*

Serbia Convention Bureau (SCB)

SERBIA CONVENTION BUREAU

History

Established in 2007, Serbia Convention Bureau (SCB) was at the time ranked 73rd on ICCA statistics and did not even appear in European rankings, with just 6 international association conventions and congresses in 2006.[10]

Performance

Serbia has been the fastest growing meeting destination in Europe in the last 7 years. The number of international association conventions and congresses in the country has increased 11 times in a period of 7 years, from 6 in 2006 to 66 in 2013. This positions Serbia as 42nd on world rankings and 23rd European destination. Additionally, Serbia is amongst the top-5 Eastern European countries for MCCI events, after Poland, Czech Republic, Hungary and levelled with the Russian Federation and Croatia. In 2013 Serbia has achieved 2.2 million arrivals and 6.6 million overnights, and the share of international visitors has increased continually in the last 7 years (9% annually). While Serbia is not a tourism-focused country, and most arrivals are centred in the capital, it is estimated that at least one third of total international arrivals are business tourists.

While Serbia only has one local convention bureau – Belgrade Convention Bureau (BCB) – SCB can play a pivotal role in increasing the number of regional and local convention bureaux across the country.

Governance

Serbia Convention Bureau (SCB) was established in 2007, as a department within the National Tourism Organization of Serbia (NTOS), fully governmental driven. NTOS is highly involved in all SCB activities and NTOS' managing director is also a permanent member of SCB's Advisory Board.

Local support/resources

As a department of NTOS, Serbia Convention Bureau receives important support from NTOS. Communication with public institutions and politicians is developed through NTOS and through

---

10 Serbia Convention Bureau (2015), official website: http://m.scb.travel/.

regular communication with the Ministry responsible for tourism, which has one representative in the SCB Advisory Board.

SCB and NTOS are also partners of the Education and Industry Advancing Together (EIAT) Conference, which allows SCB to connect the MCCI industry with the best students and is also a platform for communication with politicians, the business sector and ministries, as well as an opportunity to invite international industry leaders.

–   **Funding:** SCB's annual budget reaches an average of EUR 300,000, making it one of the most under resourced national convention bureaux in Europe. This excludes the salaries of three employees, but includes renting of space in the major trade shows (IMEX and EIBTM, which takes around one third of the total annual budget).
    Industry partners do not pay fees and participation for trade shows is mainly symbolic. Nonetheless, industry partners, especially hotels are supportive, offering discounts for hotel rooms for site inspections and familiarisation trips;

–   **Subvention:** there is no "Subvention Programme" for international meeting planners in order to attract them to hold their events in Serbia. Event support is limited to logistical activities such as site inspections, promotional material, information desks and welcome drinks;

–   **Staff:** SCB has three employees, including a CEO, however there is no clear structure or departments within the bureau itself. Roles are given to the different employees: one focuses on the association market, bidding and communication with the meeting ambassadors, while the other focuses on marketing activities, membership and the corporate market;

–   **Membership/partnership:** in 2008, SCB developed a Partnership programme with a goal to involve the private sector in all its activities and to attract as many major industry players as possible. The programme includes 76 industry partners in different categories of business, including 4 meeting venues, 45 hotels (4- and 5-star), 14 event organizers (PCOs and DMCs) as well as other service providers (airline company, media, education, meeting equipment). In order to enhance communication between partners and SCB's performance, industry partners meet once a year to discuss marketing activities; and

–   **Ambassador programme:** the Serbia Ambassador Programme was implemented in 2014. SCB decided to implement a restrictive model of ambassador programme, meaning that ambassadors must have experience in hosting international conventions and congresses and are available for five years. Potential meeting ambassadors are members of Association Development Programmes, and take part in a number of events.

Strategy

Cooperation between private and public sector is achieved through the SCB Advisory Board, a body responsible for discussions of strategic directions and developments for the MCCI industry. This includes representatives of private and public sectors comprising government representatives, the tourism Ministry, the managing director of NTOS and other industry partners.

The first four years of SCB were used to increase education and awareness of the MCCI industry. In 2012, Serbia Convention Bureau started with new strategic directions including (1) the promotion of new technologies and innovative ideas (2) bringing support to local associations and thought leaders and (3) regional cooperation, all of which are still implemented today.

Research and development/innovation

Serbia is a technologically advanced country with a booming industry and strong universities in IT. SCB decided to support new, start-up companies of young people and students in Serbia and to engage them in joint marketing projects in order to promote Serbia as a destination for innovation. SCB is staying ahead in the market, being amongst the first to launch a tailor-made mobile application for meeting planners, in 2011 and Facebook games to promote Serbia as an attractive meeting destination. In this strive to use new technologies and innovation to stimulate the MCCI industry, SCB also developed solar charger and Wi-Fi spots for meeting venues.

Marketing/promotion/brand

SCB has been very active in promoting Serbia as an attractive meeting destination, engaging in various activities to represent the Serbian meeting industry and works on destination sales and business development. Generally speaking, SCB partakes in various events to promote itself on an international basis and is also active in the IMEX Politician's Forum. Because of limited budget, SCB uses new technology projects developed in cooperation with student companies or regional projects, which allows SCB to get more media coverage for less money invested.

Serbia Destination Alliance Programme: this programme promotes its members on international markets. At the moment the programme only includes five members, which are local destinations. However this has the possibility to further enhance the local MCCI industry, while also increasing international and local awareness of destination Serbia.

Bidding/bid support

SCB has a leading role in the country in the process of bidding for international meetings and events. Because the industry in Serbia is mainly focused on the capital city and because local bureaux do not have enough resources, SCB is now taking on the role of destination sales for the entire country. Most active PCOs are members of SCB Bid Alliance, which is an internal body that discusses bidding processes, potential association clients and/or meeting ambassadors.

Useful information

Serbia Convention Bureau (2015), official website: www.scb.travel.

Vienna Convention Bureau (VCB): "Central Europe's leading conference city"

History

Driven by a joint initiative from the Vienna Chamber of Commerce and the Municipality of Vienna, the Vienna Convention Bureau was founded in 1969.[11] Both parties provided the initial funding that enabled the bureau to get started as the official marketing and sales organization for building the business events industry in Austria's capital.

Performance

The city of Vienna has been one of the most consistent performers in terms of hosting international association conventions and congresses over the last decade. According to ICCA statistics, Vienna has even been the highest ranked city for 6 of the last 10 years. In the other years, it has consistently been in the top-3.

Local support/resources

- **Structure/governance:** the Vienna Convention Bureau is a department of the City Tourism Office. However, the convention bureau operates in a very independent manner. It has a 10 member Board of Directors, who oversees its activities.
  This Board, who meet on a quarterly basis, is made up of people from the local industry, but also includes other profiles, such as the Head of International Relations for the City of Vienna. The Board officially reports back to the City Tourism Board;
- **Resources:** the convention bureau receives its own budget from public sources, which represents EUR 2.6 million on an annual basis. Approximately 45% comes from the municipality and the Chamber of Commerce, 40% from the Tourism Office, with the balance coming from sponsorships and cooperative marketing efforts.
  In terms of spending, the bureau devotes 30% of its budget to staff costs, approximately 10% to general and administrative costs, and around 60% on marketing and sales activities;
- **Subvention:** Vienna Convention Bureau have developed a programme of financial incentives that they offer event planners who are willing to organize meetings or conventions at certain times of the year. Although not an official subvention programme, or fund, as is the case in many destinations, the programme has well-defined criteria and protocols in place for this incentive programme.
  In addition, for large, international events, the city of Vienna often proposes "in-kind" subventions, such as offering the city hall free of charge for special events, such as opening receptions;
- **Staff:** including its Director, the Vienna Convention Bureau has 11 full-time staff members. This makes the VCB one of the largest in Europe. However, the Vienna Convention Bureau team really distinguishes itself by the quality of its personnel. Of the 11 staff members, 7 have received official Certified Meeting Planner (CMP) status. In addition, the average time of presence at the Bureau is more than 11 years, which makes the team one of the most experienced in the world;

---

11 Vienna Convention Bureau (2015), official website: www.vienna.convention.at.

- **Membership/partnership:** the Vienna Convention Bureau has strong working relationships set up with its MCCI industry stakeholders. However, the bureau has decided not to establish a formal, paying member programme.

  When questioned, the bureau states that the 'partnership' style working relationships are already working well, so they do not feel the need to formalise them through a partner or membership programme. As an example, the Vienna Convention Bureau has managed in implement one of the most effective meetings/events data collection systems in the industry, thanks to the active contribution of the local MCCI industry. This is unique in the industry, and is only possible when there is a strong level of trust between the convention bureau and local stakeholders.

  In addition, the fact that there is not a member programme leaves large latitude to make strategic decisions about bureau activities; and

- **Business development – partnership with Barcelona:** an interesting approach to international business development has been implemented by Vienna Convention Bureau, in cooperation with Barcelona Convention Bureau. The two cities have decided to work together to undertake promotional and sales activities in long-haul markets, such as China. This approach, which can be referred to as "coopetition", has proved to be very effective for the two parties.

Business development/sales activities/bidding assistance/ambassadors

- **Market and sales activities:** the Vienna Convention Bureau allocates over 60% of its budget to marketing and sales activities. It has a truly global approach to sales, and is involved in activities in all key markets around the world. The bureau participates in over 25 trade shows or workshops on an annual basis, including events in Europe, the Americas, China, India and Australia.

  In addition, the Vienna Convention Bureau is particularly present in the market of the United States of America through its long-standing collaboration with one of the biggest representation companies in the business;

- **Leadership:** one of the key elements that creates a successful organization in any sector of activity is the quality of its leadership over the long term. The Vienna Convention Bureau has been managed by the same Director for the last 20 years. Not only is Mr. Mutschlechner a recognised and respected professional in the MICE industry (former president of ICCA), but his operational commitment within the VCB is exemplary. Extremely hands-on, he has created excellent working relationships with political and industry stakeholders within Vienna (and Austria).

  It is interesting to note that he was the only convention bureau executive to be cited by name during the survey of meeting planners for this study;

- **Bidding assistance:** VCB offers bidding assistance for association events. Mr. Mutschlechner gets personally involved in the bidding process for the city, and works closely with clients; and

- **Ambassador programme:** the Vienna Convention Bureau has strong established relationships with potential local hosts, or contacts who can help the bureau to secure large events for the destination, however it does not have a formal ambassador programme. Approximately 70% of international association events that are held in Vienna are done so thanks to a close working relationship that exists between the Bureau and the local members of the international association in question.

Marketing/promotion/brand: destination promotion

VCB is very active in promoting its destination, using more than half of its total budget, 60%, marketing activities. The bureau uses various tools such as advertising, trade fairs, workshops, study groups and individual site inspections.

Vienna CB promotes Vienna as Central Europe's leading conference city. Moreover, VCB is raising awareness for responsible and sustainable actions, supporting initiatives and projects taken in the field of Green Meetings.

Useful information

Vienna Convention Bureau official website: www.vienna.convention.at.

Prague Convention Bureau (PCB): "Wow, Prague InSpires"

History

As a city with strong destination appeal, good value for money and a number of hotels and historical venues, Prague has become one of the most popular European destinations for meetings and incentives. A key reason for the city's success is the well-organized industry under Prague Convention Bureau's leadership. Prague Convention Bureau (PCB) is established in 2008 as a non-profit, public private partnership, destination marketing organization and represents a predominantly industry-driven body.[12]

Performance

Prague is one of the world-class congress cities in the world. According to the ICCA statistics, the city ranks 11th by the number of international association meetings in 2013.[13]

Local support/resources

- **Structure/governance:** Prague Convention Bureau works in close collaboration with the City Government and Czech Tourism. PCB has nine members on the board of directors, who have extensive experience in the industry, coming from various sectors such as congress centres, hotels and restaurants/catering;
- **Resources:** half of PCB's resources come from public funds, 40% from Prague City Authorities and 10 % from Czech Tourism, all of which represents EUR 97,000. Members finance around 50% of PCB's budget through membership and marketing fees. Other funds come from sponsorship;
- **Subvention:** Prague Convention Bureau has a subvention programme, 'grants', which includes financial support for meetings, under certain criteria. On the basis of Prague City Council support, grants for congress tourism are solely intended to support events in the capital city. This can only be assigned to congresses with 1,200 or more delegates, at least half being from abroad, who spend at least two nights in Prague;
- **Staff:** Prague convention bureau is a large convention bureau, with five full-time experienced employees, one of which representing PCB in North America, and three contracted employees. PCB actively supports the employment of women. This is clearly visible as all staff members are women; and

---

12 Prague Convention Bureau (2015), official website: www.pragueconvention.cz.

13 International Congress and Convention Association (2013a).

- **Membership/partnership:** PCB has a large membership base of over 70 members, including leading hotels, conference and exhibition centres, service suppliers, catering and restaurants. The membership programme is a formal paying member programme.

Business development/sales activities/bidding assistance/ambassadors

- **Business development:** in 2013, PCB strengthened the position of Prague by opening the North American representation office. The expansion to the American market has increased sales and acquisition activities in both the United States of America and Canada;
- **Sales Activities:** project management represents the most important expenditure for Prague convention bureau. PCB's budget has been increasing mainly due to significant increase in revenues from sales activities from EUR 10,000 in 2012 to EUR 46,000 in 2013;
- PCB regularly attends and participates, every year, in a number of trade shows. In 2013, PCB organized or participated in 33 sales and marketing events in Europe, Asia and the Americas;
- **Bidding assistance:** PCB actively bids for international meetings, prepares and supports bidding processes, and offers consulting and advice for meeting planners, assisting them with attendance building for events. PCB also organizes educational and networking events such as 'Why and how to bid for an international congress to Prague' to inform potential congress ambassadors about the importance of organizing international congresses for both their discipline and the destinations;
- **Ambassador programme:** the PCB Ambassador Programme was established in 2010 in partnership with public and academic institutions with the aim to engage local thought leaders to secure conventions and congresses for the City (one of the most successful); and
- PCB underlines that ambassadors are not only able to attract a certain audience to the destination, but also are valuable assets for sharing their experience and expertise for the organization of the event, for instance, choosing the programmes' content.

Marketing/promotion/brand

The third most important source of expenditure for PCB comes from marketing activities. PCB has an extensive list of domestic and international media that released articles on Prague, based on PCB's output. This media coverage is helping increase knowledge of the destination.

- **Destination promotion:** marketing communication is increasingly being focused on foreign MCCI media using regular distribution of press releases and e-newsletters, direct communication and cooperation with journalists to feature Prague as a MCCI destination. Additional communication on the local market includes media partnership with publishers and media. The total value of media coverage is estimated at EUR 249,000. In general, PCB is putting efforts in obtaining a uniform presentation of the destination; and
- **Brand:** under the brand "Wow, Prague InSpires" PCB promotes the city as rich in cultural heritage, with many archaeological monuments and historical sites; a beautiful, mysterious place that inspired the most famous artists, scientists.

Useful information

Prague Convention Bureau official website: www.pragueconvention.cz.

9.2 American landscape: North and Latin America

9.2.1 North America

The North American market (United States of America and Canada) has the largest number of CBs, also known as Destination Marketing Organizations (DMOs), with each state, and almost every city and county having their own. The first CBs were established in North America, as a means of destination promotion. There is a total of approximately 1,800 Canadian and United States CBs, who either engage in both convention promotion, or just in tourism activities, or both. United States of America and Canadian convention and visitor bureaux (CVBs) are generally financed through bed taxes or member fees, in order to perform their role of destination marketing.

Most North American convention and visitor bureaux are independent not-for-profit organizations. They receive the largest part of their funding from the public sector, especially smaller-budget CBs, which rely on public-sector sources for almost 90% of their total funding.[14] CBs rely primarily on a combination of public and private funds. Almost 90% receive hotel room tax/bed tax, which is the most important source of public funding, while most private funding comes from membership dues, especially for larger DMOs.[15] Other sources of private funds include advertising, donations, event hosting, convention centre revenues and more. Unites States' and Canadian DMOs have an average staff number of 13 employees, and are generally much larger than in other parts of the world. 46% are membership-based, with an average of 100 members and 38% have partnership programmes.[16]

CBs work with tourists and meeting planners to provide valuable information on their local area. In many locations, they work closely with a convention centres. In large destinations CBs often market nationally and globally, while smaller cities may focus on their state, region, or specific niche tourism markets.

Following is a description of best practices for Vancouver.

---

14 Destination Marketing Association International (2011), *2011 DMO Organizational & Financial Profile Study,* DMAI (online), available at: www.destinationmarketing.org (08-06/2015).

15 Ibid.

16 Destination Marketing Association International (2013), *2013 North American DMO Organizational & Financial Profile Study,* DMAI (online), available at: www.destinationmarketing.org and (08-06/2015).

Tourism Vancouver: "Vancouver – Spectacular by Nature"

History

Founded in 1902, Tourism Vancouver is one of the oldest Destination Marketing Organizations in North America.[17] Initially set up as an association to provide services to visitors of the city, it became an important part of the city's tourism and business events development programme in the mid-1980's when Vancouver geared up to host the World Expo in 1986. Since then it has evolved into one of the leading DMOs in Canada and North America.

Performance

The city of Vancouver has been one of the most consistent performers in terms of hosting international association conventions and congresses in the North American market.

Although ICCA statistics are not as significant on the North American market (compared to Europe and Asia), Vancouver has been in the top-5 among North American destination every year.

In addition, Tourism Vancouver tracks its performance closely, focusing on measurement indicators such as room nights, convention delegates, confirmed business on the books, etc. For example, they anticipate that 2015 will be a record-setting year for tourism and business events in the city. In addition, the forecasts for Vancouver up through 2020 (based on business on the books) are very positive.

Customer satisfaction

In order to enable the convention bureau and the city to consistently deliver high quality service to large meetings and conventions and congresses, Tourism Vancouver has set up a customer advisory board. The group of leading meeting planners and buyers meets on a regular basis to provide insights into trends in the demands and requirements from the marketplace. At the heart of all good DMOs is developing and maintaining relationships with customers, whether they are members, stakeholders, consumers, meeting planners, travel trade, or the travel media. Tourism Vancouver has in place an integrated, cross-organizational, web-based CRM system to manage these relationships.

---

17   Tourism Vancouver (2015), official website: www.tourismvancouver.com/meetings.

Local support/resources

- **Structure/governance:** Tourism Vancouver is an independent, not-for-profit association that is governed by a 15-member board. It has the responsibility for promoting Vancouver as a leisure and business events destination;
- Board members are elected by overall membership, and the president is elected by the board. Tourism Vancouver has close working relationships with city and regional elected officials, although it has no official connection with local government. The convention bureau is a department within Tourism Vancouver, and represents approximately a third of its personnel, and 25% of its budget;
- **Resources:** Tourism Vancouver has an annual budget of approximately CAD 16 million. Approximately 80% of its resources come from the local "bed tax" collected by hotels in the city. The remaining 20% come from its membership programme and some local sponsors. The staff at TourVan represents about 60 full time employees (FTE);
- **Subvention:** the city of Vancouver has set up an official subvention programme, which operates as a three-way partnership between Tourism Vancouver, the local hotel association and the Vancouver Convention Centre. The hotel association has implemented a "destination marketing fee" which it collects from overnight stays. Sums collected from this "fee" are directed to the subvention fund, which is used to support organizations that want to bring an event to the city. A strict series of criteria is used to allocate funds, such as group size, potential delegate pick-up, etc. or fund, as is the case in many destinations. There are well-defined protocols in place for this incentive programme;
- **Staff:** the convention bureau has a budget of CAD 3.5 million and a staff of 20 FTE. Three of the members of the bureau are actively involved in convention services, working on activities such as event servicing and delegate boosting; and
- **Membership/partnership:** Tourism Vancouver has a strong and active membership programme, with over 1,000 paying members from local industry, and from the community.

Business development/sales activities/bidding assistance/ambassadors

- **Business development:** Tourism Vancouver manages an on-going strategic planning process, which includes its key members and stakeholders. For example, after the city successfully hosted the Winter Olympics in 2010, Tourism Vancouver embarked on a major strategic planning exercise, entitled "Re-Think Vancouver". The resulting plan outlined the key directions for the DMO for the next decade. Since then they have worked closely with local city government to develop a city-wide tourism master plan, which incorporates their strategic goals;
- **Tourism master plan:** Vancouver's Tourism Master Plan provides specific prescriptions for the policy and planning framework that will ensure that the tourism sector grows in a manner that is economically, socially and environmentally sustainable and thus able to meet the future needs of residents, visitors, investors and other stakeholders. The master plan guides the tourism sector's development through ensuring a consensus on future direction and establishing an enabling environment to help it realize that direction;

- **Market and sales activities:** Tourism Vancouver Convention Bureau focuses on three key markets:
  1. Domestic (Canada);
  2. The market of the United States of America; and
  3. The international market.

  TourVan is present at all the key international MICE trade shows around the world, and has a very active sales and marketing presence in key markets; and
- **Ambassador programme:** Tourism Vancouver has an active ambassador programme, called "Be a Host", which provides a number of support services to local members of international associations who want to invite their events to the city. The programme proposes an array of training opportunities to potential local hosts, and "Be a Host" programme also strives to bring recognition to those who have helped attract large events to the city. There are currently over 300 "ambassadors" in Vancouver.

Marketing/promotion/brand

Communication/branding: Tourism Vancouver has developed a strong brand around the notion of its by-line: "Vancouver – Spectacular by Nature". Building on that positioning statement, the convention bureau promotes the city around the quality of service delivery when it comes to hosting large professional events. The brand promise for Vancouver hinges on exceeding expectations from meeting planners, providing "spectacular service" thanks to a tightly aligned community of business events professionals that work hand in hand to propose seamless operations in event organization.

Useful information

Tourism Vancouver official website: www.tourismvancouver.com.

9.2.2 Latin America

The Latin American and Caribbean CBs – Asociación Latinoamericana y del Caribe de CBs (ALACVB) was recently created as a non-for-profit organization, to contribute to the sustainable growth of the meetings industry in Latin America and the Caribbean. Developing public and private policies that strengthen destinations and promotional activities have become integral parts of the strategy. ALACVB is responsible for promoting interaction among its members, international promotion – trade shows exhibition – and education – organizes annual meeting to discuss CBs' interests and challenges.

Local convention bureaux: most local CBs in the region are independent not-for-profit organizations, representing a city (or a small region in some cases) and are usually focused on the attraction of meetings. There are just about 24 local convention bureaux in Latin America. These are mainly funded by membership fees and room tax collected in hotels, but the models vary a lot across countries – for example, in Brazilian cities it is a levy, an 'optional tax' that guests may or may not pay, representing 80% of the CBs' annual budget; in Mexican cities it is a legal tax with similar structure to the models of the United States of America, while in Argentinian cities the CBs do not charge room tax. Local CBs in the region count on full institutional support (and eventually also finance) from their governments, only a small part of them get a regular financial support from the government. As a result, the main concern among Latin American CBs is their sustainability and global competitiveness.

National convention bureaux: there are very few examples of National CBs in the region. Some examples include Paraguay and Costa Rica that operate under limited resources and standard procedures, promoting the capital city as main destination. So far, NTOs – National Tourism Organizations, work the hardest at developing the tourist industry (legally, infrastructure, research, education). The NTOs frequently partner with local and regional CBs and tourism boards to support bids, to cooperate on international trade shows and promotion, sometimes providing a small dedicated staff focused on the MCCI market. Most countries now understand the importance of the MCCI industry and are developing the necessary alliances and infrastructure.

Following is a description of best practices for Bogotá.

Greater Bogotá Convention Bureau (GBCB): "Bogotá: MICE Destination of Choice"

History

The Bureau de Convenciones y Visitantes de Bogotá was officially established in 2004 as an initiative of private hoteliers.[18] Its initial role was to work both the MCCI industry and holiday/leisure tourism. In 2010 the organization was redefined to focus solely on the MCCI industry, and the District Institute of Tourism focusing on the leisure and vacations market. From that moment on, the Bureau strengthened its membership and increased the contributions received by the Chamber of Commerce of Bogotá. In 2012, the state of Cundinamarca (where the city of Bogotá is located) made a few studies to identify the potential of the region to offer complementary attractions to conferences, conventions and incentives, to become more competitive as a meetings destination. The organization was then renamed as Greater Bogotá Convention Bureau.

Performance

With recent social and economic reforms, the city has transformed its living standards and business environment with enormous market potential. Recent ICCA statistics rank Bogota 50th holding 47 international events.

Local support/resources

- **Structure/governance:** the bureau is a public-private institution which has three fundamental support sources:
    1. The Chamber of Commerce of Bogotá;
    2. The industry-business sector/bureau members; and
    3. The district, which supports the CB through interagency agreements.
  They do not depend on any national entity or district level, but they work very closely with Procolombia (the promotion and exportation federal agency) and the District Institute of Tourism. The bureau has an executive director and three managers in charge of the Communications and Meetings Attraction and Development departments, who handle all relationships with affiliates and the public sector. With six main representatives, chosen during assembly, the Board of Directors is autonomous;
- **Resources:** resources come from three main sources:
    1. 1/3 from the Chamber of Commerce of Bogotá;
    2. 1/3 from affiliate members (through membership and maintenance fees); and
    3. 1/3 from public sector (through special agreements and Cundinamarca).
  For each dollar that comes from the private sector, the public sector must match it (Cundinamarca needs to provide 50% of it). GBCB's annual budget is around USD 600.000. 50% is used for administrative costs and the other half for international MCCI programmes. The city government, through its Tourism Institute, also provides USD 50.000 every year to allow GBCB to support specific meetings of shared interest, such as "Rio+20" or international government – and investment-related meetings. For these events, additional support can be provided if needed, via a covenant between the government and local chambers.

---

18   Greater Bogota Convention Bureau (2015), official website: www.bogotacb.com/?lang=en.

"FONTUR – Fondo de Promoción Turística de Colombia" is a fund for tourism promotion and competitiveness, that all entrepreneurs and trade associations can benefit from if they present projects related to business development improvements of infrastructure, industry education and specific studies. Even though the GBCB cannot directly ask for these grants, any industry association (hotels, restaurants, travel agencies etc.) can ask for them, if they can justify the benefits for the whole community and industry. These funds are taxes collected on related services;

– **Subvention:** GBCB does not have an official subvention programme, however it offers some support for meetings on the basis of three criteria: number of delegates, national or international meeting, priority sectors/segments of interest, duration of the event and economic impact. With this information in hand GBCB calculates the investments it can offer: collaterals and photos or additional city tours and cultural shows, additional closing diner for VIPs etc. The support is offered as value added, and not as financial support. Funding comes from both GBCB and ProColombia; and

– **Staff:** after experiencing a number of changes, Greater Bogotá Convention Bureau staff numbers grew from four people in 2010 to 16 people in 2015. Staff is divided between the three GBCB departments. The Communications Department has four employees. The Implementation/Development Department has four employees working on commercial links with affiliates and the public sector. The Events Department has five employees specialised for the different MCCI segments. And administration has two employees.

Business development/sales activities/bidding assistance/ambassadors

– **Business development:** GBCB develops a number of strategies to further develop itself. It aims at attracting events that positively impact the city's economy and generate business, focusing mainly on the city's strongest sectors such as oil and gas, art and culture and innovation. Moreover, since Colombia is a small country, and national conventions rotate amongst local destination, ensuring that Bogotá gets a fair share of MCCI events, GBCB mainly invests in attracting international meetings.

GBCB is looking to prospect other niches, and looks for strategic alliances with the new convention centres. GBCB invests in industry education through an alliance with the Hotels Association (Cotelco). GBCB also has an open dialogue with their stakeholders to understand the needs of the industry and provide seminars according to their expectations – such as green meetings, innovation, excellence on services etc.;

– **Sales activities:** GBCB along with its members, industry associations and tourism board, attend national and international trade shows in their respective fields of interest (IMEX, EIBTM, etc.). GBCB also organizes extra meetings and sales calls, presentations for PCOs, associations and corporations. Their main target markets are Spanish speaking and regional countries;

– **Bidding assistance:** the CB also offers support for potential meeting planners, in terms of bid strategy advices, lobby and advocacy, eventually website development and paying for the association's air tickets for the bid presentation – depending on the economic impact the event can produce. The GBCB uses its research sources such as ICCA database, partner universities, members, the chamber of commerce and other strategic partners to identify bidding opportunities. The bureau is responsible for the bigger costs on a bid campaign, such as booths, site inspections, collaterals production, letters of support, bid book and presentation development, travel related costs and more; and

- **Ambassador programme:** there is no formal ambassador programme, however GBCB has a database of key people within different industries who are sometimes invited to lead a bidding campaign and play the role of an ambassador. The local support is given by related entities that support the bid initiative, like the District Institute of Tourism, Chamber of Commerce, and Bureau of International Relations of the Mayor's Office.

Marketing/promotion/brand

Tourism in Bogotá has increased since the 2000s due to aggressive publicity campaigns showing the improvements in both infrastructure and safety. The city has worked heavily in recent years to position itself as leader in cultural offerings in South America, and it is increasingly being recognised worldwide as a hub in the region for the development of the arts.

GBCB is staying active in the promotion of its destination. Strategically, they just joined Best Cities Global Alliance and promote themselves as the only South American destination to achieve these standards.

Useful information

Greater Bogota Convention Bureau official website: www.bogotacb.com.

9.3   Asian landscape

A number of countries in Asia are still developing. Nonetheless, there are seven successful and important national convention bureaux and over 35 local convention bureaux. As the countries continue to develop, authorities understand the value of having a well-established MCCI industry. However, because the industry is still in a growing phase, some countries and cities are gaining considerable momentum and competitive advantage.

Generally established as not-for-profit organizations, CBs' main source of income is public funding, either as direct contribution from local/regional/national governments, ministries or national tourism organizations and sometimes as income from taxes.

CBs are playing an essential role in triggering economic development and are stimulating investments in research and development and innovation, as well as education. Ambassador programmes and membership/partnership programmes further allow local participation in this development.

Following is a description of best practices for Malaysia and Singapore.

Malaysia Convention & Exhibition Bureau (MyCEB): "Malaysia – Asia's Business Events Hub"

History

MyCEB was established in 2009 by the Ministry of Tourism and Culture Malaysia with the aim to further strengthen Malaysia's business tourism brand and to position it for the international MCCI market, otherwise known as business tourism.[19] A non-profit organization, MyCEB serves as a one-stop centre to assist meetings and event planners to bid and stage regional and international business tourism events in Malaysia and act as a conduit for national product development.

Performance

Malaysia has more than doubled its number of meetings over the past decade and becoming more and more successful and popular in hosting MCCI events. Although it is only 35th on ICCA world rankings, it is 9th best destination for holding MCCI events amongst Asia and the Pacific and Middle East rankings.

Governance

MyCEB has eight members on the board of directors, including industry executives, secretaries of the ministry of finance and the ministry of tourism and culture, and from Tourism Malaysia. The bureau focuses primarily on international meetings and events.

Local support/resources

– **Funding:** although Malaysia is still considered as a developing nation, the government is focusing on reaching the 'developed' status by 2020. Under the Economic Transformation Programme's NKEA project, Malaysia targets to grow business tourism arrivals from 5% to 8% of overall tourist arrivals by year 2020. In line with these efforts, MyCEB is fully supported by government funding but generates private sector revenue from cooperative marketing and educational activities. In 2011, a government funding of MYR 50 million (EUR 12 million, USD 16 million) was allocated for the business tourism sector, as part of the 10th Malaysia Plan. The funding will be channelled towards enhancing Malaysia's competitiveness in the Meetings, Incentives, Conventions and Exhibitions (MICE) arena;

---

19   Malaysia Convention & Exhibition Bureau (2015), official website: www.myceb.com.my.

–   **Subvention:** to enhance Malaysia's competitiveness, a Subvention Fund has been set aside to encourage companies, especially non-profit organizations, to bid for and host international business events in the country. The level of support is based on an assessment of the overall economic value of the proposed event and on several other criteria, such as the number of international participants.

    Other less tangible factors like the development of an on-going legacy the event may bring to the community is also considered. The support provided may apply to different stages of the event planning cycle including the bid process, event planning, event marketing and/or on-site support;

–   **Staff:** MyCEB currently has 82 staff members, including CEO's office (2), the Business Events Team (25), the Marketing and Communications Team (17), the Malaysia Major Events Team (18) and the Finance and Administration Team (20). The bureau also has a number of overseas representatives inAustralia and New Zealand, China and in North America;

–   **Membership/partnership:** MyCEB initiated the Industry Partner Programme (IPP) to create cooperative sales and marketing platforms for Malaysia's business events industry. In 2013 MyCEB had over 300 IPP members. The purpose of the programme is to strengthen Malaysia's competitive position in the international market, to grow Malaysia's international business events market and to create business opportunities for the industry. It has also been designed to help create a seamless experience for international meeting and event planners that are considering Malaysia for their next business event.

    Partners of IPP are provided with the opportunity to participate in international tradeshows and promotions, online directories and print publications, bid and sales proposals, educational and product development forums, as well as My CEB's product and service referrals programme; and

–   **Ambassador programme:** also known as the Kesatria 1Malaysia, the ambassador programme is based on similar internationally operating programmes whereby leaders of key industry sectors, who have previously hosted large scale international events, voluntarily assist in identifying and encouraging other potential local hosts to bid for and stage international conventions.

Strategy

As part of Malaysia's Economic Transformation Programme (ETP) and in line with the Ministry of Tourism's objective of focusing attention on high-yield tourism visitors, business tourism has been identified as one of the key contributors to economic growth. Moreover, through its Association Development Programme, MyCEB is continuously engaging with industry associations to become more internationally connected.

Participating in over 10 trade shows (AIME, IMEX, AIBTM, EIBTM, CIBTM, etc.), MyCEB is active in presenting its destination and increasing sales activities across the globe (America, Europe, Asia and the Pacific).

Research and development/innovation

As MyCEB continues to develop, it understands the importance of investing in R&D and innovation. The bureau has a dedicated market research team, working to determine the state of the industry, its impact on the economy and opportunities for future development.

Moreover, MyCEB supports innovation via product development workshops training and education for the industry and associations. Among the innovations was the launch of the inaugural Malaysia Business Events Week in August 2014, the Association Development Programme and the RAWR awards that recognises industry excellence.

Marketing/promotion/brand

In 2013, Malaysia Convention & Exhibition Bureau announced that Malaysia has once again proven its position as Asia's Hub by winning two international awards; Business Destinations Travel Awards 2014 for "Best Destinations for MICE, Asia 2014" and the European Asia Awards 2013 for the "Best Convention and Exhibition Bureau, Asia 2013".

- **Marketing:** MyCEB initiated the Industry Partner Programme (IPP) to create cooperative sales and marketing platforms for Malaysia's business events industry. The bureau is very active in marketing itself to be recognised as Asia's model bureau, with 16% of the annual budget dedicated to marketing and 6% to media;
- **Promotion:** MyCEB places a strong emphasis on media relations to support its sales and marketing efforts. Being a relatively new bureau it is constantly launching new programmes and initiatives at major trade shows and events. Aside from trade advertising the bureau is also developing digital platforms to actively profile the destination; and
- **Brand:** in November 2011, MyCEB unveiled its business events tagline, 'Malaysia – Asia's Business Events Hub'. This goes in line with its aim to promote Malaysia as a gateway to Asia for meetings – a blend of Asia's diverse cultures, languages and lifestyles are represented and have emerged through Malaysia's long history as a major trading route between Asia, the Middle East and the West.

Bidding/bid support

MyCEB provides a full range of support services from the initial bidding stage to the onsite staging of the event. This includes bid support, conference planning, event marketing and onsite support. In 2013, through its bid support activities, MyCEB and its partners won 134 meetings and incentive events for Malaysia.

Useful information

Malaysia Convention & Exhibition Bureau official website: www.myceb.com.my.

Singapore Exhibition & Convention Bureau (SECB): 'Your Singapore'

**SINGAPORE EXHIBITION
& CONVENTION BUREAU**

History

After declaring independence in 1965, Singapore thrived as a financial and trading hub. Through global trade links and the establishment of Free Trade Areas Singapore has become a highly developed market-based economy. Today Singapore is home to a large number of global associations and corporations, and has high quality services and infrastructure, making it a key destination for MCCI events. The board realised early on the potential for business events and formed the Singapore Convention Bureau in 1974 renamed in 1996 as the Singapore Exhibition & Convention Bureau (SECB).[20]

Performance

For over 12 consecutive years, Singapore is Asia's top convention city and is the top-6th convention city in the world, the only Asian city figuring in the top-10. Singapore has long been regarded as one of the most innovative and forward thinking destinations within the Asia and the Pacific region.

Local Support/resources

- **Structure/governance:** the Singapore Exhibition & Convention Bureau (SECB) is a not-for-profit association, part of the Singapore Tourism Board (STB). As the lead government agency for the industry, the SECB aims to establish Singapore as a dynamic business events destination, encompassing ideas, people and technology through a wide range of knowledge and networks. STB has a total of 11 board members;
- **Subvention:** Singapore has a number of financial and non-financial initiatives that support the development of the business tourism market including tailored bid support programmes, association development, incentives for business partnerships and the attraction of world or regional headquarters for associations and corporations.

   The SECB offers customised support, through the Business Events in Singapore (BEiS) subvention that may include facilitation in securing venues, introductions with leading government agencies, local associations and business partners as well as marketing and publicity support. Funding support is also given through the Business Events in Singapore (BEiS) scheme on fulfilment of its evaluation criteria and deliverables.

---

20 YourSingapore (2015), official website: www.yoursingapore.com/en.html.

Moreover, the SECB has partnered major industry players to launch "In Singapore Incentives & Rewards" (INSPIRE) – a rewards programme that leverages on Singapore's unique and world-class attractions to curate unique value-added experiences with a strong local flavour for both the Indian and Chinese markets.

The newest Singapore MICE Advantage Programme (SMAP) is yet another cost saving incentive scheme. Based on certain eligibility criteria, there are a variety of benefits to assist event organizers, including financial grants, and more, such as visa facilitation for participants;

– **Staff:** SECB's staff is part of STB's Business Development group. Within this department, SECB is categorised into three main divisions: Conventions and Meetings, Exhibition and Conferences, and Business Tourism Development, which work together to promote Singapore as a leading destination. Six members are part of SECB's management team.

Moreover, the International Group is responsible for representing Singapore on an international level as a destination for MCCI events. Each region is headed by individual covering regions across the global, including Asia, Africa, Americas, Europe and Oceania; and

– **Membership/partnership:** SECB values industry partnerships and collaborates with business event organizers, associations and MCCI industry stakeholders to identify key opportunities to grow, attract and create business events.

Business development/sales activities/bidding assistance/ambassadors

– **Business development:** the business Tourism Development division is responsible for the growth and development of the Business Travel and MCCI industry. Focusing on developing an industry ecosystem, alliances and infrastructure, it also facilitates the creation and development of new concepts and products to enhance business traveller experience.

Because Singapore has gained important experience in the industry, and is considered as an important hub for innovation and business development, it is well-positioned for developing innovative solutions for the future. SECB works closely with relevant government agencies as well as trade associations and academic/research institutions;

– **Bidding assistance:** SECB provides bidding and promotional assistance, assisting bidders in determining the next open submission date for a bid to host the event, finding the necessary information on what elements should be included in the bid, and in compiling the bid book; and

– **Ambassador programme:** an initiative of the SECB, the Conference Ambassador Programme (CAP) identifies and recognises the contributions and efforts of notable professionals and key opinion leaders that are advocates for Singapore's MCCI industry. Ambassadors are recognised experts or key opinion leaders in their field.

They typically hold regional and international affiliated positions in associations and are passionate about Singapore. With their influence and network, they play a key role in profiling Singapore and championing bids. Membership to CAP is by invitation only.

Marketing/promotion/brand

The SECB is a member of the BestCities Global Alliance, the world's first convention bureau alliance with ten partners in five continents. The Alliance has a common set of service standards, a knowledge exchange programme and business intelligence network designed to provide consistency in services for meeting and event planners that stage their events in a partner destination.

–   **Destination Promotion:** the Business Tourism Development division is also responsible for coordinating and initiating marketing and PR activities to establish Singapore's position in the MCCI industry.

Singapore and SECB have been receiving a large number of awards for the quality and success of the industry. These awards increase the destination's exposure, having some positive impact for increasing awareness and future MCCI opportunities; and

–   **Brand:** the "Your Singapore" brand identity was launched in 2010 focussing on experiences that can be easily personalised for a marketplace of more sophisticated travellers. In a business sense the brand supports Singapore's commitment to building partnerships, bring together business leaders, experts and policy makers for the exchange of ideas and development of business networks.

Useful information

YourSingapore official website: www.yoursingapore.com.

Chapter 10

Key findings and recommendations

The first phase of this report gathers a clear taxonomy and key characteristics of the MCCI segments. The association conventions and congresses segment is less affected by the economic instabilities, but is nonetheless experiencing some changes, mainly driven by a decrease in participants, shorter events and the increased focus on quality over quantity. But the segment is focusing on innovation and engagement in order to respond to the changing environment and demand. The corporate meetings segment, which is experiencing growing demand, is affected by changes in budgets, demand for closer to home locations and is influenced by a rise in the use of hybrid technology and increased focus on ROI. The corporate incentives segment is growing and increasingly valued by corporations. The segment is affected by lower per-person expenditure, demand for wellness and unique experience incentives and the need to add a meeting dimension to the programmes. In general, the MCCI industry is experiencing a number of changes as the industry expands in other markets and continues to grow in mature markets.

The second phase of the study, which evaluates planners' decision-making processes, confirms some of the trends identified in the first phase of the study. Because MCCI events play an integral part of the overall strategy of the organization, planners play a key role in organizing the events appropriately. When analysing the different segments, it is clear to see that different decision-making processes exist across segments and regions. Key findings show that convention planners' final decisions are dependent on cost and size of meeting facilities, however once basic criteria are met, advocacy for subject matter, local presence and membership growth become essential considerations for final destination choice. Planners prefer destinations that fit with their objectives and which allow freedom to discuss topics that may be political in nature. The decision-making process in corporations is very different, varying depending on the nature of the meeting – internal or external – and characterised by the desire to provide quality and high profile events. Planners' decisions are mainly influenced by destination appeal and cost. Once basic criteria are met, planners underline that destinations with local presence are preferred. Corporate incentive planners' final decisions are largely dependent on the destinations and the desire to offer the additional 'wow factor'. The decision-making process responds to the corporations' communication strategy. Moreover the survey also investigated planners' use of convention bureaux. Results show that convention planners use CBs the most and that CB services are used differently across regions, although mature markets are generally more active in using them.

The final phase of this study, which explores CBs' best practices, identifies three types of convention bureaux: local, regional and national. As differences are observed across these bureaux, more variations exist across regions. CBs share fundamental roles of developing the MCCI industry by engaging local ambassadors, partners and by providing support for MCCI events in hopes of bringig positive returns to the economy. In general, convention bureaux are not-for-profit entities where governments represent a main source of funding and engage in policy developments. The main differences between bureaux and regions exist in the structure and level of services. The European landscape has the most regional CBs, while mature markets use local CBs the most, developing markets find the greatest support from national CBs. The North American landscape is very well established, including the largest number of CBs and the most important budgets. The Latin American market is on the other still developing, overcoming difficulties of security and economic conditions. The Asian MCCI market is mainly still developing, with some destinations becoming key examples for future CBs to follow. Despite differences across regions there are a number of 'best practices' that characterise convention bureaux, including:

- Clearly defined strategy;
- Strong support from government institutions;
- Close working relationships with MCCI partners;
- Strong marketing/branding strategy;
- Presence in global markets; and
- Investment in research, development and innovation.

Recommendations

This report gathers extensive research on the MCCI industry and on the decision-making process of meeting, congresses, conventions and incentive organizers. The attractiveness of the MCCI industry has triggered many destinations to invest in this growing market and presents today many opportunities for destinations. Following are some recommendations for European destinations:

- **The importance of the MCCI Industry:** recognising and understanding the importance of the MCCI industry is key. In the wake of a global financial recovery, the MCCI industry offers many possibilities for development and offers significant return-on-investment. By investing the necessary resources destinations can truly benefit from the industry, which generates valuable social and economic contributions. Not only do MCCI events attract visitors, but they also attract investors, business opportunities, investment and sponsorship, education, employment, tax revenue and can contribute to improving destination image. Destinations need to have a full understanding of the business case that supports the development of their MCCI activity;

- **Does the destination respond to planners' needs and expectations?** Throughout the report a number of criteria were identified, to which MCCI planners pay particular attention to during their decision-making process. Planners have underscored basic criteria, such as destination attractiveness, access, cost, safety and more, which are the primary factors evaluated when looking at a destination. After that other 'value added' criteria, such as advocacy for subject matter, presence of local hosts and potential for audience and membership growth are important to decision-makers. It is therefore crucial for destinations to identify and evaluate their current offerings with respect to the key decision criteria in order to determine strategic ways to become more attractive for MCCI planners; and

- **The value of convention bureaux:** the research has underlined the important role convention bureaux play in attracting and securing MCCI events. This is particularly true for association conventions and congresses. The research has identified a number of best practices undertaken by convention bureaux, including clearly defined business strategy, support from government institutions, strong working relationships with local industry, and more. Destinations around the globe should benchmark against these case studies if they wish to develop their MCCI industry. European destinations, because of the competitiveness of their market, should look at these best practices in order to develop their convention bureaux and to position themselves within these criteria. From a sales and marketing point of view, convention bureaux can be key entities to develop and enhance the MCCI industry for destinations.

Annex 1

List of contacts for the primary research

2one2F

Abercrombie & Kent

Academy of World Business, Marketing and Management
Development – AWBMAMD

Accomplished Events Ltd

Activate Event Management – AEM

ADEVMA COMMUNICATION Ltd

AKZO Nobel Pharma

Alzheimer's Disease International – ADI

Annual International Conference of SICOT/SIROT

Annual Meeting of the International Society for Behavioral
Nutrition and Physical Activity – ISBNPA

ASN Events

Association of Critical Heritage Studies

ATP Event Experts

Avenue Events

AVVENTURA Corporate Events

BCD Meetings and Incentives

Brief to Event Solutions

BTG M.I.C.E International Service Co. Ltd.

CARREMENT !

CCD Global Events Ltd

Centre International de Liaison des Ecoles de Cinéma
et de Télévision – CILECT

CERES73

CHAIKANA

CIB W78 – IT in Construction

CITS Group Shanghai Co Ltd

Civil Air Navigation Services Organization – CANSO

Cochrane Collaboration

Collaborative International Pesticides Analytical Council – CIPAC

Conference of the International Association of Ports and Harbors
– IAPH

Congrex Holland BV

CONNECT FACTORY

CONSTELLACTION

Corporate events

CSC Consulting

Diners World Travel

Directions Conference & Incentive Management

Dress Incentive

EMDR International association

EMPHASE

EMU Events Ltd

European League of Institutes of the Arts – ELIA

European Recovered Paper Council – ERPC

Event Travel Management – ETM (Melbourne)

Eventboutique GmbH

Fédération Cynologique Internationale – FCI

Federation of Veterinarians of Europe – FVE

First Incentive BV

Fuse Consultancy

GECKO Incentives & Events

GI Travel (Group & Incentive Travel) (Amsterdam)

GI Travel (Group & Incentive Travel) (Rotterdam)

Global Business for BI Worldwide

GRG (Grass Roots Group)/Deloitte

Group Se7en Events

Hannick Reizen

HiCentives

ICEC World Congresses & Council Meetings

IECEx System

Incentive Direct BV

Incentive Europe

Incentive Partner

Incentive Promotions

IncentivePlus – Businessplus Lufthansa City Center

Inclusion International

Intelligent Transport Systems

Int. Confederation of Contamination Control Societies – ICCCS

International Abalone Society – IAS

International Academy of Ceramics – AIC

International Academy of Quantum Molecular Science – IACQMS

International Air & Shipping Association – IASA

International Apparel Federation – IAF

International Association for Earthquake Engineering – IAEE

International Association for Mathematics and Computers in Simulation

International Association for the Study of Obesity – IASO

International Association for Vegetation Science – IAVS

International Association of Costume – IAOC

International Association of Congress Centres – AIPC

International Association of Gerontology and Geriatrics – IAGG

International Association of Insolvency Practitioners – INSOL International

International Association of Institutes of Navigation – IAIN

International Association of Insurance Supervisors – IAIS

International Association of Maritime Universities – IAMU

International Association of Residential Arts Centres – RES ARTIS

International Association of Schools & Institutes of Administrations – IASIA

International Association of Science Parks – IASP

International Association of Travel and Tourism Professionals – SKÅL International

International Association of Universities – IAU

International Bar Association – IBA

International Behavioral Ecology Conference – ISBE

International Bobath Instructions Training Association – IBITA

International Canoe Federation – ICF

International Cold Forging Group – ICFG

International Conference of the International Bartenders Association – IBA

International Conference on the Genome – HGM

International Congress on Fracture – ICF

International Coral Reef Initiative – ICRI

International Council for Commercial Arbitration – ICCA

International Council of Nurses – ICN

International Council of Organizations for Folklore Festivals and Folk Art – CIOFF

International Council of Sport Science and Physical Education – ICSSPE

International Council of the Aeronautical Sciences – ICAS

International Council on Archives – ICA

International Council on Archives Section on University and Research Institution Archives – ICA/SUV

International Dairy Federation – IDF

International Diabetes Federation

International Electrotechnical Commission – IEC

International Federation of Arts Council and Culture Agencies – IFACCA

International Federation of Gynecology and Obstetrics – FIGO

International Federation of Landscape Architects Asia and the Pacific Region – IFLA APR

International Federation of Library Associations and Institutions – IFLA

International Federation of Orthopaedic Manipulative Physical Therapists – IFOMPT

International Federation of Rock Art Organizations – IFRAO

International Federation of Social Workers – IFSW

International Federation of Societies for Microscopy – IFSM

International Federation of Surveyors – FIG

International Federation of Thanatologists Associations – IFTA

International Federation of the Periodical Press – FIPP

International Federation of Warehousing Logistics Associations – IFWLA

International Fellowship of Evangelical Students – IFES

International Fiscal Association – IFA

International Glaciological Society – IGS

International Handball Federation – IHF

International Headache Society – IHS

International Ice Hockey Federation – IIHF

International Laboratory Accreditation Cooperation/International Accreditation Forum – ILAC/IAF

International Life Saving Federation – ILSF

International Network on Public Communication of Science and Technology – PCST

International Options Market Association – IOMA

International Paralympic Committee – IPC

International Philatelic Federation – FIP

International Project Management Association – IPMA

International Public Television – INPUT

International Rail Safety Council – IRSC

International Real Estate Federation – FIABCI

International Seed Federation – ISF

International Shopfitting Organization – ISO

International Society for Animal Hygiene – ISAH

International Society for Gastrointestinal Hereditary Tumours – InSIGHT

International Society for Horticultural Science

International Society for Influenza and other Respiratory Virus Diseases – ISIRV

International Society for Microbial Ecology – ISME

International Society for Music Education – ISME

International Society for New Institutional Economics – ISNIE

International Society for Skiing Safety – ISSS

International Society for Soil Mechanics and Geotechnical Engineering – ISSMGE

International Society of Behavioral Medicine – ISBM

International Society of Fertility Preservation – ISFP

International Society of Orthopaedic Surgery and Traumatology – SICOT

International Society of Ultrasound in Obstetrics and Gyneacology – ISUOG

International Sporting Press Association – AIPS

International Symposium Spatial Accuracy Assessment in Natural Resources and Environmental Sciences – Accuracy

International Team for Implantology – ITI

International Union of Architects – UIA

International Union of Crystallography – IUCr

International Union of Latin Notaries – UINL

International Union of Microbiological Societies – IUMS

International Union of Pure and Applied Physics – IUPAP

ISO/TC 164 Mechanical Testing of Metals

ISSA International Section for the Prevention of Occupational Risks in the Construction Industry

IUPAP C.8 Commission on Semiconductors

Jarvis Woodhouse Events

JCD CONSEIL

KPMG

LA FONDERIE D'EVENEMENTS

LE PUBLIC SYSTEME

Lighting Urban Community International – LUCI

Lumen Global

MARKET PLACE

MCI Australia

Meeting Makers

MMCO World

National Foundation of Educational Research

NICE (New Independent Conference Experts)

Nike Europe BV

Nuffield Farming Scholars International

Off-Site Connections

PAC Conference and Event Management

PEAM (Performance & Event Management)

Pentecostal World Fellowship – PWF

Performance In Top Travel

Prolamat 20: International Conference on Software for Discrete Manufacturing – IFIP TC5 WG 5.2–WG 5.3

PUBLIC EVENTS

rs-travelling-events

Safe2Travel Pte Ltd

Shanghai Spring International Travel Service (Group) Company Limited

Society for Worldwide Interbank Financial Telecommunication – SWIFT

Steering Committee of the International Conference on the Bioscience of Lipids – ICBL

Sunshine Tour/BCD Travel Taiwan

Technology Innovation and Industrial Management – TIIM

The World Association For Veterinary Dermatology

Thika Travel

Thought Agents

Transparency International – TI

Traventive

UFI – The Global Association of the Exhibition Industry

Uniq Luxe

Unique Attitute UK

United Nations Environment Programme Finance Initiative – UNEPFI

Women In Nuclear – WIN

World Aberdeen-Angus

World Association for Bronchology and Interventional Pulmonology – WABIP

World Confederation for Physical Therapy – WCPT

World Congress on Engineering Asset Management – WCEAM 20

World Congress on Intelligent

World Express Pte Ltd

World Federation of Advertisers – WFA

World Federation of Parasitologists – WFP

World Federation of Societies of Anaesthesiologists – WFSA

World LP Gas Association – WLPGA

World Obesity Federation

World Society of Sustainable Energy Technologies – WSSET

World Society of Victimology – WSV

World Travel & Tourism Council – WTTC

World Union of Wholesale Markets – WUWM

World Wind Energy Association – WWEA

World Wise Travel Business Events

World Youth Student & Educational Travel Confederation
      – WYSETC

Xcentive

Yellow Fish

Zero Energy Mass Customised Housing –
      ZEMCH – 20 International Conference

Zibrant

Annex 2

Sample survey for the European association conventions and congresses segment

Your role

1 **What best describes your role:**
- ☐ Association planner
- ☐ Third party meeting planner
- ☐ Association management
- ☐ Executive
- ☐ Other (please specify):

2 **What type of influence do you have in the final decision process?**
[check all that apply]
- ☐ Final decision
- ☐ Research
- ☐ Recommend
- ☐ Plan/organize

Your programme

3 **What is the average attendance of your international meeting(s):**
- ☐ 1–250 people
- ☐ 251–500 people
- ☐ 501–1,000 people
- ☐ ≥ 1,001 people

4 **What types of venues do you utilise for your events?**
[Check all that apply]
- ☐ International hotel chains with meeting facilities
- ☐ Independent hotels with meeting facilities
- ☐ Convention centres
- ☐ University based facilities
- ☐ Other (please specify):

5 **Do you incorporate technology to create hybrid meetings for the benefit of those attendees prevented from attending an international meeting?**
- ☐ Yes
- ☐ No

Regional rotation

6   **How likely are you to repeat locations for your international events?**
☐   Very likely
☐   Not likely

7   **Where are most of your events organized**
☐   Within Europe
☐   Outside Europe

8   **What non-European locations did you use in the past year for meetings**
[Check all that apply]
☐   Middle East
☐   Africa
☐   North America
☐   Latin America
☐   Asia and the Pacific

9   **Would your association consider an emerging destination?**
If yes, please state the location(s).
☐   Yes (please specify):
☐   No

Sourcing

10   **What is your typical lead time for planning an international event?**
☐   < 3 years
☐   – 6 years
☐   > 6 years

11   **What sources of information do you use to research international destinations:**
[Check all that apply]
☐   Online meeting management
    ☐   If so, which?:
☐   Destination/hotel/convention bureau websites
☐   Social networking sites (Facebook, LinkedIn, etc.)
☐   Travel blogs
☐   Other media sources (please specify):
☐   Local associations/ambassadors
☐   None

12   **What tools do you utilize when planning an international meeting:**
[Check all that apply]
☐   National tourist office or convention bureaux
☐   National sales office
☐   Local chapter assistance/ambassadors
☐   Destination management company

☐ Professional congress organizer
☐ Third party planner
☐ Site selection firms
☐ Online meeting management
  ☐ If so, which?:
☐ No additional services

13 Do you use the services of a convention bureau/tourist board?
☐ Yes
☐ No

14 If so, what services do you find most useful?
☐ Impartial advice
☐ Site visits
☐ Venue finding service
☐ Marketing material
☐ Big support
☐ Other (please specify):

Criteria

15 What are the key factors in choosing a destination?
(Please rank by order of importance, 1 = most important 9 = least important)
☐ Access
☐ Appeal of destination
☐ Range of accommodations
☐ Size of meeting facilities
☐ Cost
☐ Safety and security
☐ Potential audience and membership growth
☐ Presence of local association/local hosts
☐ Advocacy for subject matter

16 Do you require subvention?
☐ Yes
☐ No

Decision process

17 Does your association follow a formal bidding process?
☐ Yes
☐ No

18 How is the final decision made?
☐ Committee
☐ Board

□   Executive

□   Membership vote

□   Other (please specify):

19   How far in advance is the final decision made?

□   < 3 years in advance

□   3–6 years in advance

□   > 6 years in advance

Budget

20   How have your budgets for international events changed from 2013?

□   Increased

   □   By what percentage?

□   No change

□   Decreased

21   How do you expect budgets to change for your next international event?

□   Increase

□   Decrease

□   Remain the same

List of abbreviations and acronyms

AACVB	Asian Association of Convention and Visitor Bureaus
ACFORUM	Associations Conference Forum
ALACVB	Associación Lationamericana y del Caribe de CB
AMC	Association management company
AmEx	American Express
AMI	Associations Meetings International
BE	Business event
BRIC	Brazil, Russian Federation, India, and China
CB	Convention bureau
CIC	Convention Industry Council
CSR	Corporate Social Responsibility
CVB	Convention and visitors bureau
DMC	Destination management companies
DMO	Destination marketing organizations
DOS	Director of Sales
EIAT	Education and Industry Advancing Together
EMC	Event management companies
ETC	European Travel Commission
FTE	Full time employee
GBCB	Greater Bogota Convention Bureau
GCB	German Convention Bureau
GDP	Gross domestic product
GM	General Manager
HO	Head offices
HQ	Headquarters
IAPCO	International Association of Professional Congresses Organizers
ICCA	International Conventions and Congresses Association
IMC	Industry Meetings Centre
IMEX	Worldwide Exhibition for Incentive Travel, Meetings and Events
INCON	Global Partnership in Conferences and Events
IRF	Incentive Research Foundation
MCCI	Meetings, Congresses, Conventions and Incentives
MEXCON	Meeting Experts Conference
MNC	Multinational Corporation
MPI	Meeting Professionals International

MyCEB	Malaysia Convention & Exhibition Bureau
NCB	National convention bureau
NTO	National tourism organization
PCB	Prague Convention Bureau
PCMA	Professional Convention Management Association
PCO	Professional conference organizer
PEO	Professional Employer Organization
R&D	Research and development
RFP	request for proposal
ROI	Return on investment
ROO	Return on objective
SCB	Serbia Convention Bureau
SECB	Singapore Exhibition & Convention Bureau
SITE	Society for Incentive Travel Excellence
UIA	Union of International Associations
UNWTO	World Tourism Organization
VCB	Vienna Convention Bureau
WTTC	World Travel & Tourism Council
B2B	Business to Business
G2G	Government to Government
G2B	Government to Business
G2C	Government to Customer

List of figures and tables

List of tables

References and bibliography

'2014 Incentive Safety and Wellness IQ Survey' (2014), *Incentive What Motivates,* 26-03-2014 (online), available at: www.incentivemag.com (29-09-2015).

Advito (2013), *Industry Forecast 2014* (online), available at www.vdr-service.de/fileadmin/der-verband/fachthemen/studien/advito_industryforecast2014.pdf (08-06-2015).

Advito (2014), *Industry Forecast 2015* (online), available at www.advito.com (08-06-2015).

Alexander, A. C.; **Kim,** D.-Y. and **Groves,** J. (2012), 'Individual and Organizational Characteristics Influencing Event Planners' Perceptions of Information Content and Channel Choice', *Journal of Convention & Event Tourism,* volume 13 (1), 22-02-2012, Routledge, pp. 16–38 (online), available at: www.tandfonline.com (15-09-28).

American Express (2013a), *American Express Meetings & Events Forecast Predicts Stabilization of Meetings & Events Activity in 2014,* 14-10-2013 (online), available at: http://about.americanexpress.com/ (08-06-2015).

American Express (2013b), Press Release, October (online), available at: http://about.americanexpress.com/news/pr/releases.aspx.

'American Express Forecasts "Return to Business Fundamentals" for 2015' (2014), *International Meetings Review,* 13-10-2014 (online), available at: www.internationalmeetingsreview.com (08-06-2015).

American Express Meetings & Events (2013), *2014 Global Meetings and Events Forecast* (online), available at: www.congreswereld.nl/files/documents_upload/documents_upload_2013/2014_Meetings_Forecast_FINAL_US.pdf (08-06-2015).

Asian Association of Convention and Visitor Bureaus (2014), Background and History, AACVB (online), available at: www.aacvb.org.

Association Trends (2013), *Association mergers: Where are they headed now?,* 24-12-2013 (online), available at: www.associationtrends.com (08-06-2015).

Bair, B. (2014), *New Tri-City Alliance Offers Rotating Association Meetings Value Pricing, Added Services,* MeetingsNet, 18-08-2014 (online), available at: www.meetingsnet.com (09-06-2015).

Chon, K. S. and **Weber,** K. (2002), *Convention Tourism: International Research and Industry Perspective,* Haworth Press, New York.

Comas, M. and **Moscardo,** G. (2005), 'Understanding Associations and Their Conference Decision-Making Processes', *Journal of Convention and Event Tourism,* volume 7 (3/4), pp. 117–138.

Convention Industry Council (2011), *APEX Industry Glossary,* CIC (online), available at: www.conventionindustry.org/StandardsPractices/APEX/glossary.aspx (08-06-2015).

Cvent (2015), *Europe CVB Directory* (online), available at: www.cvent.com/rfp/europe-cvb-directory-18129d1549184b9a8117deee791ae01a.aspx (08-06-2015).

Cvent (2014), *Strategic Meetings Management Software* (online), available at: www.cvent.com/uk/strategic-meetings-management/ (08-06-2015).

Davidson, R. (2013), *EIBTM 2013 Trends Watch Report,* The Global Meetings & Events Expo, Read Travel Exhibitions, Elsevir.

Davidson, T. (2013), '2014 Meetings Focus Trends Survey', *Meetings Focus,* December 2013 (online), available at: www.meetingsfocus.com (08-06-2015).

Davidson, T. (2012), '2012 Meetings Market Trends Survey', *Meetings Focus,* January 2012 (online), available at: www.meetingsfocus.com (08-06-2015).

Destination Marketing Association International (2013), *2013 North American DMO Organizational & Financial Profile Study,* DMAI (online), available at: www.destinationmarketing.org and (08-06/2015).

Destination Marketing Association International (2011), *2011 DMO Organizational & Financial Profile Study,* DMAI (online), available at: www.destinationmarketing.org 08-06/2015).

'EIBTM Trend Watch Report Indicates Growth for 2014' (2014), *International Meetings Review,* 18-11-2014 (online), available at: www.internationalmeetingsreview.com (08-06-2015).

'European National Convention Bureaux Form Strategic Alliance' (2014), *International Meetings Review,* 16-10-2014 (online), available at: www.internationalmeetingsreview.com (08-06-2015).

European Travel Commission and **World Tourism Organization** (2010), *Budgets of National Tourism Organizations, 2008–2009,* UNWTO, Madrid.

European Travel Commission and **World Tourism Organization** (2003), *Evaluating NTO Marketing Activities,* UNWTO, Madrid.

Fox, J. T. (2014), 'Why Virtual Conferences will not Replace Face-to-Face Meetings', *International Meetings Review,* 08-10-2014 (online), available at: www.internationalmeetingsreview.com (08-06-2015).

German Convention Bureau (2015), *Recently Launched European National Convention Bureaux Alliance Experiencing New Growth & Strong Interest,* newsblog, 03-03-2015, GCB, Frankfurt (online), available at: www.gcb.de/article/newsroom/newsblog/recently-launched-european-national-convention-bureaux-alliance-experiencing-new-growth-strong-interest (29-09-2015).

Global Incentive Council and **Incentive Marketing Association Europe** (2013), *Recognition and Incentives in Europe,* White Paper (online), available at: www.incentivemarketing.org (29-09-2015).

Grimaldi, L. A. (2015), 'Third-Parties: Big Small or None at All?', *Meetings and Conventions,* 01-01-2015 (online), available at: www.meetings-conventions.com (08-06-2015).

Harwood, S. (2014), 'European Convention Bureaux Create Strategic Alliance', *Conference & Incentive Travel,* 16-10-2014 (online), available at: www.citmagazine.com (08-06-2015).

IMEX (2012), 'IMEX Group Issues 2013 Predictions for the Meetings & Events Industry – Participation, Pricing, Political Prowess and Pursuit of Green', IMEX, 03-12-2012 (online), available at: www.imex-frankfurt.com (08-06-2015).

'Incentive Travel Buyer's Focus – Program Design Structures' (2012), *Successful Meetings,* December 2012, Northstar Travel Media, pp 49–60 (online), available at: www.incentivemag.com/uploadedFiles/Travel/Travel_Buyers_Guide/incentive_buyers_handbook_1212.pdf (08-06-2015).

INCON (2012), *Fourth Annual INCON Survey of the Global Association Conference Market,* INCON.

International Association of Professional Congress Organisers (2014), *Members' Annual Review 2014,* IAPCO, Freshwater.

International Association of Professional Congress Organisers (2013), *Annual Survey 2013,* IAPCO, Freshwater.

International Congress and Convention Association (2013a), *2013 Country and City Rankings,* ICCA, Amsterdam.

International Congress and Convention Association (2013b), *A Modern History of International Association Meetings 1963–2012,* ICCA, Amsterdam.

International Congress and Convention Association (April 2014a), *Congress Ambassador Programmes,* ICCA, Amsterdam.

International Congress and Convention Association (April 2014b) *International Association Meetings: Bidding and Decision-making,* ICCA, Amsterdam.

International Congress and Convention Association, IMEX and **FastFuture** (2011), *Convention 2020* (online), available at: www.iccaworld.com and www.imex-frankfurt.com (02-10-2015).

Iwamoto, K. (2014), *Demystifying the Big Data Buzz, MeetingsNet,* 06-10-2014 (online), available at: http://meetingsnet.com/strategic-meetings-management/demystifying-big-data-buzz.

Jago, L. K. and **Deery,** M. (2005), 'Relationship and Factors Influencing Convention Decision-Making', *Journal of Convention & Event Tourism,* Vol. 7 (1), pp. 23–41, published online: 23-09-2008.

Mair, J. (2014), *Conferences and Conventions – A Research Perspective,* Routledge, Abingdon – New York.

Meeting Media (2013), *HeadQuarters Magazine* (online), available at: www.headquartersmagazine.com (access date?).

Meeting Metrics (2014), *Meetings and Events ROI,* White Paper (online), available at: www.meetingmetrics.com (08-06-2015).

Meeting Professionals International (2014), *MPI Meetings Outlook,* spring edition, MPI, Dallas.

MeetingsNet (2014), *Top 5 Emerging Incentive Destinations in 2014,* 12-02-2014 (online), available at: www.meetingsnet.com (08-06-2015).

Meetpie.com (2015), *New Members Bolster European National Bureaux Alliance,* 05-02-2015 (online), available at: www.meetpie.com/Modules/NewsModule/NewsDetails.aspx?newsid=20363 (09-06-2015).

Pricewaterhouse Coopers LLP (2014), *The Economic Significance of Meetings to the U.S. Economy – Interim Study Update for 2012,* Tampa (online), available at: www.conventionindustry.org (02-10-2015).

QRA Analytics (2015), *IRF Fall Pulse Survey – Fall 2014,* International Research Foundation, 07-02-2015 (online), available at: http://theirf.org/research/irf-full-pulse-survey---fall-2014/152/ (08-06-2015).

QRA Analytics (2013), *IRF Pulse Survey – Fall 2013,* International Research Foundation, 16-12-2013 (online), available at: (online), available at: http://theirf.org/research/irf-full-pulse-survey---fall-2013/99/ (08/06/2015).

Rogers, T. (2013), *Conferences and Conventions – A Global Industry,* 3rd edition, Routledge, Abingdon – New York.

Russell, M. (2014), 'Convene's 23rd Meetings Market Survey', *Convene,* March 2014, Professional Convention Management Association, p. 43–60 (online), available at: www.convene-digital.org (08-06-2015).

Sherry, Y. (2014), *2015 Global Meetings and Events Forecast, American Express Global Business Travel* (online), available at: www.imexamerica.com/media/517556/ Yma-Sherry-2015-Global-Meetings-Trends.pdf (08-06-2015).

Simms, P. (2014), 'Standout CVBs – Some One-stop Shops Are Better Than Others', *Corporate & Incentive Travel,* 01-09-2014, The Meeting Magazines (online), available at: www.themeetingmagazines.com/cit/cvbs-2/ (09-06-2015).

Smith, E. (2014), 'Helping Hands for Meeting Planners', *MEET,* 02-10-2014, Associations Now (online), available at: www.associationsnow.com (08-06-2015).

Society for Incentive Travel Excellence (2013), *The Annual Analysis and Forecast for the Motivational Events Industry,* SITE (online), available at: www.siteglobal.com (09-06-2015).

South Africa National Convention Bureau (2014), *South Africa Business Events: Positioning Campaign,* SANCB, Sandton, see: www.businessevents.southafrica.net.

Ting, D. (2013), 'The Top Incentive Travel Destinations of 2013', *Incentive What Motivates,* 24-09-2013, (online), available at: www.incentivemag.com (08-06-2015).

Trends in International Association Meetings from North America 2015 Survey Report (2014), Marketing Challenges International Inc., March 2014 (online), available at: https://gallery.mailchimp. com/620ef227ca4419ebb370f38d4/files/Association_ Survey_2015_MCIntl.pdf (08-06/2015).

Union of International Associations (2013), *2013 Associations Survey – International Meeting Organization and Issues – Final Report,* UIA, Brussels (online), available at: www.uia.org (09-06-2015).

van Dyke, M. (2015), *Rebounding the Recession: 10 Trends Paint a Picture of the Future of Incentive Travel 2015,* International Research Foundation, 07-02-2015 (online), available at: http://theirf.org/research/rebounding-the- recession-10-trends-paint-a-picture-of-the-future-of- incentive-travel-2015/87/ (08-06-2015).

van Dyke, M. (2014), *2014 Trends in Engagement, Incentives, and Recognition',* International Research Foundation, 30-01-2014 (online), available at: http://theirf.org/research/2014-trends-in-engagement- incentives-and-recognition/102/ (05-10-2015).

van Dyke, M. (2012), *2013 MeetingsNet IRF Annual Incentive Travel Trends Survey,* International Research Foundation, 31-12-2012 (online), available at: http://theirf.org/research/2013-meetingsnet-irf-annual- incentive-travel-trends-survey/278/ (08-06-2015).

van Dyke, M. and **May,** M. (2014), *Incentive Travel Trends for 2014 and Beyond,* Meetings and Conventions, 05-02-2014 (online), available at: www.meetings-conventions.com (08-06-2015).

World Tourism Organization (2015), *Repository of National Tourism Master and Marketing Plans – Update: May 2015,* UNWTO, Madrid.

World Tourism Organization (2014a), *AM Reports, Volume seven – Global Report on the Meetings Industry,* UNWTO, Madrid.

World Tourism Organization (2014b), *Organismos de gestión y promoción del turismo en las Américas,* UNWTO, Madrid.

World Tourism Organization (2012), *MICE Industry – An Asia-Pacific Perspective,* UNWTO, Madrid.

World Tourism Organization (2006), *Measuring the Economic Importance of the Meetings Industry – Developing a TSA Extension,* UNWTO, Madrid.

World Travel & Tourism Council (2014), *Travel and Trade Linkages: Analysis of trends worldwide & within Asia-Pacific,* WTTC, London.

Useful websites

European Travel Commission (ETC): www.etc-corporate.org.

German Convention Bureau: www.gcb.de.

Greater Bogota Convention Bureau: www.bogotacb.com.

INCON: www.incon-pco.com.

Malaysia Convention & Exhibition Bureau: www.myceb.com.my.

Prague Convention Bureau: www.pragueconvention.cz.

Serbia Convention Bureau: http://m.scb.travel.

Tourism Vancouver: www.tourismvancouver.com.

Vienna Convention Bureau: www.vienna.convention.at.

World Tourism Organization (UNWTO): www.unwto.org.

YourSingapore: www.yoursingapore.com.